Making Civics Count

Making Civics Count

Citizenship Education
for a New Generation

Edited by

David E. Campbell,
Meira Levinson, and
Frederick M. Hess

Harvard Education Press
Cambridge, Massachusetts

Library of Congress Control Number 2012937483

Paperback ISBN: 978-1-61250-476-6
Library Edition ISBN: 978-1-61250-477-3

Published by Harvard Education Press,
an imprint of the Harvard Education Publishing Group

Harvard Education Press
8 Story Street
Cambridge, MA 02138

Cover Design: Sarah Henderson

Cover Photo: sandra_javera/Flickr/Getty Images

The typefaces used in this book are Bembo and Scala Sans.

CONTENTS

INTRODUCTION

David E. Campbell

This book has one simple objective: to shine a spotlight on civic education in order to help policymakers, educators, parents, and voters better understand what American youth learn about democratic engagement and to encourage us all to ask how our schools might do better. After all, for all the attention paid to school reform in recent years, civic education has been given short shrift. Given the challenges that American children will be facing in the twenty-first century, this oversight points to a peculiar and troubling state of affairs. While there is certainly much to be learned about effective civic education, a wealth of multidisciplinary academic research offers some promising places to start. In the pages to follow, you will find various approaches that have been shown to be effective in civic education.

WHAT IS CIVIC EDUCATION?

The first order of business is to define civic education—a notoriously slippery term. For one thing, it goes by different names, including citizenship education and democratic education. Furthermore, it is taught in different classes—including social studies, civics, and government—and in extracurricular activities. Even defining civic outcomes to be measured, not to mention how to measure them, is fraught with controversy. For our purposes, we provide a working definition of civic education as *the knowledge, skills, attitudes, and experience to prepare someone to be an active, informed participant in democratic life.* In offering this definition, we concede its pliability, but this is because the parameters of civic education are ambiguous. As Peter Levine notes in chapter 2, you could say that all liberal arts education is civic education. Nonetheless, it is possible to identify specific knowledge, skills, attitudes, and experiences that uniquely prepare young people to be active citizens.

WHY WORRY ABOUT CIVIC EDUCATION?

At a time when schools are under enormous pressure to improve test scores, raise graduation rates, and prepare more students for college, perhaps it seems superfluous to concentrate on civics. To the contrary, civics is not superfluous or even secondary to the primary purpose of public schooling. It *is* the primary purpose. The irony of the inattention to civic education is that U.S. public schools were actually created for the express purpose of forming democratic citizens. Many state constitutions explicitly mention the democratic purpose of their public schools. And as Anna Saavedra notes in chapter 6, virtually all states have a civics requirement for graduation from high school. In chapter 10, I describe the emphasis on civics in both private and charter schools as well. Therefore, our call for improved civic education does not mean adding anything more to what our schools already have a mandate to do. It simply means doing it better.

Why should Americans be concerned about the current state of civic education? As detailed by Richard Niemi (chapter 1)—and many others—American high school students know relatively little about their government. And while Levine offers a more optimistic perspective in chapter 2, he nonetheless laments the inequalities in the civic knowledge of American youth. Whether you think the glass is half empty like Niemi or half full like Levine, there is still half a glass left to fill.

Civic education takes on even more significance when put in the context of three megatrends in American politics. The first has been the decline of civic engagement among all Americans, but especially the rising Millennial generation. By nearly every measure, Americans are less engaged in their communities and political activity than generations past. Some readers may question the claim: didn't the 2008 presidential election electrify the Millennial generation? Considering voter turnout, the answer is actually no or, at least, "not much." By recent standards, 2008 had a relatively high rate of turnout among Americans aged eighteen to twenty-four—12 percentage points higher than in 2000. But the sobering fact is that the turnout rate was still only 44 percent, 2 percentage points higher than in 2004. While turnout bumps up and down depending on the conditions of each election, the general trend has been downward since 1972, the first year in which eighteen- to twenty-year-olds could vote nationwide. Even worse, only 20 percent of eighteen- to twenty-four-year-olds turned out in the 2010 congressional elections, down from an average of roughly 24 to 25 percent through the 1970s and early 1980s.[1]

Voter turnout, however, is only one measure of civic engagement, and *sui generis* at that. Because the factors affecting turnout are unique, an exclusive focus on voting can distract people from all the other avenues of involvement in political and civic life. While turnout fluctuates, a wealth of other civic indicators have been in free fall. As exhaustively documented by the dean of civic engagement scholars, Robert Putnam, there has been a sharp drop-off in the percentage of Americans who participate in an array of civic activities such as rallies, political campaigns, and public meetings. And that drop-off has been most pronounced among the youngest Americans.[2]

However, a skeptic might press the case further and ask about all those online petitions, tweets, and such. Hasn't there been an upswing in political expression through new online channels? The jury is still out on the frequency of such activity but, no matter how frequent, cyber "activism" still represents an extremely thin form of civic engagement. It requires virtually no investment of time and effort to learn about the issues and no willingness or even opportunity to compromise. Clicking a check box on a Web site is a poor substitute for articulating and even defending your views in a public arena. In other words, meaningful, sustained, and substantive civic engagement is down, and precipitously so among young people.

The second megatrend in politics is polarization. Scholars debate the extent to which voters themselves are polarized—although the best evidence suggests that ideological camps are hardening—but, unquestionably, U.S. elected officials are increasingly polarized along ideological lines.[3] With elected members from the two parties pulling farther apart ideologically, compromise is harder and harder to reach. In America's system of two houses of Congress (often run by different parties) and shared power among the three branches of government, an absence of compromise results in political paralysis. Even such routine business as congressional approval for presidential appointments is met with difficulty. Much like the proxy wars fought by the United States and Soviet Union during the Cold War, members of Congress use presidential appointments as proxies for deep-seated ideological battles. And never mind the proxies. The House of Representatives, Senate, and White House often do direct battle over fundamental ideological and partisan differences, causing government to grind to a halt.

The third megatrend is a lack of trust in government, which should concern people across the political spectrum.[4] While conservatives and liberals alike may sneer that Americans ought not to trust a government run by the "other team," and libertarian-leaning conservatives especially may applaud mistrust in government as the first step to rolling back its size, deep distrust calls into question the very legitimacy of the government. Conservatives, liberals, libertarians, and progressives should all be concerned about a government viewed with suspicion. Any democratic system relies on a foundation of trust in those who govern. Who would enlist to defend a nation whose government they did not trust? Who would obey its laws? Who would pay their taxes?

These three megatrends are arguably related to one another. When civic engagement declines, it falls off most among political moderates. Those with fervently held views still get involved. Therefore, a winning electoral strategy is often to appeal to the loyal members of your base, rather than the fickle voters in the moderate middle. The base shows up at meetings, turns out for elections, and writes checks to candidates. The result? A polarized Congress filled with members who increasingly do not need to move to the middle to stay in office. With polarization comes increasing distrust of Washington, and Congress especially, which in turn leads to a further decrease in political engagement as more and more moderate voters throw up their hands in frustration and decide that politics is not for them.

In the long run, a more effective civic education could be a tonic to counteract all three of these trends. A resurgence in civics could stem—and perhaps even reverse—the nation's long-term civic recession and boost levels of engagement. More engagement, especially in the moderate middle, could tamp down the polarization of U.S. politics and thus the paralysis of the government. With less polarization and less paralysis, voters would then have less reason to distrust those elected to govern.

Improving civic education in schools will, of course, not solve all the nation's political problems. Obviously, democratic reform is not as simple as pulling the lever of civic education to fix a complex system. But neither is the civic education of young people irrelevant to the nation's current civic woes. If subpar academics in U.S. schools can cause economic problems, then couldn't subpar civics education cause political problems? So even if civic education cannot solve all of a democracy's woes, it may better prepare young voters for the realities of politics in a diverse, democratic nation. Political scientists John Hibbing and Elizabeth Theiss-Morse make a strong case that voters need to learn that conflict, and thus compromise, lies at the heart of politics:

> To the extent the climate in schools these days encourages avoiding controversial political issues rather than teaching students to be comfortable in dealing with those issues, a great disservice is done to the students and to the democratic process. Students are left with only a saccharin civic side of politics and thus made more likely to react negatively when in the real world they are exposed to the gritty, barbaric side of politics. The American educational system needs to work harder at teaching students to appreciate the difficulty of making decisions democratically.[5]

As the reader will see, the authors' call for teaching what they provocatively label "barbarics" instead of civics has a lot of theoretical and empirical support. To do democracy, citizens must appreciate that it is messy.

Thus, one reason to improve civic education is to correct the mistakes of the past. That is reason enough, but is only the start. America also needs to improve civic education to prepare for the challenges of the future.

One such challenge—and, in equal parts, opportunity—is America's increasing racial, ethnic, linguistic, and religious diversity, as the United States becomes a majority-minority nation. This demographic shift presents an unparalleled possibility for citizens to contribute their diverse knowledge, perspectives, and capacities to addressing the needs of America and the rest of the world in the twenty-first century. Yet diversity also brings challenges to any nation's civic cohesiveness. Americans need to be prepared for that reality. In the past, U.S. schools served to weave together the many strands of a diverse nation to make a stronger whole, although admittedly at a high cost to some individuals and groups. To be successful in helping new and long-standing Americans come together to create a common civic culture, schools will need new models and methods.

The United States also faces impending policy challenges that are unrivaled in their severity—ballooning public debt, a social security system facing collapse, a threatened environment, and competition in a global marketplace are only a few. Solving these problems will require a responsible electorate, perhaps even one willing to endure personal sacrifice for the public good. The nation will need a generation imbued with a sense of civic responsibility—an old-fashioned concept that should be resurrected. Thomas Jefferson put it best: "I know no safe depository of the ultimate powers of the society but the people themselves; and if we think them not enlightened enough to exercise their control with a wholesome discretion, the remedy is not to take it from them, but to inform their discretion by education."[6]

THE NEED FOR GREATER ATTENTION TO CIVICS

The irony of the inattention to civics within education circles is the nearly universal consensus on its importance. Education experts on both the left and the right give lip service to the importance of civic education. Yet even with this apparent harmony regarding its importance, civics still receives little sustained attention from education reformers, policymakers, teachers' unions, and so on. When debates rage over education policy, math and reading are in the spotlight, while science sometimes sneaks in with second billing. Civics barely warrants a mention, except perhaps for an occasional lament about young people's political ignorance.

One reason for the inattention to civic education is that it suffers from a false consensus. Everyone can agree that schools should teach young people to be civically active and politically informed. Yet move beyond bromides about good citizenship, and the consensus breaks down. The nation would be better off if it had a national conversation—a debate even—over what an effective civic education should entail. While conservatives and liberals can agree that civics should count more than it currently does, no progress will be made without a working consensus on what schools should teach and what students should learn. Ironically, the difficulty in finding consensus over civic education is arguably because of poor training in civics to begin with; finding consensus requires a familiarity with the give-and-take of democratic decision-making.

Improvement in civic education will follow from greater attention paid to it. When phrased that way, the recommendation probably sounds pretty anodyne—perhaps as innocuous as the bipartisan paeans to the virtues of civic education itself. Most everyone interested in civic education would presumably endorse the idea that it should receive greater attention. However, as with the specific meaning of civic education, there are deep, legitimate disagreements over what such attention should entail. Nonetheless, the contributors to this book—coming from many perspectives—agree that improving civic education will require developing and deploying metrics to gauge what's happening when it comes to important civic outcomes. Many contributors offer practical recommendations on this score. Peter Levine describes student portfolios, whereby the students collect their civically relevant work from across subject areas. Levine and Joseph Kahne and his colleagues describe virtual badges that students can earn for mastering specific civic skills; these badges could be awarded both by schools and by other organizations. Interestingly, if this idea were to catch on, it would be a twenty-first-century update to a twentieth-century idea. Badges of the tangible kind are, of course, most famously associated with the Boy Scouts and Girl Scouts—two civic-oriented organizations created during the Progressive Era, an earlier period rife with civic innovation.

Any discussion of assessment, civics or otherwise, cannot ignore the 800-pound gorilla of high-stakes testing. Should civics be subject to standardized testing, as math, reading, and, to some extent, science are? Some argue that the only path to improved civic education is through high-stakes testing, which puts civics on equal footing with math and reading. Only with high-stakes tests, the reasoning goes, will teachers, administrators, students, and parents get serious about civics. On the other hand, adding civics to high-stakes testing is often met with vociferous objection by educators and advocates for civic education. Some of their objections echo the general case against high-stakes testing—that the practice unfairly stigmatizes schools with hard-to-educate students, leads to rote instruction over intellectual stimulation, and causes schools to give short shrift to a well-rounded education. Another concern about high-stakes testing in civics is more distinctive, suggesting that because civics is multidimensional, an effective evaluation of a young person's preparation for active citizenship cannot be reduced to a standardized exam.

Whatever the theoretical merits of high-stakes civics testing might be, it is far more productive for advocates of civic education to focus on developing meaningful, reliable, defensible metrics and on evaluating civic outcomes that are politically feasible. That alone will require considerable political will. The debate over high-stakes testing can wait for another day.

WHAT IS KNOWN AND NOT KNOWN

Notwithstanding the relative inattention to civic education among scholars and policymakers, the waters are not entirely uncharted. As is clear from the contributors assembled for this volume, a critical mass of knowledge about what makes for effective civics instruction has begun to accumulate. As the editors of this book, we tip our hats to researchers who work in the area of civics, since the paucity of data makes such research difficult. It is all the more notable when these researchers agree on what works, given that they often come from different disciplinary backgrounds. Existing research of different types, in different places, and by different scholars converges on the importance of discussing contrasting viewpoints within the classroom and is buttressed by a strong theoretical basis for why such discussion is effective. Exposure to, and interest in, dialogue appears to lead to greater political knowledge and interest. Some of the increase in knowledge and interest likely results because conflict is intrinsically interesting and thus catches the attention of distractible teenagers. But interest in conflict is probably not the whole story. Classroom discussion is also conceivably an effective pedagogical technique because it exposes students to more information than do lectures, worksheets, movies, or other methods of civics instruction, and this greater quantity of information is matched by higher quality of instruction. In addition to its efficacy for enhancing cognitive learning, a well-moderated discussion of contentious questions also teaches students that politics is about resolving disagreements and, hopefully, models the use of civil discourse.

Classroom discussion is not the only means of civic education that works. Throughout the volume, you will find still other examples of effective tools and methods. For example, James Youniss (chapter 5) describes the evidence in favor of service-learning, while Joseph Kahne, Jacqueline Ullman, and Ellen Middaugh (chapter 9) highlight the innovative use of video games as a means of civic education.

However, for all that is known about civics, there are still gaping holes in the knowledge about what works. In chapter 10, I note that an array of studies has compared the civic education in public and private sectors and found that private schools often excel. The explanation for the "private edge" (actually, largely a Catholic edge) remains unknown. Indeed, *why* some forms of civic education are more effective than others is largely a mystery. And perhaps the largest lacuna of all is whether civic education in adolescence has a long-term effect on political engagement into adulthood. Does high school cast a long shadow? Research conducted in the 1960s suggested it did not, but much has changed since. Examining the long-term effects, if any, of civic education should be a top priority—hopefully, this volume provides direction on the design of such a study.

In addition to guiding future empirical work, we hope also to raise the normative questions of what a civic education should entail and why it ought to be a priority for educators. The false consensus around the virtues of a vague commitment to civic education without a specific vision has constrained the full-throated debate over the purpose and thus the design of civic education. A few chapters raise such issues (see, in particular, Meira Levinson's discussion of civic education and diversity in chapter 4), but the conversation is only just starting. Much more can, and should, be said.

THE ROAD MAP

Civic education is a broad topic, and so the chapters to follow cover a lot of ground. The book starts with a description of the state of civic education in America today. Interestingly, as was noted above, that subject is a matter of debate. Niemi (chapter 1) summarizes what young people know—and don't know—about politics and government. He wishes to raise the alarm about the lack of civics knowledge among young people and calls for a greater emphasis on contemporary politics in civics classes. In contrast, Levine (chapter 2) is more sanguine, arguing that young people know more than their elders give them credit for. However, Levine's position is nuanced. Even though he does not believe that civic education is as bad as often described, he still sees the need for improvement. He argues that deliberation and collaboration are the hallmarks of civil society and that schools must teach them to young people because other civic institutions are faltering. Interestingly, given his disagreement with Niemi over whether "the kids are all right," one of Levine's recommendations bears a striking resemblance to Niemi's: reform civics standards to focus on "relevance to civil society." Upon reading these two chapters, you will may very well conclude that the real story is not so much where they disagree but where they find agreement.

Next, Michael Johanek (chapter 3) offers some important historical context for a contemporary discussion of civic education. For all the current focus on America's rapidly transforming social and civic landscape, this is not the first time the United States has undergone such dramatic change. Important innovations in civic education came about during another period of civic flux, the Progressive Era. Johanek provides three compelling case studies from this era, in each of which the schools facilitated civic education for the community as a whole. He provocatively laments that today's schools generally do not fulfill that same role of community center. Whether or not you endorse such an expanded mandate for schools, Johanek's argument for the success of these cases from the past cannot be ignored, as it demonstrates that schools do not operate in isolation from the communities in which they are embedded.

Whereas Johanek describes how schools dealt with a changing social landscape in years past, Meira Levinson (chapter 4) looks to the present, and to diversity, one of the trickiest yet potentially rewarding developments facing civic educators. Levinson's chapter is a welcome contrast both to those who glibly invoke diversity without considering the difficulties it presents and to those who only disparage diversity. She stresses both the civic challenges and the opportunities presented by an increasingly diverse society. The chapter combines empirical research and philosophical analysis to frame the ways in which diversity and civic education intersect—ideally but certainly not always in productive tension with one another.

The next five chapters provide what is often missing in discussions of civic education, concrete examples of successful programs for students and teachers. No serious discussion of civic education can ignore these success stories, as they ought to inform any proposals to enhance and improve how civics is taught. James Youniss (chapter 5), for example, highlights a number of strategies that schools can use to enhance civic education, all with support from empirical research. As noted, these strategies not only include classroom discussion, but also extend to meaningful student government and community service that connects students to their communities (with whispers of the sort of school-community linkages Johanek describes in the Progressive Era). Anna Saavedra (chapter 6) provides case studies of dynamic civic education at the local, state, and national levels. While she laments most classrooms' continued reliance on dry textbooks, plodding lectures, and the dreaded worksheet, she also offers concrete recommendations for how these classrooms could be transformed with administrative and other support.

Keith Barton (chapter 7) turns the focus from education *by* teachers to the education *of* teachers. From his perspective as a teacher of teachers, Barton describes how most educators do not enter the profession with the goal of facilitating democratic civic participation. He makes a forceful case that, whatever their motivations for becoming teachers, they should be taught to be democratic exemplars in the classroom. Their training can, and should, do more to emphasize the connections between teaching and democracy. That is, a passion for democratic participation should pervade what all teachers do. Diana Hess and John Zola (chapter 8) complement Barton's chapter by emphasizing the importance of professional development for teachers throughout the course of their careers. The content of civic education is a moving target, especially if educators are to adopt the proposal to focus civics instruction on contemporary politics. Furthermore, effective civic education requires demanding pedagogical methods that require effort to master. It is thus unrealistic to think that teachers will learn everything they need to know in preservice teacher education. Hess and Zola lay out five characteristics for high-quality professional development programs centered on civics and provide case studies of three highly successful programs.

The next chapter moves beyond the classroom. Joseph Kahne, Jacqueline Ullman, and Ellen Middaugh (chapter 9) explain how civic educators should harness technology, particularly online activities and even video games, to invigorate civic learning. To bring civics into the brave new online world would be a step toward counteracting civic education's bad reputation as dry and boring. Lest you think that civics online would sacrifice content, they make a compelling argument that the innovative use of online tools need not mean short-changing substance. Finally, in chapter 10, I summarize the evidence regarding civic education in public and private schools. In doing so, I argue that it is time to move beyond the question of whether public or private schools are "better" at civic education. That question came out of the debate over school choice and has largely been settled. The empirical evidence makes clear that private schooling is not a detriment to civic education. In many cases, private schools surpass their public counterparts when it comes to civic outcomes. The education community does not need yet another study to make that point. What it needs is a new generation of research, reoriented to explain *why* schools differ in the civic education they offer. What can traditional public schools learn from the private sector or from charter schools? And what can private and charter schools learn from their traditional public counterparts?

In sum, this volume offers summary and synthesis of what is known, and not known, about civic education. The chapters are written to be accessible to a wide audience, including the general public, policymakers, and elected officials. The contributors are not just academics talking to one another in the code of technical jargon. All the contributors, and we the editors, are scholars and citizens who care about the nation's civic health and are using the tools of our trade to improve civic education. This is not a conversation only for the ivory tower or within the confines of the Washington Beltway. Civic education should be discussed in school board meetings and PTA luncheons, in living rooms and chat rooms. Indeed, the somewhat immodest hope of this volume is to help get that conversation started. A national discussion would itself be an exercise in civic education and an important step toward making civics count.

1

WHAT STUDENTS KNOW ABOUT CIVICS AND GOVERNMENT

Richard G. Niemi

Public opinion surveys and national student testing have contributed, each in their own way, to the unflattering conclusion that present and future American electorates are remarkably ill-informed about political matters. Lest we forget, we are reminded every Fourth of July, when a newspaper in one city or another finds beachgoers unable to recognize and reluctant to sign a petition consisting of the Bill of Rights or another significant American document.[1] On a more formal level, students might read in an American government text that "the results [of the 1998 National Assessment of Educational Progress] reflected a startling lack of understanding regarding basic concepts related to American government among high school seniors."[2]

Is the population—young and old—really as uninformed as these reports suggest? Yes and no is the short answer. A longer answer requires a look at what's asked on surveys and tests, how various demographic groups line up, and how responses and scores vary over time and across countries. It also requires us to ponder the importance of political knowledge—or of various specific kinds of political information—as well as why information levels are as low as they appear to be and whether and how it is possible to increase them. This chapter provides a longer look at young people, the public in general, and what they do know (and don't) about government and politics.

OVERALL KNOWLEDGE ABOUT POLITICS AND GOVERNMENT

The easiest—and most amusing—way of "proving" that citizens have low knowledge levels is through anecdotes. One of the more absurd examples is from the late novelist James Michener. While writing a nonfiction book about the U.S. presidential election process, he cited a number of person-on-the-street interviews in Philadelphia, including one informant who said, "Every boy and girl should go to college and if they can't afford Yale or Harvard, why, Electoral is just as good, if you work."[3] On a lighter but equally telling note, late-night television viewers are occasionally treated to "Jaywalking"—episodes on *The Tonight Show* in which Jay Leno asks questions about U.S. politics, history, and other subjects of individuals, often young adults, who are extraordinarily ill informed and willing to demonstrate that point on camera.

Are Americans really this ignorant? Are Michener's and Leno's interviewees truly indicative of how little the public knows about politics and government? In some respects, yes. Adult surveys demonstrating this point are legion. The most extensive, accessible collection is in a 1996 book *What Americans Know About Politics and Why It Matters.* In light of responses to fifty years' worth of factual questions, the authors summarize the results: "Only 13 percent of the more than 2,000 political questions examined could be answered correctly by 75 percent or more of those asked," and "many of the facts known by relatively small percentages of the public seem critical to understanding—let alone effectively acting in—the political world."[4] Drawing on a specially commissioned survey, the authors add that "when the answers were coded for levels of knowledge, the average percent correct for 'surface knowledge' was 41, but for 'deep knowledge,' it plummeted to 16 percent."[5]

Ignorance of facts and figures, however, is hardly the end of it. As far back as 1960, political scientists determined that American voters often fail to have anything resembling an ideological perspective on the political world. Even when presented with the concepts of liberal and conservative—terms universally used by journalists and political elites in describing political values, policies, and leaders—many voters fail to recognize or understand these concepts. Large numbers of adults fail even minimal tests of knowledge of current government policies and candidates' proposals for new policies.[6] A "golden oldie" is how much the United States spends on foreign aid; a recent poll found an average guess of 27 percent of the U.S. budget, compared with the real figure of under 1 percent.[7] Young people, beginning with secondary school students, likewise demonstrate levels of knowledge that can at best be described as inadequate and at worst "confirm that we have a crisis on our hands when it comes to civics education."[8] On the 2006 National Assessment of Educational Progress (NAEP) in civics, about one-third each of fourth-, eighth-, and twelfth-graders scored *below* basic, indicating to William Galston "near-total civic ignorance," and only 25–30 percent achieve a score indicating grade-level proficiency or above.[9] Recent NAEP tests include "constructed-response" (essay) questions as well as multiple-choice items. In either case, specific items often reveal surprising weaknesses in students' answers. When asked, for example, what occurs when state and national laws are in conflict—whether the state law is enforced, the national law is enforced, the state decides which law to enforce, or the public holds a referendum to decide which law should be enforced—only half of the seniors were able to answer correctly that the federal law takes precedence. On a question calling for a written response, only 60 percent meaningfully described "two factors besides political party identification that influence voter preference."[10]

Things are no different at the college level. In 2006, the Intercollegiate Studies Institute commissioned a survey of some fourteen thousand students from college and universities across the country, asking them sixty multiple-choice questions. Among the findings: more than half the seniors did not know that the Bill of Rights explicitly prohibits the establishment of an official religion for the United States. Overall, the institute gave students a failing grade in each of the areas on the exam (American history, government, America and the world, and a market economy). The results were no better in 2008.[11] Yet another study found, astoundingly, that only 46 percent of American college students correctly picked the *half-century* in which the U.S. Civil War was fought.[12] And in a survey of Ivy League students, only a quarter could identify the source of "a government of the people, by the people and for the people," and only half could name both of their state's senators in the weeks following an election.[13]

Can we be content, as suggested by Peter Levine in chapter 2, with the notion that knowledge levels have always been low—so there is nothing to worry about? Unfortunately, no. For one thing, adult knowledge levels by some accounts should have increased substantially over the past half-century and yet have not. Education, which is strongly correlated with knowledge levels in cross-section surveys, has risen substantially over this period.[14] Sources of news exposure have risen dramatically over the same period, first with the coming of nightly news programs, later with the genesis of cable news programs, and very recently with the Internet. Yet the best available evidence is that knowledge levels are about the same as they were five decades ago.[15]

What is especially disconcerting, however, is that knowledge levels seem actually to have *declined* among young people, at least relative to older persons. Comparing knowledge across time is fraught with difficulties. The best evidence comes from surveys or tests that use identical items over time or from tests that are carefully calibrated so as to be comparable despite changing questions. One source of such comparisons is NAEP trend studies. After examining studies done from 1976 to 1988 and again from 1988 to 1998, I, along with my colleagues Mitchell Sanders and Dale Whittington, concluded that "there was a decline in civic knowledge among 8th and 12th graders," though possibly a small increase among fourth-graders. Indeed, the decline among twelfth-graders, though small, "appears to have left high school seniors in 1998 able to answer questions only a little better than 8th graders in the mid-1970s."[16] The most recent trend study, from 1998 to 2010, shows no change among eighth-graders, a small but statistically significant decrease among twelfth-graders, and, again, a significant upward trend among fourth-graders.[17]

Evidence about young versus older adults comes from comparisons of cross-section surveys conducted between the 1940s or 1950s and the mid-2000s. In the earliest such studies, there is only a slight correlation with age; surveys show that those under thirty were equally able or slightly more often able to answer questions correctly than seniors. Over time, however, the age gap has grown such that older individuals are now considerably more often able to answer questions about politics. If one controls statistically for education levels, the results are unmistakable. As table 1.1 demonstrates, average correlations between age and knowledge by decade have become much stronger, vividly demonstrating how the political knowledge gap between young and old has accelerated over time.[18] Significantly, a growing knowledge gap is not uniquely American. Evidence from nearly a dozen countries shows the same pattern as in the United States—a growing knowledge gap between young and old.[19]

That so many countries have parallel results indicates that recent knowledge gaps are a generational, or cohort, phenomenon. Paul Howe notes that across many nations, this age gap has slowly emerged over several decades and that the trend cannot be explained by changes in the questions asked at different points in time.[20] Michael Delli Carpini and Scott Keeter compared five items asked in early surveys with

TABLE 1.1

Correlation between age and political knowledge, 1948–2000s

Year	Average correlation between age and political knowledge
1948	.03
1960s	.06
1970s	.16
1980s	.22
1990s	.23
2000s	.28

Source: Martin P. Wattenberg, *Is Voting for Young People? With a Postscript on Citizen Engagement* (New York: Pearson Longman, 2008), 79.

identical items asked in their own survey. Their conclusion: "An age gap in knowledge does not even appear . . . in the 1940s and 1950s. In 1989, however, eighteen to twenty-nine year olds were considerably less informed than older citizens."[21] The knowledge gap in recent years is thus most likely generational rather than life cycle (i.e., owing to aging itself) in origin.

A final point to glean from adult surveys is that young adults are less knowledgeable on a wide array of political subjects. One might well imagine that older adults are better able to identify long-serving political leaders because they (both older adults and long-serving leaders) have had plenty of time to become acquainted, and there is some evidence that this is the case.[22] The same reasoning does not apply to all current leaders. And one might expect the opposite of "civics" knowledge—that is, young adults would better remember things that were the subject of high school or college classes. Yet Martin Wattenberg finds unwavering results: "Regardless of whether the question concerned basic civics facts, identification of current political leaders, information about the presidential candidates, or knowledge of partisan control of Congress, the result was the same: young people were clearly less well-informed than the elderly."[23]

The United States in Global Perspective

Despite the bleak picture of popular knowledge of politics, especially among the young, not everything is so dismal. One bright spot comes from the 1999 International Association for the Evaluation of Educational Achievement (IEA) International Civic Education Study, in which comparisons were made of civic knowledge among fourteen-year-olds in twenty-eight countries.[24] From the perspective of the United States, the fact that American students scored near the top overall and significantly above the international mean is a welcome contrast to the many stories we hear about how U.S. students lag behind other nations in mathematics and science achievement.[25] However, even this good news is tempered by the fact that American students achieved the highest score of any country on interpretive skills, but only near-average scores on content knowledge.[26]

From a broader perspective, the IEA testing tells us several important things. First, cross-country differences are, in general, not very large. Fourteen-year-olds from countries as diverse as Finland, Portugal, Bulgaria, and the United States were not that divergent in their civic knowledge. Countries that differ in many ways are all conveying about the same abilities in basic content and citizenship to mid-adolescents. Second, the job many countries do in educating their students is at least in some respects a creditable one. The authors of the IEA study note that "over 75 percent of the students in most participating countries are able to answer questions dealing with the fundamental nature of laws and political rights."[27] Third, however, other results mimic strictly American studies in cautioning against too much optimism, as the authors also point out that few students could answer "more demanding questions" about elections, political reform, and the implications of policy choices. As with so many other findings about political knowledge, one can conclude that the glass is half full or half empty.

Cautionary Notes

A few caveats about the findings I have summarized: first, experts often think people should know more than they do. That is certainly so with respect to teachers, who complain endlessly about how poorly their students do or how little they seem to know. For evidence that this is not a new phenomenon with respect to young people's knowledge about politics, one can go as far back as 1905, to a paper presented at the second annual meeting of the American Political Science Association. Therein, one Professor W. A. Schaper complains that students entering college are woefully unprepared with respect to knowledge about government. His evidence, from a (nonrandom) survey of college students, leads him to this conclusion: "When case piles upon case [of erroneous answers] you begin to fear that the want of information about the government and the utter want of comprehension of our political system may be the rule, not the exception among this much favored class of the rising generation."[28]

Another example of experts thinking students should know more—an example with contemporary, serious interpretive implications—is perhaps the specification of achievement levels in the NAEP tests. I noted earlier how few students are said to be grade-level proficient in their knowledge of civics. Yet what constitutes proficiency is essentially arbitrary, a level of hoped-for achievement as determined by teachers, administrators, and others involved in designing the test. Were students to significantly increase their scores, one gets the feeling that the bar would be raised in a way that would wipe out the apparent gains.[29]

A second cautionary note asks us to consider what long-ago data tell us about the low knowledge levels we observe today. Though even the best long-term comparisons are tenuous because of differences in the tests themselves and the populations being tested, they raise doubts about whether contemporary students are less knowledgeable than those of much earlier decades. In one case, researchers compared twelfth-graders' responses to nine items on 1988 and 1998 NAEP civics tests to responses to identically or nearly identically worded questions in tests given in the 1930s through 1976. The percentages responding correctly were nearly identical in one instance (one point apart). On the other eight items, earlier students were more often correct on four items (by 6 to 11 points) and less often correct on four others (by 8 to 15 points). Other tests permitted comparisons involving more items, but earlier and later sets of items were similar only in that they covered the same nominal topics (for example, criminal and civil justice). The authors cautiously concluded that "contemporary high school seniors are not demonstrably less informed about politics and government than were students in the 1930s through the 1960s."[30] With respect to knowledge of history, others have noted that beginning in the 1910s, tests or surveys of students yielded results similar to those of contemporary tests—that is, overall poor to "middling" results and examples of "abysmal ignorance."[31] A systematic comparison of history test results yielded another cautious conclusion—that "students of the 1980s may not be demonstrably different from students in the past."[32]

Still another caveat is recognition that knowledge varies considerably by topic. In adult surveys, there are obvious variations depending on the salience of the topic or person being asked about, which can change greatly over time. But variations exist on student tests as well, where the questions are designed to be less time-sensitive. NAEP results are not reported by subject area, but an analysis of the 1988 items suggests that students are especially well versed in many aspects of the criminal justice system, especially as it pertains to their individual rights. Questions about the right to a lawyer, the right to remain silent, and the meaning of the right to counsel were answered correctly by over 90 percent of twelfth-graders; slightly more abstract questions, such as about appealing criminal cases to a higher court and the meaning of a Miranda warning, were answered correctly by two-thirds or more of the seniors. On the other hand, questions about political parties and lobbying showed considerable variability and were in general answered by lower numbers of students; just 74 percent of the seniors knew that lobbying was legal, and only 39 percent knew that the procedure for nominating presidential candidates was established by the political parties.[33] This difference is probably attributable, in part, to the fact that parties and lobbying are not mentioned in the Constitution and are therefore covered in less detail in classes; it may also be due to what students see on television and in the movies and what seems most relevant to the average teenager.

Variations Across Demographic Groups

Variations in knowledge levels also exist across demographic groups. Unsurprisingly, some of the greatest differences occur when people are grouped by their education level. Such findings were extensively documented as early as the 1950s and persist today.[34] They extend to all kinds of political knowledge and all sorts of "academic" knowledge. They persist even when other significant factors, such as income and political interest, are statistically controlled.[35]

Of greater significance, similar gaps in knowledge levels are found among adolescents when the children are divided by the level of their *parents'* education. In the most recent NAEP test, for example, eighth-graders' scores ranged from 134 for those with parents who did not finish high school, to 139 when parents had graduated from high school, to 155 when parents had some post–high school education, to 162 when parents had graduated from college. Among twelfth-graders, scores for the same groups were 128, 137, 147, and 158, respectively. To appreciate the significance of these differences, note that the students in a given grade themselves all had the same nominal amount of schooling at the time of testing.

Racial and ethnic differences are also important because they are large and persistent but normatively undesirable. Among adults, African Americans lag significantly behind whites, partly but not entirely due to lower education levels.[36] Latinos also have lower knowledge levels, with nativity and English language ability added as predictive factors.[37] Large racial and ethnic differences are also found among students. Differences between blacks and whites have changed little over the past decade. Latinos, however, have begun to close the gap. In all three grades tested, the gap between white and Hispanic students has narrowed significantly, though a substantial difference still exists. In 2010, scores for twelfth-graders were 156 for whites, 137 for Hispanics, and 127 for blacks.

Also of interest are differences in knowledge levels of males and females. Traditionally, adult males have been more knowledgeable about political matters, just as they have participated more frequently in politics. This observation holds even after controlling for possible confounding factors such as partisanship and media exposure.[38] In recent years, questions have been raised about the sources of gender differences and just how meaningful they are. Men, for example, are more likely to guess in response to knowledge questions, and this may account for some of the difference.[39] There may also be subjects, such as government services and benefits and school board matters, about which women are more knowledgeable.[40] Still, as conventionally measured, it is generally found that men retain an edge in information.

Evidence from pre-adult studies suggests that while the gender gap may at one time have dipped well into the childhood years, it is no longer visible in the school setting.[41] In the 1988 NAEP civics assessment, boys outscored girls in the twelfth grade by only a small amount, and in the last three civics assessments, girls have tended to perform as well as, or slightly better than, boys.[42] The only statistically significant difference in the past dozen years was among fourth-grade students in 2010, and that difference favored girls. Likewise, the gender gap in the NAEP U.S. history assessment has been very small or nonexistent since at least

1994.[43] It appears as if the persistent gender gap at the adult level develops after youths leave high school, perhaps as a result of greater interest and attention to politics among men.

WHY IS POLITICAL KNOWLEDGE SO LOW AMONG TODAY'S YOUNG PEOPLE?

The finding that political knowledge is lower today than in past decades and that it is especially low among today's youth runs contrary to expectations for at least two reasons. First, education levels have risen greatly over the past fifty or sixty years, approximately the time frame for which we have (reasonably) comparable estimates of overall knowledge. Given the strong cross-sectional relationship between education and knowledge, one would expect greater overall knowledge today— yet, as noted, that is not the case. Second, the media environment today is vastly richer than it was, and young people are the best equipped group to take advantage of the newest (online) portion of it. Yet today's young people appear relatively less knowledgeable (compared with older adults) than in the 1950s and 1960s. What accounts for the failure to meet these expectations?

Various hypotheses and other interesting research address these questions, but there are no definitive answers. One possible explanation is that young people today are simply less interested in politics and therefore "naturally" acquire less information. Evidence related to this point is mixed. While cross-section surveys generally find that young people express less interest in politics than do older adults, this difference may reflect life cycle changes rather than a shift toward lower interest among today's youths.[44] Thus, it is important to ask whether political interest has declined generally in recent decades and whether it has declined more among young people than among older individuals.

When posed in these more specific ways, the answer seems quite clear—aside from the United States. One study, for example, looked at over-time data from twelve countries spread across North America, Western Europe, and Australia. In every country except the United States, political interest *increased* from roughly 1970 to the mid-1990s. In the United States, however, interest in politics generally (1964–1996) and in the presidential election (1952–1996) declined.[45] The reason for this apparent U.S. exceptionalism may lie in the extraordinary events taking place in this country in the 1960s and 1970s (the Kennedy and King assassinations, the civil rights movement, and the Vietnam War). Indeed, if one limits one's view to the period from 1978 through 2008, the line representing the percentage following government and public affairs "most of the time" is essentially flat.[46] So, in the United States, interest has declined, but not progressively, and it was lower both before and after the 1960s and 1970s and thus does not seem to explain declining political knowledge.

Still, interest may have declined disproportionately among young people. Here also the evidence is mixed, though perhaps more suggestive of a meaningful change among American youths. In a repeated nationwide survey of college freshmen, for example, the percentage saying that "keeping up with political affairs" is essential or very important hovered in the mid- to high forties even after 1978; but after 1992, it dropped rapidly, reaching into the low thirties.[47] In a number of countries in which comparisons between younger and older people could be made, most countries show no growing gap between young and old in levels of political interest.[48] In the United States, however, the gap appears to have widened.

Overall, whether the change in political interest among young people has been consistent enough and large enough to account for the decline in political knowledge is a matter of interpretation.[49] Among other things, interest can vary sharply and quickly, as it did both overall and among young adults during the presidential election contest in 2008, while knowledge levels change slowly.[50]

Even if *interest* in politics has not declined in recent decades, *attentiveness* to politics may well have dropped. Despite remaining interested, people may be getting less news about politics. This drop in attentiveness is especially apparent with respect to newspaper reading. Newspaper circulation in the United States peaked at about 35 percent of the population between 1925 and 1963. It then began a steady slide to about half that rate in recent years.[51] Percentages saying they read about election campaigns also show a decline.[52] Moreover, the decline in readership is especially concentrated among the young and has been observed in surveys gathered across multiple countries.[53] Thus, as one researcher put it, "the timing of these [cohort] changes is consistent with the proposition that a drop in newspaper reading was a significant contributor to the decline in political knowledge among young people that became clearly evident by about 1980."[54]

Of course, there could have simply been a substitution effect, with television and, more lately, other media taking the place of newspapers as a primary source of political information. In fact, this does not seem to have happened. Instead, there has been a coincidental and substantial decline in viewing the news on television, with young people again at the forefront of the decline. As with newspapers, the age gap for TV news viewing has grown from a relatively small margin between young and old in the 1960s to a much more visible gap in the 1980s and beyond.[55]

Moreover, reduced attention to television news did not coincide with the increase in viewing options brought about by the expansion of broadcast networks and then cable television. Viewing habits of people born in different eras show a cross-national pattern of steadily declining attention to TV news—a decline that extends back to those born in the 1930s (thus coming of age as early as 1950).[56] Changes in viewership options on television do not effectively account for this change.

Despite this evidence, the last word on the effects of the media revolution has not yet been written, even with respect to television. Some research, for example, suggests that "soft news" programs such as *Dateline* and *Inside Edition* to some extent make up for lack of attention to regular news programs, though it is hard to imagine that the weekly shows provide the depth, breath, and continuity of coverage of regular daily news shows.[57] Others note suggestively the appearance of presidential candidates—and now even a sitting president—on talk shows such as *The Tonight Show with Jay Leno*. At the same time, still other powerful evidence suggests that the enormous expansion of non-news programs has transformed some viewers into entertainment specialists, with negative consequences for their knowledge of political news.[58]

In the past fifteen years, people have been able to go online for news. Though careful analyses of online news viewing have only begun, it is unlikely to make up for the declines in the traditional media. Online viewing would not simply have to retain the attention of young people;

it would have to make up for their diminished attention to newspapers and television. Though youths are technologically more adept than older citizens, evidence so far does not suggest a disproportionate inclination on the part of young people to use those skills for political information-gathering. When asked in 2008 whether they got any news "online through the Internet yesterday, or not," some 31 percent of 18- to 29-year-olds said yes. But an even higher percentage of 30- to 49-year-olds said yes (36 percent), with 50- to 64-year-olds trailing only slightly behind (29%). Only those over 65 lagged seriously behind, at 13 percent.[59]

In sum, despite undiminished interest in politics, an apparent decline in attentiveness to the news over the second half of the twentieth century has probably continued into the first decade of the new century. The decline hit especially hard among young people, contributing to a larger age-related gap in political knowledge. Despite overlapping with significant technological changes in the media, it appears unlikely that the introduction of television broadcasting and then cable TV and the Internet were the main force underlying that change.

CIVIC EDUCATION

A rather different possible explanation for the decline in political knowledge—one that focuses especially on young people—is that civic education is no longer doing the job it once did. Civics teaching underwent considerable change beginning in the 1960s. Indeed, while people continue to talk about "Civics" courses as if that were the name of the relevant secondary school classes, courses by that name as well as others of the pre-1960s era (especially, "Problems of Democracy") rapidly gave way to "American Government" classes.[60] Likewise, there has been considerable discussion about changes in the content of these courses from an effort to explain and encourage citizen participation to more antiseptic descriptions of the structure of government.[61]

Whether these changes contributed to a decline in political knowledge, however, is far from certain. Based on a less-than-complete record, it appears that there was a drop in civics-type enrollments in the 1960s and 1970s and that it perhaps extended into the 1980s. The demise of civics courses per se, reductions in the number of social studies courses required for high school graduation, a rise in social studies electives such as economics and psychology, and a generally greater permissiveness about course selection all contributed to the decrease. Yet this situation turned around quickly as American government courses took hold. By 1987, 72 percent of graduating seniors had taken an American government course (up from 62 percent in 1982). By 1990, the figure stood at 77 percent, and it has hovered around that figure through the latest available reading in 2000.[62] (A much higher number of students, 97 percent, self-report having studied civics or government in high school.)[63] These percentages compare favorably with estimates of coverage in the 1920s through the 1940s, perhaps even surpassing coverage in those times. And, of course, these estimates are based on students in school, and the number of students staying in school went up dramatically over this period.

Thus, simply in terms of course taking, one cannot argue that changes in civics classes account for a post-1960s decline in political knowledge.[64] Still, there is the added fact that traditional civics classes were often taken in the ninth grade, while American government classes are most often taught in the twelfth grade. Seniors in high school might already be so jaded by their familiarity with the outside world that the material falls more frequently on deaf ears or is even met with hostility and disbelief. Moreover, though systematic evidence is nonexistent, anecdotal evidence suggests that the length of many government classes declined as well, from a full year to one semester. It is also likely that attention to social studies in the elementary grades dropped precipitously about the same time that civics courses declined in later grades.[65]

Similarly, changes in the type of civics coursework do not necessarily connect to a decline in political knowledge. Tests given to high school students tend to focus on textbook descriptions of government structures and processes. But that is precisely what American government courses are likely to emphasize. Despite some greater attention to skills of inquiry as opposed to straightforward facts in more recent NAEP civics tests, there is still a good deal of emphasis on the Constitution and Supreme Court interpretations thereof. Thus, while a declining emphasis on participation in secondary school courses indirectly might have reduced attentiveness to politics, assertions of this sort are little more than speculation.

We are left with no clear explanation for declining knowledge levels generally or among young people in particular. It may be some combination of changing interests, perverse effects of the media revolution, and unintended consequences of classroom teaching. Or, perhaps as Paul Howe speculates, it is something less tangible but at the same time more substantial, such as the "entrenchment of the adolescent state of life" and altered "transitions from youth to adulthood."[66] If the latter is true, reversing the pattern of stagnant or declining knowledge will be a tall order indeed.

INCREASING POLITICAL KNOWLEDGE

Given the complex set of causes that appears to underlie today's knowledge problem—low overall knowledge levels, no increase in knowledge despite greatly increased education, and apparent declines in youthful knowledge, at least relative to older adults—it is not surprising that multiple authors and groups have weighed in on the question of how to increase political knowledge. Proposals range from institutional changes such as shifting to a proportional representation election system, requiring and enhancing community service for young adults, transforming media output and improving political party and individual candidate communications, deliberative opinion polls, and continuing (adult) education.[67] The most frequent suggestions, however, surround civic education—often calling for more of it but also for improving the way it is carried out.[68]

Calls for changes in civic education have themselves been highly varied. Some have focused on experiential learning, including simulations, debates, and mock elections.[69] Others have pointed to the benefits of an open classroom style, while still others have touted the benefits of bringing politics into the classroom by encouraging visits from community leaders and elected officials.[70] The content of instruction has been directly addressed with frequent calls for more emphasis on teaching the realities of politics with all its controversy, conflict, and compromise.[71]

To all of these suggestions, I add my own modest proposal. It stems from a comparison of student test items, especially those in the NAEP assessment, with the kinds of knowledge questions generally asked in adult surveys. There is, in my view, a deep disjuncture between the foci of student tests and adult surveys, and therein lies an important lesson for civics teaching.

The NAEP questions, of which fifty-seven from the 2010 twelfth-grade test are publicly available, draw heavily on the National Standards for Civics and Government developed in the 1990s by the Center for Civic Education.[72] NAEP's own classification is expressed in the form of five questions, and nowhere is there any reference to contemporary politics.[73] Nevertheless, some questions do touch on topics (such as immigration) that are currently in the news, and a few others deal with political parties and interest groups. In creating my own classification, I have been generous in placing items in these two categories.

Even so, when compared with the classification of repeated adult survey items compiled by Delli Carpini and Keeter, the differences are stark.[74] As noted in table 1.2, 30 percent of the adult survey items are about public figures or political parties. Most of the former are identifications, asking about the president's cabinet members, Supreme Court justices, names of "your" senators, foreign heads of state, and so on. Questions about parties include names of nominees as well as frequently asked questions about which party has the most members in the U.S. House or Senate and which of the major parties is more conservative. All these relate to current politics. In contrast, only 7 percent of the NAEP items fall into the same category. None ask for names of current officeholders or other prominent persons. The lone question about political parties asks only for "two important functions that are performed by political parties."

Adult surveys include a relatively large proportion of questions about domestic and foreign policies, some 42 percent of all repeated questions in Delli Carpini and Keeter's compilation. Student tests contain only about half that number. Examination of individual questions suggests that the difference in focus is even greater than this comparison indicates. On the student test, the item asking for a summary of the views of Franklin D. Roosevelt and Ronald Reagan is based on quotations that are provided in the question stem; a good reader could answer the question without knowing anything about the speakers or their policies.

TABLE 1.2

Comparison of item content in student National Assessment of Educational Progress (NAEP) test and adult surveys about government and politics

Question category	2010 NAEP Civics Test	Adult surveys 1943–1992
Public figures, political parties, policies	30%	72%
Public figures, political parties	(7)	(30)
Domestic and foreign policies	(23)	(42)
Government institutions and processes	30	28
Historical developments	35	—
Misc.	5	—
Total	100%	100%

Sources: National Center for Education Statistics, U.S. Department of Education, "NAEP Questions Tool for Civics 2010," http://nces.ed.gov/nationsreportcard/ itmrlsx/search.aspx?subject=civics; Michael X. Delli Carpini and Scott Keeter, *What Americans Know About Politics and Why It Matters* (New Haven, CT: Yale University Press, 1996).

Note: The categories and classification of NAEP items are the author's. The categories and classification of adult survey items are from Delli Carpini and Keeter, *What Americans Know About Politics*, appendix 3.

The first of two questions about U.S. dependence on foreign oil is an exercise on graph reading (did the line go up or down?). The two questions about possible military action ask about conflict between "Teresia" and "Corollia." Adult items, in contrast, ask about the size of the federal budget; whether various named, real countries are democracies; which country is the largest trading partner of the United States; and so on.

Adults are often asked about government institutions and processes, including such items as how many times an individual can be elected president, what is in the Bill of Rights, and so on. Even in this category, many items on adult surveys are somewhat policy related, asking about tariffs, farm subsidies, a balanced budget, and NATO, whereas NAEP items ask more about constitutional provisions. Nevertheless, on this broad dimension, coverage is about the same for the two age groups.

The student test, finally, devotes more than a third of its items to historical developments, especially constitutional doctrines as represented in Supreme Court interpretations. This topic is virtually unrepresented in adult surveys.

My suggestion flows directly from the distribution of coverage shown in the table: increase the emphasis on public figures, parties, and policies—on contemporary politics, in other words—in civics and government classes. Recognizing that time spent on civics and government instruction is not likely to increase in the foreseeable future, space for this greater emphasis should come from that currently devoted to historical development. It is not that the latter is unimportant, but one needs to prioritize, and a greater focus on contemporary politics will result in more knowledge of the sort we value among adults than exists at present. In part, this will occur from the greater interest that will flow from the focus on the present versus the historical world.

Is this the same as suggesting that students be introduced to controversial issues and spend more time discussing them? To some extent, yes. The moment one talks about contemporary politics, controversy will arise. It is hard to imagine how one could discuss the high cost of Social Security or Medicare and steer completely clear of debate over whether and how these costs can or should be reduced. Talking about Afghanistan inevitably means talking about how long and how large the U.S. presence there should be.

Yet my point is not simply that such issues should be discussed or that there exist ways of having relatively calm and neutral discussions about them (such as assigning students to argue for one side or the other, regardless of what they personally believe).[75] More importantly, high school students should learn what issues are currently controversial, why they are controversial, what alternative proposals have been made for dealing with them, who is in favor and who is opposed to the various alternatives (including both individual and party positions), and so on. And, coincidentally, high school tests of civic and political knowledge should include questions about these topics—perhaps even as a major focus.

Knowledge of structures and formal processes is not unimportant, of course; nor should test questions about these topics be altogether eliminated from tests. Indeed, the "basic structure of government," however phrased, clearly deserves a place in the pantheon of useful, sometimes essential knowledge.[76] But it is not enough. Besides knowing how the government is supposed to operate, one needs to know about what it is actually doing—as well as about the persons who are presently in power and those who want to succeed these leaders. Governments do not operate in the abstract; people operate them. Conflicts over issues are not simply theoretical; they exist over specific, intensely felt matters. Knowing only about government structures leaves one unaware of what contemporary politics is actually about. Even authors who claim that not all citizens have to be civics experts emphasize knowledge of issues, alternatives, and individual and party support.[77] Thus, questions in adult surveys have regularly inquired about people's knowledge of contemporary leaders, parties, and policies. So, too, should students' tests—and their classes should give them the knowledge needed to do well on those tests.

Of course, contemporary politicians and politics change, so the information students would learn might become outdated relatively quickly. Can we create lessons and batteries of test items that will stand up over time? It will be difficult and perhaps even impossible in any strict sense. But the lack of strict continuity is a price we have to pay in order to focus on what ought to be the lessons of secondary school civics and government classes. And, of course, we confront this challenge all the time in creating adult surveys. Though it may be difficult, meaningful long-term lessons and comparisons can be made—even over quite long periods—as shown by the comparisons made by Delli Carpini and Keeter.

CONCLUSION

Attentiveness to politics may be one key to increasing political knowledge. A commonplace observation about voting is that it is habitual: once people get in the habit of voting, they are likely to continue.[78] Perhaps the same is true, to a degree, with following public affairs. If students get in the habit of paying attention to politics at a relatively early age (say, in eighth grade), they may continue to do so.[79] Note, however, how this is connected to my proposal about topics needing coverage.

Having an eighth-grade (or ninth- or tenth-grade) civics class is not enough. What is required is a class in which students are asked to follow what is going on in the outside world. It means asking fourteen-year-olds to pay attention to what is happening in politics, to learn some of the language used in discussing political matters, and to get a grasp of the political actors and issues involved. The hope is that students will continue to do so when the class ends. This approach requires paying more attention to the age at which young people can understand political matters. If experience shows that age fourteen is too early, one might instead try fifteen- or sixteen-year-olds.[80] But in general, earlier is better. If attentiveness to politics is truly habitual, then forming that habit at a young age should be a major priority.

2

EDUCATION FOR A CIVIL SOCIETY

Peter Levine

When Americans turn their attention to civic education, they often make the following claims: Kids today don't know anything about government and civics! Kids today don't participate! Schools today don't teach civics! Whatever happened to the civics class that I had to take when I was young? For example, when the U.S. Department of Education released its 2011 National Assessment of Educational Progress (NAEP) Civics Report Card, the *New York Times* headline read, "Failing Grades on Civics Exam Called a 'Crisis.'" The article quoted Charles N. Quigley, director of the Center for Civic Education, who said, "The results confirm an alarming and continuing trend that civics in America is in decline . . . During the past decade or so, educational policy and practice appear to have focused more and more upon developing the worker at the expense of developing the citizen."[1] The *Washington Post* editorialized, "Clearly, young people are not getting enough education in American history or civics."[2]

The urgency of this problem may seem even worse if one believes that young Americans have ceased to participate in democracy. As Catherine Rampell writes in the *New York Times*, "Generation Y—or Millennials, the Facebook Generation or whatever you want to call today's

cohort of young people—has been accused of being the laziest generation ever. They feel entitled and are coddled, disrespectful, narcissis-
tic and impatient, say authors of books like 'The Dumbest Generation'
and 'Generation Me.'"[3] Given these premises, it would be reasonable to
conclude that states should begin (or resume) requiring and testing civics for all our young people.

But all these premises are myths. First, students know quite a bit
about civics. The main evidence of a knowledge "crisis" is the observation that only 24 percent of twelfth-graders score at "proficient" on the
NAEP Civics Assessment. But the cutoffs for "basic," "proficient," and
"advanced" are essentially arbitrary, set originally by a committee of
teachers and subject-matter experts. A different committee could easily have set the standards differently and concluded that most American
students are proficient. Compared with fourteen-year-olds in a sample
of twenty-eight other countries, American students perform substantially above average, although they know less about some specific topics than do others.[4] In any case, the term *crisis* implies decline, but the
mean NAEP scores at eighth and twelfth grade have stayed flat, and the
fourth-grade scores have risen.[5]

In chapter 1, Richard Niemi assembles a strong argument that students' knowledge is inadequate. I fully share his concerns about young
Americans' weak grasp of current events and politics, and I will argue
that many young people lack the skills and experience they need to participate effectively in civil society. But current events and civic skills are
not well measured by the NAEP. In fact, a no-stakes test taken by seniors during their final semester is not a particularly reliable measure of
even the abstract and procedural knowledge that dominates the NAEP.
Many participants lack motivation to do their best on this particular
test. If, as former Treasury Secretary Larry Summers said, no one in the
history of the world has ever washed a rental car, then no one has ever
studied for the NAEP or revised an answer.

Even so, students do well on some NAEP items. For example, in
2010, 74 percent of American twelfth-graders could identify the main
ruling of *Schenck v. The United States* (1919). On the other hand, only 9
percent could (or took the trouble to) describe in their own words two
satisfactory examples of "ways that democratic society benefits from

citizens actively participating in the political process."[6] Although the NAEP provides a mix of items, its framework puts a heavy emphasis on students' understanding of constitutional issues and other abstract and perennial aspects of formal political systems.[7] On those items, students perform reasonably well, and adults would find these NAEP questions surprisingly hard. (For example, how many adults could correctly identify the constitutional basis of a search-and-seizure decision, as 72 percent of high school seniors could in 2010?)[8] In sum, the NAEP provides no evidence of declining knowledge; nor does it support the conclusion that policymakers should be requiring more attention to the Constitution and political systems.

Second, just as there is no decline in NAEP-style civic knowledge, neither is youth political participation heading downward. The voter turnout rate for ages eighteen to twenty-nine was near a record high in 2008. Turnout has not been rising in midterm years, so the trend is mixed, but there is no evidence of systematic decline when turnout is compared with the 1980s and 1990s. Volunteering, meanwhile, reached record levels in the early 2000s and remains considerably higher than it was in the 1970s.

Third, schools do teach civics. Every state has civics standards.[9] Most states require courses. Regardless of the presence or absence of course requirements, 97 percent of high school seniors reported in 2011 that they had taken classes in civics or American government.[10] Contrary to widespread reports that social studies disappeared as a result of the No Child Left Behind Act of 2001 and its emphasis on reading and mathematics, the amount of time devoted to social studies fell only in the early grades (from a low baseline) while remaining constant in middle school. In high school, the number of credits earned in social studies has substantially increased.[11] Further challenging the thesis that civics is in crisis because of cuts in time and money, the NAEP civics scores rose in fourth grade even though it was only in grades one through four that time devoted to civics was reduced.

The social studies curriculum has changed. In the mid-twentieth century, three courses were common: American Government, Civics (which emphasized the role of individuals in their own communities), and Problems of Democracy (which involved reading and discussing the news).[12] The latter two courses basically disappeared, but economics and other social sciences have become far more common. Overall, the shift is not from more social studies to less, but rather from courses about current events and citizens' roles in their communities to courses based on college-level academic disciplines. (That shift, however, is countered by the rise of *service-learning*: courses that combine hands-on community service with research and reflection learning.)[13]

Secretary of Education Arne Duncan deplores the fact that "a staggering number of Americans do not know much of the basic history and traditions of our nation."[14] He cites information that many adults fail to know—information ranging from the three branches of government to the names of today's Supreme Court justices. The structure of the federal government is included in state standards, taught in mandatory courses, and included on standardized tests. In other words, education policy is already designed to ensure that young people know the three branches of government, and 69 percent of high school seniors can correctly answer a question about *Marbury v. Madison* (relevant to relations between two of the branches).[15] The main problem is probably that adults tend not to remember such information even though they knew it when they were teenagers. On the other hand, the names of individuals who currently serve on the Supreme Court and hold other public offices are virtually never included on standardized tests. News and current events are not common areas of emphasis in social studies classes. In short, as Niemi also notes, how policymakers and educators assess policies for civic education depends essentially on what they think is most important for young people to learn.

REAL WEAKNESSES IN CIVIC EDUCATION

Instead of focusing on the three myths listed above, a discussion of civic education should begin with concerns that are based in evidence. A first serious problem is inequality of both opportunities and outcomes. Although average levels of civic knowledge are moderate and not in decline, U.S. schools permit vast gaps in both civic opportunities and civic engagement. Within a school of mixed demographics, the most socio-economically advantaged students usually dominate the opportunities for civic learning, such as the school newspaper and social studies electives. When we compare schools whose student bodies differ demographically, the ones with the most affluent families provide many more such opportunities.[16] Universal public schooling was established to create universal civic engagement, but it actually exacerbates inequality.

This gap is especially unfortunate since civic education can be a pathway to better outcomes for young people. For instance, reading texts about history and social studies seems to boost literacy as measured on standard reading tests.[17] Students who perform required service in courses are much more likely to graduate, even when the numbers are adjust for demographics.[18] In one randomized experiment, teenage girls who performed service and discussed social or political issues with their peers were half as likely to become pregnant as the control group. Participants in YouthBuild, which combines job training, preparation for the GED, and explicit civic education, are much more likely to think they will live a full life when they exit the program than when they enter it. Their own estimates of their life expectancies rise by an average of thirty-nine years over the course of a ten-month program: evidence that they have gained optimism and purpose and have seen ways to escape from violence.[19] Given these psychological and educational benefits of civic engagement, it is particularly unjust to reserve the most engaging opportunities for people who need them the least.

Finally, Americans must invest more time and effort in civic education (for all students, including relatively privileged ones) because other educative institutions have lost the capacity or will to recruit young citizens into public life. As figure 2.1 demonstrates, participation in unions, religious congregations, and neighborhood and membership organizations has shrunk dramatically. People are substantially less likely to work on community projects and to attend meetings than they were a generation ago. Newspaper readership has fallen at a similar pace, and no alternative source of reported and edited political news comes close to replacing the traditional daily newspaper.

Unions, fraternal and neighborhood associations, churches and other religious congregations, and newspapers are not primarily known for teaching the kinds of knowledge and academic skills measured on the NAEP, such as the division of powers in the U.S. Constitution. But

FIGURE 2.1

Civic participation and newspaper readership, 1975–2005

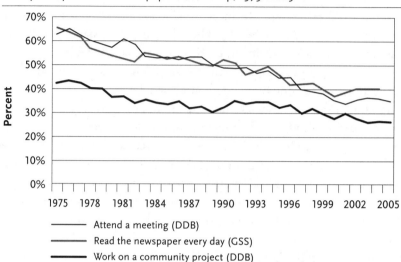

Source: Data from General Social Survey (GSS) and DDB Needham Life Style Survey (DDB). Age range of survey population is eighteen years and older. Analysis by the author.

these institutions teach the arts and habits of association that Alexis de Tocqueville thought were essential to the success of democracy in America, such as how to organize a meeting, listen to someone else's perspective, build collective will, and deal with free-riders. Elinor Ostrom, who won the 2009 Nobel Prize in Economic Sciences for her work on the organization and governance of voluntary groups, argues that civic skills must be intentionally taught to each generation because many of the most effective techniques are counterintuitive. Modest penalties for free-riders work better than draconian penalties; the most persuasive participants may be the ones who talk the least in meetings. We learn these lessons from experience. Schools must deliberately teach these concepts and provide practice in applying them, for citizens can no longer count on unions, churches, or fraternal associations to recruit and train most of the nation's youth.

It is worth recalling why participation in voluntary associations is important in any democracy. A strong civil society reduces the burdens on the state to provide public goods. It monitors and holds accountable both the state and the market. It permits groups with a diversity of norms and mores to form, so that the whole population need not agree about everything to cooperate effectively. And it enhances the political power of individuals who lack money, offices, and connections.

Civil society has characteristic norms distinct from those of families, markets, and governments. In civic associations, people are supposed to come together as rough equals to discuss matters of common or public concern. Unable to coerce, buy, or order action from their fellow citizens, they must offer reasons to which others can voluntarily assent. In the private sphere of home and family, emotional bonds and shared self-interests may (in the best cases) generate harmony. In formal systems, such as governmental bureaucracies and firms, employees are required to employ efficient means to attain ends already fixed by the purposes or leader of the organizations. But in civil society, individuals who are only loosely connected emotionally are supposed to decide collectively what ends and what means are best. Strategic rhetoric (trying to persuade someone to do what you want) is deprecated in favor of deliberative communication (trying to decide together what is best). Instrumental reasoning (calculating how to achieve a given outcome most efficiently) is supposed to be secondary to moral reasoning (deciding which outcomes to pursue).

Civil society is the venue for a host of separate conversations inside particular associations and networks. The *public sphere* forms when communications media disseminate perspectives and information from various organizations and associations to the broader public, and vice versa. The public sphere should not be dominated by firms' and governments' official representatives, who enter conversations with fixed goals set by their organizations, or by technical experts, who employ instrumental reason. Public issues always involve values as well as facts. Thus, everyone has a right to enter the public sphere by virtue of membership in the community. That is the essence of citizenship. As Pericles said in 431 BC, "Our ordinary citizens, though occupied with the pursuits of industry, are still fair judges of public matters."

Readers may recognize the philosophy of Jürgen Habermas in the previous paragraphs. Habermas emphasizes that the norms of the public sphere are regulatory ideals whose influence is always limited, because power and inequality interfere. There is no perfect public sphere, but some societies honor its norms better than others do.[20]

I endorse Habermas's normative theory with the reservation that it is excessively cognitive. Habermas understands the public sphere as basically the domain of thinking and exchanging thoughts with other people. One problem with that theory is motivational: most people are not drawn to lengthy conversations about public issues. Whether the forum is an eighteenth-century coffeehouse or a twenty-first-century political blog, participation is always a minority taste. A different problem is epistemic: we do not have very good ideas about how to address common or public issues unless we have personal experience working on these matters. The business leader who enters public debates having struggled to meet a payroll while paying taxes speaks from authentic experience. So does the soup kitchen volunteer who has faced a long line of homeless people with insufficient welfare benefits. Civil society functions best when both kinds of people (and many others) bring their experience into a common conversation and then take what they learn from discussions back to their work, in an iterative cycle. Although the business leader's perspective belongs in the conversation, society particularly needs the experience of people who have tried to manage not-for-profit and public institutions, because these organizations have distinctive goals and constraints. They are not organized to maximize efficiency but rather to *balance* efficiency with inclusiveness, equity, and deliberation. Unless many people have had direct experience working in such organizations, the public debate will lack an important set of values.

In short, the public sphere composed of voluntary associations is a venue for communication informed by work (whether paid or unpaid) and is distinct at least formally from the systems that are organized mainly by money or power. An important premise of this chapter is the poor condition of our public sphere today. As illustrated earlier in figure 2.1, the sheer frequency of participation in the traditional institutions that once formed American civil society has declined substantially. In addition, the composition of the participants has shifted: the people who continue to engage are disproportionately well educated and wealthy.

In 1952, some 15 percent of adult Americans were professionals or managers. According to the American National Election Study, they constituted about one-quarter of all the people who attended political meetings.[21] Thus they were substantially overrepresented in the nation's meetings, yet outnumbered three to one. More than 40 percent of the nation's meeting participants worked in other occupational categories—clerical, sales and service jobs, laborers, and farmers—and the rest were mostly female homemakers. They were, as Pericles would say, "occupied by industry." By 2004, however, nearly 30 percent of all adult Americans held professional or managerial jobs and represented 44 percent of the people who attended political meetings. Another 48.5 percent of meeting attendees held other jobs. Professionals now provide almost half of the participants for meetings, and much more than half in affluent communities.

Those statistics do not tell us how people talk in meetings today, but they are consistent with Habermas's thesis that civil society and the public sphere have been "colonized" by the "systems" of government and corporations that employ managers and professionals to pursue their interests. When the public sphere was predominantly composed of local voluntary associations and newspapers, civic discourse was mainly an interchange among independent citizens about what should be done. Participants brought roughly equal levels of expertise, personal experience, and values into the public sphere. Today, a substantial proportion of the individuals who enter public discussions come with instructions from the organizations that employ them—organizations that have fixed goals, such as to maximize returns for their shareholders. Another large proportion brings specialized expertise, jargon, and techniques that they can apply to public issues.

For example, community-level discussions of educational issues may be dominated today by representatives of the teachers' union and the chamber of commerce, lawyers, educational psychologists, and advocacy groups. A central topic is accountability, defined as the objective and quantifiable assessment of the impact of schools on individual children. Unions, professors of education, and reform groups may seek different measures and uses of assessment data, but all speak the same language. Meanwhile, nonexpert citizens understand accountability very differently: as a matter of the values that educators hold and the relationships that form between individual educators and parents.[22] But nonprofessionals are marginal in the public discussion about education. They may literally be outnumbered in meetings, and the ways they think and talk about education seem irrelevant to the important decisions about testing, funding, and management.

Meanwhile, in a crowded and splintered media environment, the techniques required to reach and persuade large numbers of fellow citizens are becoming increasingly sophisticated and expensive. Attending meetings may not be particularly important anymore. Instead, advocacy groups of all stripes develop short, simplified messages that test well with focus groups, and the advocates then try to disseminate these messages through the mass media or social media forums. Discourse that is open-ended and dialogic has little chance of influencing people. Instrumental reason and strategic communications prevail.

To make matters worse, most Americans have sorted themselves into relatively homogeneous communities and conversations in which a person need not engage with people who think differently. Liberals live with liberals; professionals live with professionals. Bill Bishop argues in *The Big Sort* that Americans now live in counties—and other fixed geographical jurisdictions—that are far more politically homogeneous than they were in previous generations, because we "vote with our feet."[23]

These observations about the parlous state of civil society suggest that civic education has special value today. Civic education is not just the name of a course, but refers to discussions of social issues in any school context, service-learning projects, extracurricular groups, and student government. At their best, these experiences embody the ideals of the public sphere that are being lost elsewhere, and they can teach students core skills and values to take into civil society when they graduate.

For example, despite the ideological homogeneity of many large political jurisdictions, surveys detect ideological and philosophical diversity in almost all social studies classes.[24] Good classes are places where, thanks to skillful moderation, diverse young people can learn from one another. While our political and media leaders offer shouting matches, social studies classes are places where civility can be taught and required.

For the most part, citizens' discourse about public issues is separated from action, because large public institutions fail to engage ordinary people in important work. But service-learning, extracurricular participation, and other forms of excellent civic education encourage young people to discuss and study issues and then take constructive action.

U.S. politics is largely manipulative. Politicians, interest groups, and pundits use sophisticated techniques to persuade a large audience to adopt views they have chosen. But civic education, at its best, is open-ended. Civic educators do not try to manipulate their students or neighbors into adopting opinions or solutions that they as educators think are right—at least, they shouldn't. They give young people opportunities to deliberate and reflect and then act in ways that seem best to the students themselves. In a time of increasingly sophisticated manipulative politics, these opportunities are precious.

WHAT IS TO BE DONE?

The previous sections suggest implications for what should be taught, how to teach it, and how to measure success. I now focus on those topics in turn.

Standards

The first question is what should be taught. I will use the word *standards* to refer to any official and influential list of priorities for a subject or field of education. As noted above, all states have adopted standards for the social studies. These documents have the force of law, but usually lack sanctions for failure or noncompliance. The National Council for the Social Studies provides voluntary national standards, as does the Center for Civic Education (the latter supported by the U.S. Department of Education and The Pew Charitable Trusts).[25] Many schools and school districts have policies that determine what is the most important to teach and learn.

The challenge of developing standards is not to find facts, concepts, and skills worth learning and even worth requiring students to learn. The difficulty is reducing the list of worthy topics to a manageable length to establish realistic priorities, while allowing teachers and classes to explore nonmandatory topics as well. A 2003 study by the Albert Shanker Institute found that most state social studies standards contained far more material than would be possible to cover in the amount of time allotted for social studies.[26] Most observers believe that the problem has worsened since 2003.

One can sympathize with the writers of standards, because a truly competent and mature citizen should possess a wide range of facts and concepts. Some candidates for what citizens should know or understand include the following: the Constitution; statistics; the carbon cycle; the Holocaust; the positions of powerful politicians; the chief principles of Islam; the biography of Abraham Lincoln; macroeconomics; the Atlantic slave trade; accounting principles; the geography of Afghanistan; the contents of the recent health-care reform; the major components of the federal, state, and local budgets; evolutionary biology; the tenets of classical liberalism and civic republicanism; Spanish; the causes of AIDS; the rudiments of criminal procedure; influential interest groups and what they stand for; the mechanics of voting; the economic theories of Keynes versus Hayek; *Brown v. Board of Education*; how a bill becomes a law; the King James Version; citizens' rights; the global poverty rate (half the world's population lives on less than two dollars per day); *Letter from Birmingham Jail*; and how to moderate a meeting.

If Americans' chief concern is to encourage young people to participate in civil society and the public sphere (with its distinctive norms), then certain of these topics emerge as priorities. For example, anyone active in civil society should understand that the First Amendment protects freedom of association, assembly, and speech. To comprehend the First Amendment implies an understanding of the Constitution and the idea of judicial review.

Meanwhile, various other bodies of knowledge are relevant to associational life and are worthy of study. For example, religious congregations play a substantial role in American civil society, and each congregation is guided by its own denomination's doctrines and founders. Thus a mature, sensitive, and effective participant in American civil society would do well to study the religious views of people like Augustine, Mohammed, Luther, Calvin, Loyola, Wesley, and Gandhi. To mention another example, anyone who acts as a steward of a physical building or an urban neighborhood should be aware of its architectural styles, where they originated, what they signify, and why they might be valuable to preserve. These topics go beyond even the extensive list offered above, because they are not conventionally seen as part of civics or social studies. In a sense, all liberal education is education for citizenship.

On the other hand, much about politics and the Constitution is not especially relevant to participation in civil society. One could play a constructive leadership role in civic associations without knowing that the U.S. Congress has two houses and without recognizing James Madison's role as an author of the Constitution. I do not mean that these are trivial topics. As someone who has taught Madison at the graduate level and has written NAEP items about the separation of powers, I am proud that I have some grasp of these matters. A highly educated adult should be informed about them. Standards for civic education, however, don't need to include voluminous facts about the Constitution and American political history. Turning standards into long lists can lead to micromanaging teachers, favoring breadth over depth, and even trivializing important topics. As Paul Gagnon wrote in his study of state standards, "the most common failure is not deciding on priorities." History and social studies offer "mountains of content," he writes, because "rather than battle over what to put in and leave out, writers [of state standards] put in everything, either in the form of endless specifics or vast headings that could 'cover' any and all unnamed essentials."[27]

I would favor reforming the existing standards in the social studies, which generally focus on the U.S. Constitution and perennial issues in political philosophy, such as classical republicanism versus liberalism. These are, for example, the major topics assessed by the NAEP. I would shorten these lists, using *relevance to civil society* as the main criterion of inclusion. Diverse people will then bring different and complementary knowledge to bear in a thriving civil society. Not everyone need understand James Madison, Victorian gothic architecture, or Catholicism, as long as some people do and the venues for discussion and collective action function well. The chief purpose of civic education is to prepare people to strengthen those venues, which are civic associations, networks, and media of communication.

Pedagogy

Once policymakers, educators, and citizens know what students should learn, they must decide how to teach it. I argued above that the purpose of civic education is to prepare students for participation in civil society. That is not necessarily a popular position; a recent survey found that most American citizens want schools to teach facts about history and government, not to promote civic values or behaviors (although most social studies teachers have the opposite priorities).[28] The idea that education should promote civic participation is, however, a traditional one, with roots in the thought of Jefferson, Tocqueville, John Stewart Mill, Horace Mann, John Dewey, and other classic thinkers. In 1915, the U.S. Bureau of Education formally endorsed a movement for "community civics" that was by then quite widespread. Its aim was "to help the child know his community—not merely a lot about it, but the meaning of community life, what it does for him and how it does it, what the community has a right to expect from him, and how he may fulfill his obligations, meanwhile cultivating in him the essential qualities and habits of good citizenship."[29] This was the era in which social studies classes, student governments and newspapers, and service clubs were widely introduced.

Dewey and many of his followers have asserted that to learn active citizenship, one must *be* an active citizen: civic education must be experiential.[30] A strong manifesto for the Deweyan approach to education is the 2011 Action Civics Declaration, which recommends "an authentic, experiential approach in which students address problems through real-world experiences that apply to their lives, can be a powerful motivating experience setting them on a path towards lifelong civic and political engagement. In practice, Action Civics is an iterative process typically comprised of issue identification, research, constituency building, action, and reflection."[31]

Recent research finds that experiential civic education works: it leads to significant changes in what students know and do. For example, moderated discussions of current events in school increase students' interest in politics and their political and civic knowledge.[32] A norm of civic participation by students within a high school boosts both voting and volunteering fifteen years later.[33] Service-learning of high quality has a positive impact on students' civic knowledge, skills, dispositions, and engagement.[34] Participation in extracurricular activities has been found to predict civic actions such as voting.[35] It also predicts participation in civil society even decades later.[36]

These experiences of real—but guided—civic engagement may or may not work better than alternatives, such as reading about exemplary citizens or listening to lectures about civil society. It is not a logical truth that education *for* democracy must *be* democratic. How best to teach active engagement is an empirical question, and the answer probably varies, depending on the age, interests, and backgrounds of the students and the nature of the teacher, school, and community. There is a need for research on the effects of a wide variety of pedagogies. Also needed is research that investigates outcomes more central to civil society: not only voting but also skills for effective participation in voluntary groups.

On the other hand, there is evidence that experiential civic education is effective. Most people probably learn and retain skills of active citizenship best from practice. And honoring young people's moral status as active citizens seems the right thing to do, unless it should prove actually damaging to their education. On those grounds, I endorse experiential civic education, including both extracurricular activities and project-oriented work in classrooms.

Assessment

Once society has decided what to teach and how to teach it, a third issue is how to know whether schools have succeeded. Assessments are tools for influencing policy, curricula, and instruction; they also create incentives for teachers and students.

When teachers assess their own students' skills, knowledge, and values in civics, they use a wide range of methods and data, including oral presentations and debates, group projects, journals, and lengthy reports as well as written tests. But the only civics assessments currently required by state laws are standardized pencil-and-paper tests. The federal government requires no civics exams, but funds and manages the NAEP, which is also a written instrument.

Standardized tests have the advantage of being relatively valid and reliable. In particular, they are reasonably invulnerable to bias by teachers, who might want their own students to pass even if the children are not qualified. But these instruments have particular limitations for civic education, which is defined as education for civil society.

First, because the tests are standardized instruments, all their questions must be equally relevant for very large numbers of students in numerous communities. Thus, the content is limited to broad, perennial topics or hypothetical cases. A student gets no benefit from having learned a lot about his or her particular community.

Second, because the tests are standardized, they take years to develop. The NAEP, for example, has a three-year development cycle. Thus, even if the test designers wanted to include current events, they could not predict which events would be current when the test was fielded. Instead, the content is limited to distant historical examples and timeless issues. A student gets no benefit from knowing what is going on currently.

Third, because they are written tests in conventional formats, they are strictly measures of individuals' knowledge and certain kinds of individual skills, such as interpreting a written speech, a law, or a cartoon. They are not measures of how people work in groups, persuade others, or otherwise interact. A student gets no benefit from being good at problem solving with others. The test taker is not even permitted to look at a neighbor's paper, let alone collaborate.

Finally, because the state-mandated tests are used to award grades and credits, they cannot assess values. If students were asked, for example, whether they believe voting is a duty, the results could not be used to award grades without involving the state in the oversight of personal beliefs. Besides, students could knowingly give false answers to pass. The NAEP, having no stakes for students, could ask respondents about their values, but Congress has deemed that it may not do so. If teaching civic values is a purpose of civic education, then standardized tests are not a means to evaluate success or to create incentives for good teaching and learning.

Some students do not face consequential tests in civics. The education system probably sends them and their teachers the message that civics has lower importance than the subjects that are tested. A survey of administrators found that most believed their own districts had reduced attention to social studies and civics because of greater testing pressure in other fields.[37] Secretary Duncan cited this finding as troubling evidence of a narrowed curriculum.[38]

In some states and districts, however, students are required to pass standardized, pencil-and-paper civics exams. Those instruments are heavily tilted toward factual information and academic skills related to American history and constitutional law, with almost no items about current events, values, strategies for social change, or local issues. To the extent that such tests influence curricula and pedagogy, they presumably encourage teachers to focus on historical and constitutional facts rather than discussions of current issues or group projects.

If the only option for a civics assessment is a standardized, written test, then policymakers face a dilemma. Doing without tests means marginalizing civics, but adding an exam may drive the curriculum toward facts and abstract concepts. Fortunately, assessment may be on the verge of breakthroughs. Multiplayer computer games and computer-based simulations allow students to work together in complex, fictional scenarios. In the simulations that David Williamson Shaffer calls "epistemic games," students play the roles of adult professionals.[39] For example, an epistemic game that colleagues and I tested in Tampa schools allowed students to play the roles of legislative aides to a fictional U.S. congresswoman in their real district.[40] InterroBang, a game produced by Nuvana, allows young people to undertake service "missions" in their communities, and iCivics, an organization founded by Justice Sandra Day O'Connor, provides a whole suite of games in which students role-play such characters as attorneys arguing before the Supreme Court. The purpose of all these games is educational: to teach knowledge and skills. But games can also be used for assessment; in fact, assessment can be built into game play and not treated as an extra, time-consuming task. A game can capture data about an individual's contribution to the collective effort and thereby assign appropriate scores to each player. Because all the civic games mentioned so far require considerable amounts of persuasive and analytic writing, they could serve as assessments of literacy as well as civics.

Nuvana and the international educational organization called Global Kids are awarding badges to students who complete specified projects to a satisfactory standard. The use of badges represents a bold, alternative approach to assessment and has caught the attention of the MacArthur Foundation, the Mozilla Foundation, and senior federal officials.[41] Awarding badges provides an incentive for students to learn the specified skill without creating a different way for them to fail. It allows various institutions, not just schools, to develop and award credentials. And it disaggregates high school and college diplomas, allowing individuals to demonstrate particular skills that have value in civil society or in the workforce. Badging holds special promise for civics because the applied aspects of civics are not well measured by traditional assessments; because graduation requirements rarely encompass civic knowledge and skills; and because organizations outside of schools and colleges could also offer the badges. (As Michael Johanek argues in chapter 3, civic education is a community function, not just the province of schools.) For example, students could earn badges for knowing how to chair a meeting, for understanding the Bill of Rights, or for making an accurate map of their community.

Badges can be connected to portfolios: archives of individual students' work that they can share with prospective employees, college admissions officers, or civic leaders. If students were encouraged to build online civic portfolios, the young people might display their own badges along with essays, audio and video files, testimonials from community leaders, and other qualitative evidence of their achievements.

Finally, students are beginning to provide data about how their schools educate them. Consider, for example, the "Constructive Feedback Forms" that all Boston high school students complete for each teacher each semester. These carefully constructed surveys do not ask the students to rate their teachers subjectively. Instead, they ask a series of specific questions about teaching practices. How soon after the bell does the class get down to work? How many students participate in discussions? In what ways does the teacher provide feedback on home-work? The purpose of the Boston assessment is not primarily to evaluate *civic* education, but similar efforts could focus on whether students have opportunities to discuss current events, whether diverse perspectives are expressed in class, and whether students are required to cite verifiable information in making arguments.[42]

Evaluating inputs (such as whether students discuss current events in class) has a limitation: such experiences might be provided and yet might not teach the students anything. Hence education policymakers have generally shifted to outcome assessments. However, adding new outcome assessments for civics is problematic for the reasons summarized above, whereas new input assessments might at least give educators and parents feedback on how well schools are educating for citizenship. Such assessments could be especially helpful in conjunction with badges, portfolios, and games or simulations that assess achievement.

Perhaps the most important point is that all these approaches to evaluation are relatively new and undeveloped. Instead of repeating the stale debates about civics tests (pro or con), the education community should be looking for opportunities to develop entirely new methods. Then civics would not be a subject late and reluctant to join the testing wave, but would instead be a source of innovative practices for education as a whole.

CONCLUSION

Civic education should help to strengthen and sustain a civil society in which young people participate as citizens and learn the skills, knowledge, and values they need in the broader public sphere dominated by adults. I have criticized the leading policy reform proposal—require and test civics—because it is basically already in place but tends to push civic education toward content, pedagogy, and assessments that are *not* especially valuable for civil society. It produces young people who know a fair amount about the three branches of government, but who do not know how to run a meeting.

No alternative reform, by itself, can guarantee adequate and fair civic education in American schools. What students experience is affected by a whole range of factors, including academic requirements, opportunities, standards, evaluations, curricula, textbooks and other materials, local civic associations, and teachers' education and certification for civics. My colleagues and I investigated the impact of extant state laws and policies on one hundred thousand students surveyed by the Knight Foundation. We found no statistically significant effects at all.[43] This does not mean that state laws cannot enhance civic knowledge and engagement. But quality is essential: the requirement of a course and test is less important than their effectiveness. Each input must be well designed, thoughtful, ideologically balanced, mutually consistent, developmentally appropriate, and broadly and equitably implemented in all of the diverse and largely self-governing school systems in the United States.

In that case, reforming civics is a marathon, not a sprint. It cannot be solved with a single intervention but requires constant attention to the quality of the curriculum, pedagogy, teacher preparation, and assessment. Rather than expect any state or national reform to solve the civic education problem, Americans should change the way that the government continuously addresses civics. At the federal level, an important step would be to move civic education from a suboffice within the Department of Education's Office of Safe and Drug-Free Schools to a prominent new office with an empowered director who could also convene representatives from other federal agencies that are involved with civic learning: the Corporation for National and Community Service, the Corporation for Public Broadcasting, the National Park Service, and others. States and districts should similarly make civic learning a more important priority and should charge the people responsible for it to think of themselves as the stewards of America's future civil society.

3

PREPARING PLURIBUS FOR UNUM

Historical Perspectives on Civic Education

Michael C. Johanek

Earthworms and caterpillars and ants and bees and wild horses and primitives do not rationalize the advantages of aggregation, but they utilize them, though they say little.

—Charles Merriam, *The Making of Citizens: A Comparative Study of Methods of Civic Training*

The true starting point of history is always some present situation with its problems.

—John Dewey, *Democracy and Education*

We begin with an alleged problem—a "civics recession." There are troubling levels of disengagement in the polis, limited civic knowledge, poor civic dispositions, and a dysfunctional political landscape just at a time of pressing national challenges. With such urgent concerns tweeting all around Americans, why turn to the nation's history, beyond a polite nod as filler for policy report introductions?[1]

History expands people's present imagination for solutions, taking into account the distinctive perspectives of those who faced related challenges in far different worlds. For example, many argue today that U.S. educational policies overly emphasize narrow academic outcomes, to the detriment of civic and cultural goals. Yet all sides generally agree that the publicly financed school should essentially function as an educational service provider to its attending students. The school's relationship to its wider community comes into play only to the degree that the community advances the school's delivery of educational services. Even in the matter of civic education, the job of schools is to develop the civic skills, knowledge, and dispositions of its students. Period. Yet many of our forebears would find this a peculiarly private twist indeed when discussing the public's schools, and especially so considering how Americans support and develop their roles as citizens and build the public square. For, of course, we Americans educate ourselves to be citizens through a great many means—family, community agencies, media, religious organizations, and so on. Many in the past, though, have presumed for the public school, as perhaps the most democratic tool in the collective kit, a rather assertive role on behalf of the republic and in coordination with these other, largely private civic educators. Across the past and continuing today, many citizens have creatively crafted a mix of school and nonschool organizations to advance common civic education goals.

Our colleagues in the past wrestled with distinctive civic roles for the public school as they wrestled also with fundamental questions underlying civic education, including the meaning of citizenship, the skills and knowledge required of citizens, and the desired level of their civic engagement.[2] We turn briefly to those questions below, simply to frame them. As schools struggled with both ends and means, the expectations for schools, amid the mix of civic institutions, shifted and emerged, as they still do.[3] Finally, with a vigilant eye to the lures of presentism, we examine three cases where schools took on particularly active roles as civic agents within their communities.

BUILDING "REPUBLICAN MACHINES" IN SCHOOLS

The chief end is to make GOOD CITIZENS. Not to make precocious scholars . . . not to impart the secret of acquiring wealth . . . not to qualify directly for professional success . . . but simply to make good citizens.

—Superintendent of Public Instruction, Illinois, 1862

For a long time all boys were trained to be President. Then for a while we trained them all to be professional men. Now we are training boys to get jobs.

—School Board President, Muncie, Indiana, 1929

Raising upright and responsible youth has always challenged adults, including men and women during the early days of the American colonies.[4] Imagine the early European settlers making their way in a strange new land, a world in which they sought, often in vain, to preserve prior patterns of family life, community structures and organizations, and, in particular, the education of their young. Long an understood process of extended family and close community, prior practices of child-rearing broke down as settlers adjusted to a new land, new neighbors, and a new economy. "The jarring multiplicity, the raw economy, and the barren environment of America," claims historian Bernard Bailyn, dramatically upended education in the colonies from its "half-instinctive workings of a homogeneous, integrated society," transforming "the whole enterprise" into something "controversial, conscious, constructed: a matter of decision, will and effort."[5] Slowly the school would take on a more explicit role as a supplementary institution to family and community and, in the process, take on questions of what that larger community meant to become and what shared values it sought for its young. As small communities became colonies and colonies formed a new republic, what role would the school play—should it play—in forming citizens of this new collective entity? For physician and founder Benjamin Rush, it was clear: the school should "convert men into republican machines," fitting them "to each other by means of education" so that, as well-crafted civic gears, they could "perform their parts properly . . .

to produce regularity and unison in government."[6] At least since that point, Americans have fiercely contested what the role of school should be in civic education; the debate has been shaped by their disagreements over the meaning of citizenship, the skills and knowledge of citizens, and the desired level of civic engagement.

What do we mean by *U.S. citizen*, and to whom does it apply? This has been a moving target for whatever institution would prepare citizens. American founding documents dodged the issue, as the contents of citizenship—what it means, who is included, and at what governance level—remained undefined in the new republic's constitution. Expansion to the present understanding took the greater part of U.S. national existence; most people in the world would have been ineligible for full citizenship for 80 percent of U.S. history, owing to national origins, gender, or race. For most of the nation's existence, most U.S. adults have not enjoyed full citizenship.[7] Further, as political scientist Rogers Smith argues, "pervasive . . . forms of civic hierarchy," informal understandings ordering public interactions in the United States, have plagued the republic.[8] Even among full citizens, of course, conflicts arose as Americans, a "difficult people," sought to maximize conflicting values of civic virtue and personal liberty among citizens. "Americans want both," Amy Gutmann contends, "although some people seem willing to settle for freedom for themselves and civic virtue for others."[9] Schools' efforts in civic education often became the hot putty of public debate and conflict over who and what society understood to be full citizens.

Even with some shared understanding of the term *citizen*, what should citizens know and be able to do? School curricula, formal and informal, often reflected these evolving controversies, especially during the Progressive Era, a key period for civic education.[10] A new phenomenon, the social studies, arose as a critical curricular home for many of these debates about the content of citizenship preparation. In the late nineteenth and early twentieth century, various social science disciplines began to organize themselves, and full citizenship expanded for many (e.g., less propertied males) while it remained restricted for others (e.g., women, African Americans). At the same time, the challenges of industrialization, urbanization, and immigration pressed themselves upon rapidly growing public schools, while educators developed the social studies as a central curricular remedy.[11] The new curricula would reflect the emerging social sciences (economics, sociology, etc.) as it attempted to address the pressing social problems of a rapidly industrializing nation. The resulting tensions and trade-offs were evident in a series of national reports—especially the National Education Association's (NEA) Committee of Ten (1892), the American Historical Association's Committee of Seven (1884), and the NEA's Committee on Social Studies (1916).[12] What was the content of study most needed by the republic in this new era? By its citizens? For children as they prepared to take on adult citizen roles, at least for those who would? Who would decide? Was there a fixed civics content arising from the disciplines, or should the day's problems dictate curriculum? Or as one contemporary civics educator asked, to what degree should school reflect "inquiry suited to problems arising from states of mind and inquiry suited to problems arising from states of affairs"?[13] Two new civics courses—Problems of Democracy and Community Civics—illustrate some of the trade-offs involved in answering these questions through curricular changes.

The NEA's 1916 report produced a signature new civics course for the third or fourth year of high school, Problems of Democracy, an effort to integrate history and the newer social sciences in understanding contemporary societal challenges. The NEA commission argued for reorganizing instruction "not on the basis of the formal social sciences but on the basis of concrete problems of vital importance to society and of immediate interest to the pupil."[14] Persisting for most of the twentieth century and remembered fondly by some, the course also came under critique as superficial, "denatured by external forces," or un–American in its emphasis on national weaknesses.[15] Some saw it as building a more relevant curriculum; others saw a dangerous flight from core disciplinary content. The reality in the classroom may have been more prosaic in its civic and academic impact, as a high school teacher in East Orange, New Jersey, shared in 1930:

> At first, bigotry and prejudice will crop out in the discussions. The pupils will repeat parrot-like the information secured from the textbook. Conclusions obvious to the teacher will at times wholly escape the

class. Only about 20 per cent of the pupils will really try to reason things out for themselves; the others will look around for a leader whom they can follow. A few will do most of the talking and say little. However, as the weeks go by, these difficulties will be less and less in evidence. The teacher will occasionally be startled by the maturity of thought of some of the pupils.[16]

During the same period, a community civics approach became popular in the elementary years, eventually endorsed by the NEA, the U.S. Bureau of Education, and the American Political Science Association.[17] Part of an effort by newly professionalizing educators to move beyond passive pedagogies and an emphasis on the machinery of government, the courses were organized instead around "community welfare," including health, civic beauty, recreation, and communication. Children, without suffrage, would become good citizens through "proper social deportment," learning "habits of cleanliness, neatness, obedience, regard for others . . . self-control, honesty, truthfulness, kindness and fair play . . . modesty, promptness, cooperation, punctuality, thrift, industry and accuracy."[18] Citizenship broadened beyond political participation and collective activism, now encompassing correct human relations and neighborliness. "Upright behavior," claims historian Julie Reuben, "not political participation, became the defining mark of a good citizen."[19] Further, given the complexity of social issues, community civics courses emphasized the need for expert-guided collective action and, in particular, deferent cooperation with the needed government programs of a more activist state in the early twentieth century. Did this effort for greater relevance in young student lives train youth in a domesticated notion of citizenry just as the parent state grew in stature? In sum, while "the new community civics course was designed as a radical departure from earlier forms of citizenship education . . . [t]he most striking change was its new political philosophy inherent in its apolitical definition of citizenship . . . Despite their desire to prepare students for their political responsibilities, the educators who designed civics programs could not envision both an active citizenry and a strong, active state."[20]

Even if we presume a shared understanding of citizenship and the school curriculum to support its development, what level of engagement do Americans seek in adults in the exercise of their citizenship? What should schools do accordingly? The range of engagement is shown in table 3.1.[21]

Leaning toward one end of the spectrum, many schools simply addressed the transmission of basic civic content, operating as an educational service center for their client students and neighborhood adults, with a sprinkle of community activities that might qualify vaguely as civic, or at least social. Civics was part of the course of study, citizen preparation classes were occasionally included for adults, and the neighborhood used the school facility for community events, including occasional civic ones like voting. On a continuum with personally responsible good neighbors on one end and actively engaged, "public work" citizens on the other, U.S. schools have tended to the former over the last century.[22]

Yet equally evident in U.S. history have been persistent efforts to position the school as a civic agent beyond the classroom walls, with schools playing diverse roles as public-work civic educators within their wider communities. Three historical cases below describe instances of

TABLE 3.1

What do we mean by *citizen?* A continuum

Personally responsible citizen	Participatory citizen	Public work citizen
Helping citizen who obeys laws and performs individual acts that demonstrate social responsibility, kindness, and compassion	*Corporate citizen* who participates in collective action to address a need or alleviate a crisis—action that typically involves a self-selected "little public," i.e., one that is collectively not equivalent to the larger public in its range of interests and perspectives	*Public-building citizen* who engages with members of diverse groups constituting a non–self-selected "larger public" to address and resolve a problem by dealing with underlying causes—a resolution that requires the cooperation and resources of all groups with a vested interest in the problem
Volunteers in a homeless shelter	Helps organize a clothing drive on behalf of the shelter	Engages with members of diverse groups to address and resolve the problem of access to quality housing in a community

this more civically engaged institutional role for schools, drawing from twentieth-century experiences in Rochester, New York; rural West Virginia; and East Harlem, New York City. In the present U.S. civics recession, revisiting prior investments in the full range of school roles may assist in growing people's present imagination.[23]

PUBLIC SCHOOL AS CIVIC AGENT: THREE CASES

Last century, particularly during the early Progressive Era through World War II, the United States dramatically expanded its investment in school facilities. As a result, many educators and advocates endorsed a wider use of schools, positing them as efficient and convenient centers of community life.[24] Often, this had little to do with civic engagement; the advocates justified schools as community centers to use efficiently the hard-won public funds during a period of dramatically growing enrollments. Health care, recreation, and other community needs could be productively met by tapping existing public school facilities. As early as 1897, Superintendent Aaron Gove of Denver, Colorado, asked, "Is it not reasonable and proper so to construct a schoolhouse, and with very little increased cost, as to afford to the people who pay for it, a literary home, an educational center for adults, including library where possible?"[25]

Yet across a several century span, U.S. history also features significant examples of schools' acting more aggressively to *develop* local civic life. Such work—including research, intergroup relations, community development, and public advocacy—was integral to the school's role as the public's educational utility, a means for enhancing the school's principal mission of the education of youth. Civic education was understood to encompass the school's role as an *actor* within neighborhood life, indeed, as the "common gathering place, the head-and-heart quarters" of the community.

Progressive reformers saw schools as centers for cultivating a common democratic life, facilitating political participation, and developing the common civic ties so strained by the advances of urbanization, immigration, and industrialization. These proponents often drew upon the settlement movements in England (e.g., Toynbee Hall) and the

United States (e.g., Hull House) and sought both solidarity and service in addressing social challenges. John Dewey, influenced by Jane Addams and others, translated this strategy in proposing how public schools could advance democratic development more broadly. In his address to the National Council of Education in 1902, "The School As Social Centre," Dewey argued that the school must shift from being "a place of instruction for children" to "a centre of life for all ages and classes," an evolution "born of our entire democratic movement."[26] Just as concerns for our common life generated a call for enhanced civics instruction in classrooms, claimed Dewey, the "rapidly changing environment" of that time required that the school "interpret to [the individual] the intellectual and social meaning of the work in which he is engaged . . . It must make up to him in part for the decay of dogmatic and fixed methods of social discipline . . . supply him compensation for the loss of reverence and the influence of authority. And . . . provide means for bringing people and their ideas and beliefs together, in such ways as will lessen friction and instability, and introduce deeper sympathy and wider understanding."[27] Schools, claimed reformers, comprised part of the "machinery" of democracy, often speaking of the need to engineer civic participation institutionally, as both means and motivation of civic education.

Rochester Schools As Social Centers

One grassroots progressive, for example, inspired by Dewey's social center vision, sought to "connect the primary bonds of familial association to the entire neighborhood through the local schools" in Rochester, New York.[28] Edward J. Ward, local minister and community activist, helped develop self-governing adult centers and civic clubs that were notable for active political discussion and exchange.[29] Growing from a handful of centers in 1907, eighteen centers operated by 1910 for "the discussion and understanding of civic questions and the development of a good community spirit."[30] Governor Charles Hughes praised them for "buttressing the foundations of democracy," as the civic clubs bridged across Rochester's many political, social, and ethnic groups, tapping women's clubs, settlement workers, trade unionists, socialists, and even the Daughters of the American Revolution.[31] Elites met their humbler neighbors in a public square; a Polish washwoman joined the president of the Women's Christian Temperance Union to debate a college professor and a house cleaner. The centers were locally organized by club participants, and observers noted a flurry of bottom-up civic participation at school sites.[32]

Noting broadly the "urgent calls" for "citizenship organization" and the "imperative necessity of vitalizing the common bond of civic obligation," Ward argued on civic and pedagogical grounds for "making the schoolhouse the headquarters of the district voting body, self-organized into a deliberative body, and then the center of such community expression as the neighboring citizens may desire to focus there." The "average man," claimed Ward, still bowed to authority and understood political authority as "above" him. Ask him to name the headquarters of his government, and he will point to the state or national capital; his relation to the national entity is one still of "filial subordination" in a paternalistic hierarchical system "quite contrary to the democratic idea."[33]

To help citizens develop from a "unity of a family," with citizens as the fatherland's children, to a "unity of fellowship" among equals required thinking through the mechanics of how this happens in daily life. This practice goes back to the nation's founding, claimed Ward: "The colonies did not just try to like each other; they established a social center, wherein it would be possible to get together on common ground, to disagree agreeably under rules which guaranteed each an opportunity to be heard." The school, argued reformers, is democracy's social center for the wider community. In addition to its convenience and economy, no other building could "gather about itself the significance of common obligation for the future which is embodied in the schoolhouse." Simply moving the voting booths to the school advanced the schools' central mission of training citizens, as this would provide a concrete example to children. Since "the great difficulty is in the visualizing of the business of democracy," bringing in voting booths, as well as community forums and local decision-making, would enhance the "meaning, dignity and significance" of school to students.[34]

Further, the school as a civic center would allow occasional participation by citizens in actual governance, both organizing the public

interest in the face of well-organized private interests and elevating individuals locked in daily grinds of economic survival. Citing J. S. Mill,
Ward argued that only through actual participation, when an individual
was forced to "weigh interest not his own," will "the private citizen . . .
feel himself one of the public." Ward continued:

> Where this school of public spirit does not exist scarcely any sense is
> entertained that private persons . . . owe any duties to society, except
> to obey the laws and submit to the government . . . The man never
> thinks of any collective interests, of any objects to be purchased jointly
> with others, but only in competition with them, and in some measure at
> their expense. A neighbor not being an ally or any associate, since he is
> never engaged in any common undertaking for joint benefit, is, there-
> fore, only a rival. Thus, even private morality suffers, while public is
> actually extinct.[35]

In the end, schools as social centers advanced the core mission of educating children, facilitating the meeting of parents and teachers, supplementing resources from the community, opening up project work
options, and so on. Most critically for civic education, says Ward, the
"magnified school" moves past "so-called instruction . . . devoted to
the mouthing of mere form of civic existence. Vital instruction in the
civic virtues means contact with the real pulsating civic life." In other
words, "the citizenship of the future must be trained in the civic forums
of to-day. And the civic forum contemplated in the organization of the
social center gives more promise of contributing virility and strength to
civic education than any effort has sought to bulwark political institutions since the days when the Athenian boy became a Greek through
vitalizing contact with the life of his elders and the Roman boy was educated with and by Roman citizens."[36]

The history of the social-center movement also testifies to the bare-
knuckled local battles often contesting the view of schools as fraternal centers of civic development. Existing political interests resisted the
assertion of a more participatory democratic life. Even putting voting
booths in schools aroused opposition. In New York City, despite an
appeal by three national parties, a member of the Board of Education

opposed a proposal to use schools "as polling places and as common pre-election meeting places," since "schoolhouses were built for education, and they'll not be used for politics." A senior board colleague agreed that "schoolhouses were built for education—and *politics is education*, and the appropriate place for political expression is, therefore, the schoolhouse."[37] Yet Ward lost the battle in Rochester. Precisely at their peak enrollments in 1910, the centers generated stiff opposition from several local interests that were apparently threatened by the outpouring of participation by some fifteen hundred members of the Citywide Federation of Civic Clubs and several years of dramatic growth. After resistance from members of the business community, newspapers, local political "boss" George Aldridge and others, City Hall suddenly slashed budgets and sent Ward packing. Soon the centers fell into line with other social centers across the nation, which "increasingly emphasized recreational programs to the virtual exclusion of adult civic participation."[38] The civic education function of the Rochester public schools withdrew into narrower bounds, though Ward continued his efforts from the University of Wisconsin, eventually gaining recognition from national figures like William Howard Taft, Woodrow Wilson, and Theodore Roosevelt, along with the NEA.[39]

Seeding Social Capital in West Virginia

As Ward moved out to Wisconsin, West Virginian educational leaders embarked upon a wave of school improvement efforts under a new state superintendent, M. P. Shawkey. In the process, they developed the school's role as a civic agent within declining rural communities.

Inspired by wider reform trends in the 1910s, West Virginia worked to consolidate rural schools, improve sanitation, enforce a state curriculum, organize schools into grades, and reduce teacher turnover. In a series of efforts foreshadowing more recent initiatives, Shawkey also established uniform student report cards, instituted a standard "School Efficiency Report Card" for all schools (figure 3.1), published annual county test scores side-by-side in all basic subjects (figure 3.2), and increased supervision of schools from district and state levels.[40]

FIGURE 3.1

"School Efficiency Report Card" established by Superintendent M. P. Shawkey for West Virginia schools in the 1910s

Rural and Graded School Score Card.

(Scoring to be done by visiting supt.)

Scale of points TEACHER AND PUPILS.	Possible Score
I. Grounds (16 points).	
1. Yard, playgrounds and outbuildings clean......	8
2. Cinder, stone or board walks....	4
3. Trees and shrubbery well kept...	4
II. Condition of Room (16 points).	
1. Floor and walls clean.........	6
2. Windows clean and used for ventilation	3
3. All furniture and apparatus clean	3
4. Room decorated with approved pictures and flags...........	4
III. Signs of a good school at work (68 pts.).	
1. Drinking cup law enforced.......	3
2. Library of at least 50 volumes well kept and well used........	5
3. School graded according to State Manual	10
4. Teacher pursuing State Reading Circle Course..........	5
5. Social Center Meetings held at least once a month..........	5
6. Approved methods of teaching...	12
7. Attendance 85 per cent. or over based on enrollment..........	10
8. Order and courtesy among pupils	8
9. Keen interest in play manifested	5
10. Accurate records and reports....	5
Total 100	

Boards and Trustees	Score
1. Grounds of at least ½ acre fenced	8
2. Two separate outbuildings at least 30 ft. apart.........	6
3. House ceiled or plastered and painted	8
4. Floors tight and roof without leaks	8
5. Cloak rooms............	6
6. Windows whole, with none in front of pupils.........	6
7. Window shades furnished........	4
8. Good water supply and water jar or cooler.........	10
9. Patent desks of right sizes including teacher's desk and chair..	10
10. Slate, woodpulp or combination blackboard, at least 60 sq. ft. of surface	8
11. Improved heater or jacketed stove	6
12. Dictionary, wall maps, globes, charts and other appliances necessary	8
13. Satisfactory janitor service......	6
14. Good, close-fitting doors with locks and keys............	6
Total 100	

Source: Used with permission from the West Virginia State Archives.

In 1908, most West Virginia students still attended rural schools, and rural communities were under considerable duress. President Theodore Roosevelt appointed the blue-ribbon Commission of Country Life to "seriously . . . consider the problems of farm life."[41] The relative role of farming in the economy was declining, and farmers' income did not seem to rise relative to many urban professions. Perhaps most visibly, the countryside was losing population to the cities, whether lured by their glittering attractions or pushed by poor rural conditions or both. As the nation expanded, the percentage employed in farming dropped precipitously, from roughly half in 1870 to under a quarter in the 1920s.[42] As rural sociologist E. A. Ross worried, states like Michigan and Illinois were turning into "fished out ponds populated chiefly by bullheads and

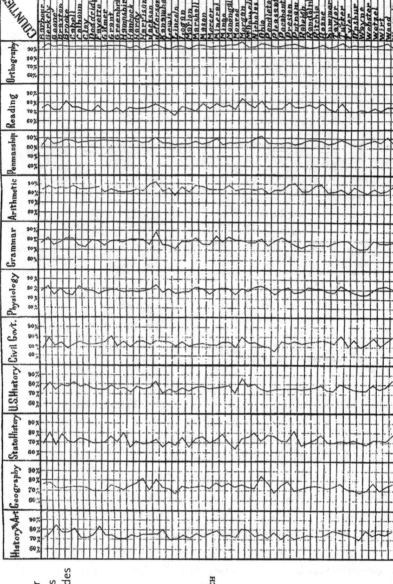

FIGURE 3.2

Annual county test
score comparison for
West Virginia schools
in the 1910s with grades
ranging from 60- to
90-plus percent

THIS CHART SHOWS THE
AVERAGE GRADE ON EACH
SUBJECT, BY COUNTIES,
FOR THE EXAMINATION
SEASON OF 1914.

Source: Used with
permission from the
West Virginia State
Archives.

suckers."[43] "The work before us," declared the commission, "is nothing more or less than the gradual rebuilding of a new agriculture and new rural life . . . The entire people need to be roused" to build a "new and permanent rural civilization."[44] This revitalized countryside, argued the commission, would require a new cadre of local leaders—especially teachers, farmers, and clergy.

This new rural society would depend mightily upon "redirecting the rural schools. There is no such unanimity on any other subject," claimed the commission. Rural schools "are held largely responsible for ineffective farming, lack of ideals, and the drift to town." While not declining per se, the schools "are in a state of arrested development and have not yet put themselves in consonance with all the recently changed conditions of life."[45] As the commission's report arrived at Congress, Shawkey appointed his first supervisor of rural schools in West Virginia, Lyda J. Hanifan, then principal of Charleston High School.

Charged to improve rural schools, Hanifan found many of them in desperate, declining shape or, at best, in static conditions within the deteriorating communities the commission described. This reality urged the reconsideration of a school-centric approach to educational improvement focused on pedagogy and curricula. Insisting that teachers follow the state curriculum—when young, underprepared teachers often fled decrepit, unsanitary one-room schoolhouses in unstable, isolated, poor communities midterm—was, in Hanifan's experience, of limited effect. To help sustain school improvement, the school would need to take on the civic role of leading community improvement. Here was a role for the school as civic educator: the rebuilding of social and civic ties torn by years of economic, social, and demographic tremors. In order to sustain school improvement, Hanifan sought to address the deteriorating conditions of rural community life, to break the dull isolation of individuals and families, and to bring neighbors together in common cause.

There was another example of the creative role schools could play civically: Hanifan hailed the arrival of the Hesperia Movement in Marshall County, a movement he felt "should spread all over West Virginia."[46] Years earlier, during the winter of 1885–1886 in the small country village of Hesperia in western Michigan, teachers and farmers began to meet, generally in the schoolhouse, on Saturdays (figure 3.3). The effort grew into annual gatherings organized evenly around educational topics and farmers' interests. The "big meeting," as it came to be known, became a local yearly tradition, running three evenings and two days and drawing standing-room-only crowds to hear "some of the best speakers in America." In 1906 (the meeting's fourteenth year), for

FIGURE 3.3

The schoolhouse at Hesperia, Michigan, late 1880s

Source: Used with permission from the West Virginia State Archives.

example, Michigan Governor Fred Warner braved zero-degree weather to join J. T. McCutcheon of the *Chicago Tribune*, noted "Dean of American Cartoonists" and future Pulitzer Prize winner, on the program. According to then state commissioner D. E. McClure, known as the father of the movement, this close working association of teachers and "patrons" would promote cooperation, "wholesome entertainment . . . [a] taste for good American literature . . . and higher ideals of citizenship."[47] The community association's "midwinter Chautauqua . . . [in] a one-street village . . . in a ramshackle building" would draw over eight hundred participants in a "great union of educational and farmer forces."[48] In its overall impact on the community, according to its chief promoter, it served to "make the rural schools character builders, to rid the districts of surroundings which destroy character, such as unkept school yards, foul, nasty outhouses, poor unfit teachers. These reforms, you understand, come only through a healthy educational sentiment which is aroused by a sympathetic cooperation of farm, home, and school."[49]

The Hesperia Movement argued for a wider view of education, fervently egalitarian and democratic, with the school at the center of a community's cultural and civic life. McClure urged that "into the lives of the toilers on the farm, in the shop, kitchen, and factory, store, and schoolroom, or wherever employed, or of whatever employment, shall come the culture spirit of song, poem, oration and painting that their children, too, may stand upon the same level of educational advantages as the children of the rich."[50]

Hanifan's enthusiasm for the Hesperia Movement signaled the larger role many understood for the school, as a public agent for revitalizing a diminished community life through an expanded sense of democracy. Walter Page, editor of *The World's Work*, noted the need to expand from a notion of "political freedom and equality" and "democracy of our fathers" to a "new democracy" in which Americans also address a citizen's social conditions. "It is not enough that a man's vote shall count for as much as his neighbor's vote," argued Hanifan. "He must also have a chance to live comfortably and bring up his children decently."[51] The parallel in education was evident in the expansion of schooling as the privilege of a few to broadened access to an increasing level of education; the challenge for Hanifan was to equalize the quality of that education for the distressed communities he served.

Experiences in the cities pointed to a shift in approach consistent with this "new democracy," said Hanifan. Instead of seeking to "improve their citizenship . . . by punishing wrong doers," leading thinkers had learned to remove the causes of poverty and crime or, in other words, not to "punish the victim of bad conditions." Applied to the rural school, this required treatment of the rural school within the context of "many related rural problems." Using a fitting metaphor, Hanifan argued that "we have merely scratched the surface, instead of plowing deep into the soil where the roots of the larger problems have their hold."[52] To do otherwise was to prescribe failure. Hanifan drew upon the recent work of rural sociologist Warren H. Wilson, who argued that the country churches depended on the local economic conditions. If you want to improve rural churches, Wilson argued, help the farmers grow better crops and get them to market. The local agricultural colleges must assist, better roads would need to be built, and schools would need to include agriculture within their studies. Otherwise, low income would drive down all the institutions of the community—school, church, Grange—moral and intellectual life would decline, superstitions would deepen, and all means of recreation would dry up.

To improve the schools, then, rural communities needed the "wise co-operation of all the forces at work for rural betterment," the establishment of some new center to community life.[53] If no other center was viable, schools needed to exercise the civic leadership necessary to stimulate community development, to create the social bonds upon which a collective and civic focus could be engendered. Improving the rural schools became an exercise in rural community building, and the community-center idea became the guiding construct. Extending Ward's social-center premises, Hanifan's efforts positioned the school as the public's default utility player in community analysis and self-recovery, modeling civic leadership by stimulating civic leadership across the community. For Hanifan, this built out to the community itself the intention of the new "community civics" materials, including the textbook *Lessons in Community and National Life*, produced by University of Chicago professors Charles H. Judd and Leon C. Marshall. "What these lessons aim to teach children in the schools, the community center aims to teach all the people as they assemble at their schoolhouses," Hanifan explained. "This partially compensates those of a previous generation for the loss they sustained by the shortcomings of the schools of their day."[54]

For Hanifan, the community center essentially sought to revive the means for social interactions and civic engagement that had been abandoned over the years. The industrializing economy's impact on the rural economy and corresponding out-migration had devastated many community organizations, from families to churches to schools. Country social traditions often fell victim, abandoning events and rituals that wove isolated farmers together. Without the corn husking socials, spelling bees, old-time "literaries," bean-stringing parties, and the like, rural life became dull, less attractive daily for those who remained. The human need for recreation, amusement, and social life would continue to drive people away from country life unless something were done, felt Hanifan.

The school became a civic leader, at least until it could stimulate other local leadership for school and community improvement. In this, Hanifan said, it carried on a tradition "as old as democracy itself."[55] As Chicago sociologist Charles Zeublin argued, "the larger use of the schoolhouse and the organization of school centers are not novelties. They are the twentieth-century revival and expression of that democratic spirit which has been vital at intervals for more than two thousand years."[56] Hanifan saw the need for the teacher to make the first move in most communities. First efforts would most likely be social or recreational and not even school-related, so that the community might strengthen the social bonds that would ultimately help the community better itself. Of the thirty programs outlined in Hanifan's handbook, all but three concerned holidays, farm programs (e.g., "Alfalfa Evening"), or miscellaneous entertainment (e.g., "Bible Story Evening").[57]

Indeed, the source of the common interest or purpose was secondary to the need to accumulate what he coined "social capital," the first modern use of the term.[58] Hanifan noted, for example, the civic work in New England, where the YMCA, the Boy Scouts, Grange, Chautauqua, and others were "conceiving *recreation* as the basal factor in the community center movement and by correlating about recreation all the other phases of this general movement." The school would often be in a "strategic position" to provide initial local leadership in rural revitalization. It had the advantages of being "free from partisan and sectarian influences"; it was public and accessible to all and had a paid employee "from whom the people may well expect a reasonable service in addition to his classroom work."[59] Yet the intent must be to help the community "discover for themselves what ought to be done . . . the more the people do for themselves the larger will community social capital become, and the greater will be the dividends upon the social investment."[60]

Hanifan then provided a good deal of guidance to the rural teacher in rebuilding local rural community life. Step one was to "teach a good school"; community cooperation would not be forthcoming if the teacher failed in this.[61] But the next steps involved a systematic approach to community organizing, starting with an inventory of community resources—"social, moral and intellectual."[62] This included identifying local organizations, community factions, local attitudes, and past experiences, among other things. A more formal survey or scientific approach might follow eventually. The teacher should also then begin to become acquainted with local leadership and call upon leaders to discuss ideas for local betterment. From there, the teacher should expand the circle further, meeting others in the community, and, to the degree possible, visiting parents in their homes. In all this data collection, given the larger framework of country life concerns, the teacher would be attempting to understand the "changing conditions" of the specific rural community that the teacher served. Much like a scientist, the rural leader must thus "study carefully the new organism in order to determine what readjustments shall be made in its economic outlook and in its moral, religious, and social life, to make it once more a normal unit of society."[63] In the exercises Hanifan provided at the end of each chapter in *The Community Center*—meant to assist teachers in implementing local community centers in their schools—he included making inventories of recreation facilities, summaries of leisure activities, maps of the community, and studies of local social habits.[64] Local teachers would become junior sociologists in their civic educational efforts.[65]

Under this expanded view of the school's role in the community's education and development, consistent with the larger trend for the wider use of school facilities, State Superintendent Shawkey officially launched in the summer of 1913 the social-center movement in West Virginia, calling for a thousand volunteer teachers to hold several community meetings at their schoolhouses over the next year. Shawkey was clear that this was a "summons to service and to opportunity" as "there is nothing in the law of West Virginia to require any teacher to undertake the service herein suggested."[66] Over a thousand teachers responded, and Hanifan was asked to publish a handbook, which went through several editions and thousands of copies.[67] In 1914, reportedly two thousand teachers held community meetings at their schoolhouses.[68] The work appears to have gained significant momentum prior to U.S. involvement in World War I.[69]

Social Living in East Harlem

A decade after Hanifan left the West Virginia statehouse, community activists in East Harlem, New York City, modeled a particularly assertive role for the school in the community's civic development. Positioning the public school as the community's "coordinating agency in all educational enterprises," Leonard Covello, principal of Benjamin Franklin High School, emphasized the school as a means for social problem solving and for training students in effective democratic citizenship.[70] A southern Italian immigrant who believed in "education for social living," Covello saw despair in East Harlem's diverse ethnic neighborhoods and worked to foster the community's social and democratic development.[71] The school had to lead the neighborhood's educational development because "the surging life of the community as a whole, its motion-picture houses, its dance halls, its streets, its gangs, its churches, its community houses, its community codes of behavior and morals—these will either promote or destroy the work of the school."[72]

Educated in the New York City schools and at Columbia University, a longtime teacher of Romance languages at Manhattan's DeWitt Clinton High School, and a local community organizer, Covello was an ethnic insider in East Harlem. Trained as a sociologist at New York University (NYU), Principal Covello used "social base" maps of East Harlem's neighborhoods to identify every apartment building

77

(including the ethnicity of its residents), store, church, empty lot, park, school, social club, and so on. To serve his students, he sought to understand the social geography in which they lived, and in turn, he understood community problem solving as a curricular and cocurricular means to prepare students to be active, publicly engaged citizens.[73] Here was civic education modeled at the institutional level, more comprehensive and explicit than the efforts of Ward and Hanifan. From 8:30 a.m. to 10 p.m., from the high school and from several off-site street units, Covello and his allies strove to build school-community partnerships across East Harlem.[74]

In what contemporary democratic theorists label *public work*—activity that harnesses the cooperative efforts of diverse groups of people (groups that are often in conflict) to accomplish shared social and civic goals—Covello spearheaded a community organizing strategy.[75] For East Harlem to effectively press its claims on the city and state for housing reform, health care, education, and economic development, Covello and his allies recognized that the diverse ethnic and racial groups would have to speak with one voice.[76] To build a shared democratic vision (and the means to attain it) among East Harlem's thirty-four ethnic and racial groups, students and teachers at Franklin mobilized citizen action (public work) campaigns around education, health and sanitation, citizenship and naturalization, and housing. Students carried out research, wrote essays, taught peers, demonstrated, and lobbied public officials (even arguing one case to Mayor Fiorello LaGuardia).

The four-year housing campaign from 1937 to 1941, the school's most notable activity, brought the first low-income housing to East Harlem: the East River Houses. The often squalid, congested, and dilapidated housing of East Harlem reduced the impact the school could have in the lives of its students. Covello knew from personal experience the toll poor housing could take on families. As a young man, amid the dark squalor of an East Harlem tenement, he had watched his chronically depressed mother wither away. He dropped out of school to help the family cover mounting bills. As one of six school-community committees involving students, teachers, and community leaders, the school's housing committee led the campaign. Franklin High School sponsored public exhibits and films of housing models; discussions in civics, economics, and history classes; essay contests through the English department; studies of local land values and use; public rallies; radio broadcasts; scale modeling of housing options through the art department; forums with local experts; and translations in Italian and Spanish through the modern languages department.[77]

As the campaigns were coordinated through the school, students learned civics by playing key roles in the campaigns targeting community problems. One problem involved East Harlem's reputation, fed by negative press accounts, as a dirty and unkempt community. In 1948, a student group took matters into its own hands and took to the streets to determine the state of the community. The students did not like what they saw: "frightful" sanitation levels (as described by the mayor) that only exacerbated high rates of illness in the neighborhood and diminished student development in school and out. Neighbors would send garbage flying out windows from upper floors—labeled East Harlem "airmail delivery" and a source of infestations. In the summer, complained one resident, "the flies are everywhere. They breed in the garbage in the gutters and backyards." "The truth is the truth," one student responded, "and instead of complaining about the press, we should see if we can do something to clean up our neighborhood." Collaborating with local agencies and community groups, the students organized a sanitation parade (complete with a fifty-piece band and five thousand leaflets), a conference led by the local congressional representative, a cleanup contest sponsored by the *Daily News*, an educational campaign complete with roving sound-truck broadcasts, and a science and social science lesson plan for the school (figure 3.4). To preserve the progress, the students achieved a change in the city sanitary code so as to enforce more frequent and more effective garbage collection.[78]

Inspired by early urban sociology that originated in Chicago but was translated via NYU, Covello approached community problem solving through an emerging, multimethod approach to urban sociological research—a more comprehensive antecedent to present-day data-based decision making. In an effort to understand the underlying dynamics of the community in which his students lived, staff and students conducted surveys, case studies, home visits, and interviews; took photographs; and made other observations. Social-base maps displayed rich

FIGURE 3.4

Students at Benjamin Franklin High School, East Harlem, leading a "sanitation parade" in 1948

Source: Used with permission from the Historical Society of Pennsylvania.

local data. One of them adorned Covello's office, providing a detailed picture of both the environment in which these educational initiatives operated and the factors supporting or frustrating success. The map identified every institution, from residence to deli. The dominant ethnicity of each block was identified, and every student residence was represented by a pushpin indicating ethnicity and whether the student was a first-generation immigrant.

Covello knew that such details mattered. When fights broke out between Puerto Rican and Italian youth along Third Avenue, with bricks tossed from rooftops, he not only knew which students lived where, but with whom he could work on those blocks to resolve tensions. To operate as an agent of civic educational development, the school must first serve as a "diagnostician," claimed Covello. Surface understanding would not suffice. School staff must "penetrate . . . into the 'sphere of intimacy' of community life and . . . follow, as far as possible, changes in the emotional life, as well as changes of a more material nature." He knew this understanding depended upon deep, respectful relationships with the community; such analysis, he claimed, "depends upon sincere friendliness in the approach, rather than upon sheer technical skill in making a physical or sociological survey."[79]

Covello's community-centered approach developed a distinctive civic engagement tactic, the "street unit . . . a unit that functions literally in the street." These street units (which were often in storefronts) directly challenged and bridged the spatial distinction between school and community. They housed recreation, research, and educational activities that encouraged community members, business owners, parents, teachers, and students (including dropouts) to work together to improve the quality of neighborhood life. Knowing that many in his immigrant community would never set foot in the school building, Covello tapped the off-site units to address issues he knew were deeply embedded within the fabric of the community. Informal leaders could be cultivated, and the relatively neutral ground allowed the school to establish a sphere of intimacy with the community it sought to understand and serve. One unit, the Association of Parents, Teachers, and Friends, had 240 members in the autumn of the year the school opened (1934) and supported the growth of other units, such as the Friends and Neighbors Club. The latter was open to any reputable community organization and held meetings of the housing committee, school social clubs, and adult education classes, which were part of an extensive Works Progress Administration (WPA) adult school program, enrolling over seventeen hundred adults by early 1938. Another street unit housed the Old Friendship Club, an association of Franklin students and dropouts and part of the community web Covello wove to support youth development within and beyond school walls. The community volunteers staffing the Friends and Neighbors Library, a third street unit, experienced strong demand despite their original set of only four hundred books.[80]

A fourth and fifth street unit, the Italo-American Educational Bureau and Hispano-American Educational Bureau, provided services to Italian- and Spanish-speaking community members while organizing local social research efforts. Over twenty-five research projects were carried out in the first eight years of the school. They included a block-by-block study of ethnic distribution, a study of motion pictures in the life of the school's students, a study of the home backgrounds of "problem" students, and a study of leisure-time patterns of high school students. As the research and services of the street units grew, Covello integrated them under an umbrella nonprofit, the East Harlem Educational and Research Bureau, also initiating the *East Harlem News*, a school-based local newspaper, staffed with faculty, community members, and students. Across research, support services, community outreach, and advocacy, the street units reflected Covello's effort to address the various factors affecting the education of the boys under his charge at Benjamin Franklin, an all-boys high school.[81] The public school both studied and developed the mix of educating agencies in the community, formal and informal, to advance its core mission of the civic education of its charges.

From 1934 to 1956, Covello's community school project focused on addressing community and civic educational needs. He drew from a wellspring of social, cultural, and political capital built up over years of involvement in neighborhood affairs. As part of the engagement process, he recognized that the curriculum could play a role in solving community problems. Covello created a participatory mechanism—community advisory committees—for jointly involving community organizations, teachers, parents, students, and at-large community members in community problem-solving initiatives. While the work of these committees sometimes penetrated the academic curriculum, especially during East Harlem crises, Covello struggled with balancing traditional disciplinary studies with his community problem-solving approach—a perennial tension in community schools. By the 1950s, after bearing the brunt of World War II and the social forces it unleashed, Covello's project in civic education within a dramatically altered East Harlem began to fade.[82]

SCHOOLS IN THE CIVIC EDUCATION ECOLOGY

Covello, Hanifan, and Ward recognized that Americans develop citizens intentionally in school and in multiple institutions beyond the school and have done so throughout U.S. history. Many institutions appear to produce more powerful civic outcomes than do schools, and each group mediates the influence of other educating agencies. What you learn in a civics class is mediated by peers after school and adults at home; these lessons are mediated by what is learned in church, and so on. "To be concerned solely with schools in the kind of educational world we are living in today is to have a kind of fortress mentality in contending with a very fluid and dynamic situation," claimed historian Lawrence Cremin, over a dozen years before Google or MoveOn.org existed.[83] To educate citizens well across the myriad of public and private educating agencies, Cremin says, educational policy must look across its citizens' lives "so that wise choices can be made as to *where* to invest *what* effort to achieve *which* goals with respect to *which* clienteles."[84] Ward sought to understand and link these different goals and clienteles via social center school sites, with an eye to political discussion. Hanifan guided rural teachers in the study of local educational influences, with the intent of forming the bonds and local leadership needed for development. Covello developed active school-community committees, assisted by local research entities staffed by WPA workers, and trained students through active participation in public problem-solving—all to build and inform the neighborhood's next set of civic leaders, student and adult. Each of these three men sought to build relational trust and a sense of collective efficacy across the configuration of civic educators, conscious of the mix of educating agents in their communities.[85]

Yet what are the implications for the school's role if this civic ecology changes significantly? If nonschool organizations that are key to civic education decline precipitously, should schools take on a more public-works approach, as in the above cases, to compensate for lost civic capacity in the wider ecology? Take the case of voluntary associations in the recent U.S. past. Sociologist Theda Skocpol and colleagues point to the steep decline of translocal federated voluntary associations (e.g., Knights of Pythias) since the 1960s and the rise of professionally managed advocacy associations run out of Washington, D.C., or New York.[86] Part of what historian Arthur Schlesinger calls "the greatest school of self-government," these voluntary groups served across U.S. history as "nationally ramified networks of membership organizers recruiting other membership organizers," reinforcing local ties while allowing participants a voice in broader movements. Within each organization, members practiced skills of deliberation and collective decision-making, learned the ropes of federated governance, and assimilated the norms of participatory discussion; in other words, these associations provided hands-on civic education to countless citizens. At Sons of Temperance meetings across five thousand divisions in the mid-nineteenth century, for example, some 250,000 men gained a civic education through this self-described "school for popular debate and eloquence," a "self-education of citizens" not limited to the elite or well-heeled. Members quickly learned "collectedness, promptness, and that enviable faculty of the right debater and orator . . . the power of 'thinking whilst on their feet,' and speaking their thoughts firmly whilst looking in the eyes of their audience."[87]

Voluntary organizations promulgated "the art of associating together," which, claimed Alexis de Tocqueville, "must grow and improve in the same ratio in which the equality of conditions is increased."[88] As individualists favoring limited government, Americans, explains Schlesinger in a seminal essay tracing the history of Americans as "joiners," "actually created the necessity for self-constituted associations to do things beyond the capacity of a single person, and by reverse effect the success of such endeavors proved a continuing argument against the growth of stronger government."[89] "Remarkably," Skocpol and her colleagues note, "U.S. voluntary associations achieved this synthesis of representative governance and moral purpose without becoming captives of either church or state."[90] With the sharp decline in these cross-class civic workshops, have Americans lost a critical place for building participatory skills for a democratic republic? As Skocpol and coauthors argue, "perhaps the best aspects of America's past are not being perpetuated or replaced in today's civic world, where market models are displacing representative arrangements, and where civic leadership no longer entails popular mobilization or the organization of interactive associations . . . Americans who better understand their civic past may need to reimagine their democratic future and look to revitalize shared and representative institutions not just in national politics but in associational life as well."[91]

That schools need to adjust their role within an evolving mix of civic institutions was evident also to school leaders during various waves of immigration, as new ethnic organizations arose and took on civic functions. During the complex history of Americanization efforts in the late nineteenth and early twentieth centuries, ethnic voluntary associations both resisted and shaped those same efforts. In challenging the "monolithic and culturally imperialistic" perceptions of such efforts, historian Jeffrey Mirel describes how Americanization resulted not in a narrow civic nationalism or balkanized ethnic loyalty, but rather in a "patriotic pluralism."[92] Immigrants balanced U.S. political allegiance with maintenance of their own cultural identity in an emerging American composite. Key to this "negotiated exchange" were various ethnic community-based organizations that stepped in to educate the new Americans, alongside the public schools.[93] "Immigrant communities succeeded where American educators failed because they provided education planned and executed by immigrants themselves," says historian Maxine Seller. "The single most influential educational force in the immigrant community, more influential than the Church, the labor movement, or any single organization was the foreign language press."[94] A young Slovenian immigrant girl, seven years in the United States, understood this mix of educators in her new world in Cleveland. She probably read the *Ameriska Domovina* or *Enakopravnost* newspaper at home, with articles supporting both Americanization and ethnic pride. She experienced firsthand the mix of civic educators. America meant "schools where you are given every opportunity for self-expression and self-government, [public libraries where you could] actually choose a book on any subject," and newspapers of differing political views.[95] State and ethnic organizations interacted to educate immigrants about the United States, "in ways that broadened inclusiveness and enriched the culture of this country."[96]

Does the recent decline of many voluntary associations, ethnic and otherwise, imply anything for the role of schools as institutional actors within the civic education ecology? For all their contributions to civic education, many associations also bonded culturally similar citizens together more than they bridged diverse neighbors to a common polis.

Does that historical tendency point to a necessary and complementary community organization, the public school, to do the work of citizenship development across group interests?

MAKING U.S. CITIZENS

In this accountability era in the United States, schools are generally given a pass on civic outcomes. If 50 percent of a school district's graduates could not read, the district would fire the superintendent. Yet regularly less than half of U.S. graduates vote, a minimal barometer of civic performance.[97] No superintendent has been fired recently for failing in this core mission of the public school, the "guardian of democracy."[98]

During the Great Depression, an era often cited in commentaries of late, sociologist George Counts dared progressive educators to "build a new social order" through the schools, taking on, without fear of the "bogeyman of indoctrination," the central public issues of the day. Most educators, apparently, demurred.[99] Some educators like Ward, Hanifan, and Covello, however, managed a distinctive middle ground, with the school serving as public problem-solver, a community utility in studying and acting upon shared challenges. It mirrored practices in voluntary associations of various stripes, provided hands-on opportunities for civic participation, and actively linked community organizations representing distinct local interests. Each school leader understood well the dangers of appearing too activist or partisan in his or her development of civic leadership, student and adult; each faced resistance from entrenched interests satisfied with the status quo. From the present "civics recession," these leaders' approaches resonate with both efficiency and effectiveness. Theirs was not the victor of history, though, as over time, most schools settled into a more subdued and largely private mission. Schools became client-focused educational service providers. Civics education meant school-based civics, and school-based civic education generally adopted an apolitical, good-neighbor approach that Reuben found in the birth of community civics.[100] With one arrow in the quiver and a weak bow at that, schools have had a well-bounded impact on civic engagement goals.

U.S. civic educational history should provoke Americans' present imagination, recalling the distinct perspectives and untidy array of approaches through which American predecessors struggled with the contested goals of civic education. In an era of privatized, partisan, and polarized politics, this history suggests exploring an enhanced public work role for the republic's schools in pursuit of common civic education in this nation, building out community places where all could "visualize the business of democracy" and learn to "disagree agreeably," as Ward put it. Amid a rapidly shifting civic educational ecology, schools might then well serve as effective and efficient agents of the public's interest in more robust citizenship development.

4

DIVERSITY AND CIVIC EDUCATION

Meira Levinson

Educators in the United States are contending with unprecedented levels of diversity in their classrooms as measured by language, culture, race and ethnicity, class, learning and other special needs, ability, motivation, family composition and background, gender and sexual identity, nationality, religion, political ideology, and citizenship status, among other dimensions. These dimensions of diversity present exciting opportunities to help students encounter and wrestle with multiple perspectives, work collaboratively across lines of difference, develop equitable and inclusive habits of interaction, and prepare for globalized life in the twenty-first century. They also present immense challenges. It is hard to figure out how to teach long division to students with vastly different experiences, interests, and capacities. It is even harder to figure out how to teach what it means to be a good citizen, how to act in service of the common good, or how to discuss controversial public issues in such a setting—especially when the polity as a whole disagrees about the answers to these questions. These tasks are further complicated by public rancor over which diverse others should even be included in the civic fold. Muslims, immigrants, those on the ideological far right or left, and those seen as having deviant lifestyles, for example, have all

89

found themselves having to defend their membership in, and identification with, the American polity.

Schools are not unique in grappling with the civic consequences of diversity. But public schools represent especially important and interesting sites for thinking about these consequences and more broadly about the acceptable boundaries of civic diversity and the challenges and opportunities that arise within those limits. Public schools are far and away the most inclusive state institutions that exist in the early twenty-first century. By law, they must accept and attempt to educate virtually every child who lives in their catchment area and is between the ages of approximately six to twenty-one years old. All children in the territorial United States are at least initially guaranteed access to the public schools, regardless of whether they are residents legally or illegally, whether they are citizens, what languages they speak, what resources they have, or what abilities or disabilities they have been diagnosed as possessing.[1] This level of inclusivity means that schools have to navigate among U.S. residents' wildly diverse beliefs, experiences, practices, and values on a regular, even daily basis. Schools have to figure out how to accommodate differences and how to teach students about navigating these differences, in ways that are developmentally appropriate, civically constructive, respectful of members' disagreement over these very questions, and legal. They also have to foster students' civic-mindedness—a sense of civic identity, an understanding of the rights and responsibilities of citizenship, and a motivation to become civically and politically involved—despite not knowing if their students even are citizens or have the opportunity ever to become citizens. Furthermore, educators are tasked with achieving these goals despite little public support for, or understanding of, such civic responsibilities, which have become entirely subsumed by college and career preparation in contemporary discourse.

At the same time that public schools navigate the civic opportunities and consequences of being profoundly inclusive institutions, they also set far more restrictive limitations on membership than those imposed by the polity as a whole. Public schools designate many forms of behavior and even speech as off-limits, using these limits to justify students' temporary removal or permanent expulsion from school. Two obvious and presumably uncontroversial examples include severe bullying and packing heat: students are automatically suspended or expelled for bringing guns, knives, or other weapons to school, despite gun possession's frequently being permitted in other locations. But other examples are far less obvious. Students may be excluded from school for using profanity or lewd language or otherwise disrespecting teachers and other students, violating "zero tolerance" policies by bringing drugs like ibuprofen or a plastic knife to school, wearing clothing or jewelry that is vaguely suspected of being gang-affiliated, or hoisting a "Bong HiTS 4 Jesus" banner at a school-sanctioned off-campus activity.[2] These exclusions have been upheld on grounds of furthering schools' educational mission—including schools' civic mission to "promote the shared values of a civilized social order" and "a democratic political system."[3] In other cases, students with nonmainstream religious beliefs have felt compelled to withdraw from school because their requests for exemption from a piece of the required curriculum were denied. In the *Mozert* case denying children from born-again Christian fundamentalist families the right to sit out a required reading program and complete alternative work in the library, for example, a judge's concurring opinion again relied on civic considerations: "Teaching students about complex and controversial social and moral issues is just as essential for preparing public school students for citizenship and self-government as inculcating in the students the habits and manners of civility."[4]

Public schools thus simultaneously welcome within their walls a more diverse array of students and families than are legally recognized in the polity as a whole, and exclude students and families for behaviors, beliefs, and values that are not only fully legal but even respected in the broader civil society. Both of these approaches to diversity have civic justifications and civic consequences; they are key to any consideration of schools as engines of civic education. Oddly, however, these characteristics have also been remarkably neglected by those who try to establish principles governing civic education and especially civic membership in schools. The vast majority of writing about civic diversity in public schools tends to equate educational inclusion within the school with political inclusion within the state—a fundamental misunderstanding—and then to obsess around the margins over who is to be included versus excluded.

The basic format is as follows: we encounter an example of a person, family, or group who has anticivic, isolationist, or otherwise off-putting views and ways of life. We are then asked, should we welcome these people in and accommodate them, either because they reveal to us that our own civic values are askew or in the hopes that their children will imbibe some of what we're trying to teach, despite their parents' opposition? Or should we be clear that there are certain givens that anyone who attends public school must accept? Are there families and groups that just can't be accommodated? Alternatively, are there families or groups that must be accommodated—in fact, assimilated—if they are to remain among us? Who are these, and why? Classic cases often focus on religious minorities, such as the Amish in *Yoder v. Wisconsin*, in which Amish teenagers were exempted from state school attendance laws in part on the grounds that the Amish exempted themselves from political life. These cases may also, however, focus on linguistic, political (white supremacist, say), cultural, or other minorities.

Not only are these border-policing cases relatively rare in practice, but they also distract us from the key question surrounding civic diversity in public schools: namely, how to manage such diversity in a developmentally and democratically appropriate way. Diverse schools present an incomparable civic resource for developing democratically oriented, globally competent citizens who collaborate across lines of difference (habits and skills that we could use more of in Congress these days!). The mere fact of diversity, however, is not enough to promote desirable civic outcomes; to the contrary, as Congress itself demonstrates, citizens often respond to diversity by hardening their own positions and taking refuge in their own presumed superiority. Diverse schools must therefore be intentional and transparent in converting diversity from a potential challenge to a civic educational opportunity.

Even the most intentional and capable school, however, cannot resolve all diversity-related challenges in ways that are civically empowering for all. Perhaps the most potent examples of such challenges are disputes over membership in the civic fold itself. Since many public schools include students who either personally or through family are excluded from broader civic or political membership in some way, public school educators find themselves in the unenviable position of acknowledging diverse voices (many within the school's own walls) raised against some of the very students they are attempting to serve. In such cases, schools cannot remain neutral by staying silent. Rather, they must establish a respectful, welcoming environment in which all students and families feel at home, even if this is denounced as advocacy by those who oppose such inclusion. Schools are responsible for nurturing the children in their care and should assert the value of, and respect due, to each child, independent of the civic consequences.

At times, however, educators, students, and families alike may become exhausted by the constant process of negotiating across lines of difference. Although schools can and should leverage their diversity as a civic resource, the aims of civic education may sometimes be well served through less diversity-oriented and more solidaristic approaches. In such situations, schools' affirmative engagement with diverse students entails the proactive creation of an environment to which especially minority students can retreat. Students, like adults, need spaces in which they feel normal and at home, where they don't constantly feel that their differences are on display. Solidaristic classes and affinity groups can provide such spaces and, in so doing, support youths' development of a secure and engaged civic identity.

LEVERAGING DIVERSITY AS A CIVIC RESOURCE

Diversity does not magically breed civic virtue. Diverse schools do not even necessarily help students develop the capacities for peaceful coexistence, the most basic element of citizenship.[5] Schools can readily end up exacerbating tensions and prejudices among their diverse members rather than resolving or eliminating the conflicts, as is evidenced by the occurrence of racially or ethnically motivated fights, even "race riots" in some highly diverse schools. South Philadelphia High School, for example, was wracked a couple of years ago by intense violence by its majority African American student population against the minority Asian and Asian American students. Asian students and families, who make up a little under a fifth of the total student body, had been complaining for years about being harassed by their African American peers, with teachers either ignoring the problem or even egging it on. Events finally came to a head when as many as seventy mostly African American students attacked dozens of Asian and Asian American students, sending thirteen to the hospital. At a school board meeting following the incident, Ellen Somekawa, the executive director of Asian Americans United, reported the following taunts: "'Where are you from?' 'Hey, Chinese.' 'Yo, Bruce Lee.' 'Who are you, Dragonballz?' 'Speak English.'" She continued, "Those aren't the words of the bad kids. Those are the words of adult staff at South Philadelphia High. So stop blaming the children and start owning the responsibility."[6] This is, one hopes, an extreme case. But the lack of news coverage of this incident and of other examples of violence among students of various ethnoracial, national, linguistic, and even religious groups suggests that the incidents are frequent enough to be ignored.

Even when actual fights are not breaking out, students may well taunt and bully those perceived as others, or self-segregate along group lines. Such self-segregation is visible in many diverse schools, whether on the playground, in the cafeteria, on sports teams and other extracurriculars, or even within the classroom. High schools have highly complex social geographies, in which students of particular ethnoracial or national origin, class, language, identified special ability or disability, or even religion inhabit starkly separate spaces, occupying their segment of school real estate as efficiently and brutally as any army controls its territory. Consider this white student's description of his school's social geography in response to a researcher's question:

> By the portables are the white skaters who hang out in the sun. They dress alike and don't care what others think. No one really pays attention to them. They listen to heavy metal and hang where no one else will bother them. The smokers hang out across the street. It's another kind of white student, bound together by their addiction. Mexicans stay far from the administration, close to the street, so they can see their friends who drive by and stop for a while. In the middle are black students, a big group who kid around a lot. They seem to know each other from junior high.[7]

Similar divisions persist in schools across the country; putative student body diversity offers no guarantee that students are actually being educated in, or making friends across, diverse groups. In response to such patterns, in fact, Teaching Tolerance, the educational branch of the Southern Poverty Law Center, now sponsors an annual Mix It Up Day, in which students and teachers are specifically encouraged to breach established social and geographic barriers.

It is not only in schools where diversity may exacerbate as opposed to mitigate social tension and unease. In communities in general, says political scientist Robert Putnam, "the more we are brought into physical proximity with people of another race or ethnic background, the more we stick to 'our own' and the less we trust the 'other.'"[8] These civic ills are not minor. Recent research shows that the mere experience of living or being educated in a diverse community may reduce all residents' civic engagement, trust, altruism, political efficacy, commitments to social justice, and realization of other potential aims of civic education. These negative reactions to diversity are frankly understandable. Diversity can pose real challenges to the achievement of communal life. These challenges are sometimes petty: "I don't like the music they listen to"; "My neighborhood smells gross now because of the spices they cook with." They may also be profound: "I think the way he treats his wife is immoral"; "If her views are enshrined in law, I'm afraid that families like mine will be destroyed." Some are eternal: "I truly believe I will suffer eternal damnation if I countenance—let alone participate in—such behavior." Any institution, including a school, that tries to promote the benefits of diversity will maintain legitimacy only if it acknowledges these difficulties forthrightly.

But diversity also can offer immense benefits, ones that schools are well-positioned both to realize and to teach if given the right support. Diverse schools hence should not only acknowledge the challenges of diversity, but also openly advocate the civic virtues of living and learning in a diverse community.[9] After all, diversity is a fact of life in the United States and increasingly in countries worldwide. Young people need guidance and experience in navigating diverse communities to develop the knowledge and skills they need to succeed in political and civil society in the future. This is true at the local and national level, but is also increasingly relevant at the global level. Students live in an interconnected, global world. Now more than ever, they need to develop the knowledge, skills, and inclinations to work together across borders and lines of difference. Furthermore, the integration and even clash of diverse perspectives ultimately benefits all Americans. Political institutions and civil society in the United States are designed for, and benefit from, diverse viewpoints, passions, areas of expertise, experiences, and ways of life. Effective, inclusive democracies create aggregate wisdom and good judgment from individual citizens' necessarily limited knowledge, skills, and viewpoints.[10] No one person—not even the greatest leader—has all the answers. American institutions are built with this (sometimes controversial) truism in mind. Americans do not believe in philosopher kings.

If diverse schools can focus on helping students learn how to respect and work collaboratively across lines of difference, therefore, they can ensure that students not only acquire a crucial set of civic and political skills, but also develop appropriate democratic attitudes about the value of diversity to a just, equal, and well-run political order. Such schools would help students become comfortable with both superficial and deep differences, which is crucial for effective participation in civic and political life. Schools could teach students that controversy does not necessarily indicate ignorance or inappropriate self-interest on the part of one or more of the parties. All too often, citizens who are frustrated by deep divides among their elected leaders or other groups withdraw from public life altogether. They cry, in effect, "a pox on both their houses!"[11] But disagreement is legitimate and necessary. A civil society or political system that consistently displayed consensus would indicate tyranny, or at least oppression of minority and dissident groups, rather than a well-functioning democracy.

In addition to becoming comfortable with controversy, students need to encounter, wrestle with, and ultimately come to value multiple perspectives. It does not advance the cause of democracy for citizens to recognize the inevitability of diverse interests and opinions but nonetheless assume that their own are automatically more valuable and accurate than those of others. Schools should thus capitalize on the diversity within their walls to facilitate highly supported conversations about controversial topics and different ways of life. They can teach students how to listen carefully, how to ask questions of one another to understand others' perspectives better, how to express their own beliefs and values in a respectful way that others can comprehend, and how to question their own initial assumptions. This isn't an easy process, especially when students' perspectives, experiences, and ways of life are profoundly different from, or even opposed to, one another. But it is essential that students should learn such skills, and hence that schools should teach them, since we cannot assume that citizens will pick up such democratic capacities and inclinations on their own. By drawing upon their schools' diversity as a resource in this way, educators, too, can help reduce Americans' self-imposed isolation within ideological, cultural, and even linguistic echo chambers.[12] Students' development of cross-cultural awareness and competencies, respect for multilingualism, and capacities for equitable and inclusive habits of interaction are crucial to prepare them for national democratic and globalized life in the twenty-first century.

Schools need to be intentional, transparent, and vigilant about achieving these goals, since the aims are not easy. But a school does not need to set aside time that is separate from the rest of its curricular and extracurricular activities. Rather, these civic educational goals should be woven throughout schools' curricula, pedagogy, and other practices. One of the most effective means of achieving many of the goals listed above, for example, is the establishment of an open classroom climate in which students feel comfortable and supported taking on controversial points of view and listening to others' perspectives. Research over the past forty years, across dozens of countries, has conclusively demonstrated that students' belief that they are "encouraged to speak openly in class" is "a powerful predictor of their knowledge of and support for democratic values, and their participation in political discussion inside and outside school."[13] Students' experiences of an open classroom climate are also positively associated with overall civic and political knowledge, intent to vote, likelihood of being an informed voter, expectation of engaging in other political and civic actions, expression of political efficacy and civic duty, comfort with civic and political conflict, interest in politics and attentiveness to current events, and critical thinking and communications skills. These findings are consistent and strong across a wide variety of schools both within the United States and around the world. They also demonstrate the effectiveness of infusing civically engaging and diversity-enhancing practices into classrooms in a way that augments, rather than displaces, other educational goals.

Unfortunately, however, research also shows that students in more diverse settings are less likely to experience an open classroom climate than students in more homogeneous settings, especially students in mostly white, upper-income classrooms or schools.[14] Perhaps open discussions are harder to have when students come in with profoundly different experiences and points of view. Or perhaps students *assume* the classroom climate is open to multiple perspectives when there is little chance that a dissenting voice will be raised, whereas they are more aware of the ways in which students are silenced in classrooms that are self-evidently diverse. Regardless of the reasons, students in diverse classrooms can explicitly be taught how to have respectful discussions about deeply controversial issues.

Project-based learning is another approach that diverse schools can use to facilitate students' capacities to take multiple perspectives and collaborate across lines of difference. In project-based learning, students work in carefully selected and mentored diverse groups to complete a complex, challenging project of mutual concern. When project-based learning is implemented well, students learn how and why to capitalize on one another's distinctive strengths to achieve their goals. A well-designed task is necessarily too great for any one student to accomplish independently (thus staving off the complaint "They're just slowing me down! Why can't I just do it myself?"). It also draws upon a wide variety of knowledge and skills to reflect the diversity present in the classroom. These may include local knowledge about a neighborhood, event, or way of life; bilingualism or biculturalism; interpersonal skills; and other contributions that enable students to discover the benefits of working in a diverse group. Still other approaches to teaching students to value diverse others include school-community partnerships that ensure the inclusion of diverse voices in school decision-making and robust extracurricular opportunities in which diverse students can get to know one another in a neutral context organized around a shared passion for, say, tennis, manga, or cooking.

ACCOMMODATING DIVERSITY AS A CIVIC EDUCATIONAL RESPONSIBILITY

The capacities to take multiple perspectives and otherwise respect diversity do not in and of themselves resolve many of the challenges surrounding diversity in schools. One of the hardest controversies for students and schools to navigate is defining the appropriate limits of diversity itself in a democratic society. Consider debates such as whether otherwise law-abiding, undocumented immigrants should be incarcerated while they await deportation hearings and appeals, whether same-sex couples should have the right to marry, whether polygamy should remain illegal, or whether Muslim girls or women should be allowed to wear full hijab in schools and other state institutions (a debate that has roiled Western Europe). These are debates not only about policy, but also about individuals' membership in the polity. Are these individuals and groups full members of civil and political society or not?

One feature that makes these debates especially tricky in schools is that those whose membership in the polity is being challenged are also often students and family members present within the school itself. For example, there are currently about 5.5 million children of undocumented immigrant parents in the United States. If they were spread evenly around the country, each classroom would have at least one child with an undocumented parent or parents. Although these students are more clustered than that—over 10 percent of students in Arizona, California, Colorado, Nevada, and Texas have undocumented parents, for example, while the percentage is much lower in most other states— schools around the country are nonetheless unaware of the legal status of children and their parents. Because they have the obligation to educate all children resident in the United States, public schools are usually forbidden from asking about families' citizenship or immigrant status, and undocumented parents certainly do not volunteer the information.[15] As a result, these children, nearly 4 million of whom are citizens themselves, constitute an invisible but unmistakable presence in many public schools.[16]

Consider what it means for these children to listen to their peers advocate for their own parents' incarceration and deportation. Similarly, consider the effects on children in school—U.S. citizens—to hear themselves described as "anchor babies" while being told that the Fourteenth Amendment should be reinterpreted to deny citizenship to other children like themselves. These young people experience such claims not just as reasonable disputes about contentious policy matters, but as a rejection of the foundations of their citizenship, their families' membership in the community, their fundamental identity. One college student describes his experience:

> The immigration debate rules my life. It goes beyond politics or law; it defines me . . . I am the child of immigrants, and I have witnessed the plight of undocumented immigration in this country . . . When I pick sides on this debate, this is what I think about. I don't think about politics, policies, laws, or statistics. I think about my family, my friends, my community, and myself . . . A close friend, the daughter of refuted immigrants, once told me that after everything she has heard about "illegal aliens destroying America," she felt so filthy, dirty and unworthy that she wanted to peel her own skin off. I don't expect sympathy, just a small understanding of the situation.[17]

In the case of undocumented immigrants and their children, youths and families find their literal citizenship challenged. In the case of gay parents and children, however, it is their symbolic and experiential citizenship that comes under attack. Current debates over gay rights offer a good example of this second kind of tussling over the limits of civic diversity. U.S. citizens and residents who are lesbian, gay, bisexual, or transgender (LGBT) are no longer at risk of being stripped of their basic citizenship rights, including their freedom of movement and association.[18] But many aspects of full civic membership have still eluded LGBT citizens. It was only in September 2011, for example, that lesbian, gay, and bisexual (although not transgender) citizens became eligible publicly to fulfill one of the most profound rites of citizenship: namely, serving in the armed forces. Furthermore, the federal government and vast majority of states continue to refuse lesbian and gay citizens the rights or recognition of civil marriage. Thanks to the federal Defense of Marriage Act (DOMA), they are hence required to declare themselves single on tax returns and other federal documents, despite in many cases being legally married according to state law. In these respects, even fully enfranchised LGBT citizens are not treated as civic equals.

Many schools recognize the bitter and damaging sense of exclusion that LGBT youth, and children with LGBT parents and other family members, may feel in response to these limitations and to the severe bullying that often accompanies these more symbolic exclusions from civic membership. The 2009 National School Climate Survey, for example, found that 85 percent of LGBT students reported being verbally harassed, four in ten were physically harassed, and almost one in five reported being physically assaulted at school because of their sexual orientation. LGBT youth are also known to have significantly higher rates of depression and attempted and actual suicide. In response, over four thousand U.S. middle and high schools host Gay-Straight Alliances and other support groups intent on building positive, inclusive, and welcoming contexts for LGBT students, families, and allied straight friends. On the other hand, this number represents less than 15 percent of the thirty-seven thousand middle and high schools nationwide.[19] Especially in communities with a diverse array of views ranging from pro-LGBT families to a belief that homosexuality is an illness or sin from which individuals can "recover" by becoming straight, schools often take refuge in silence.[20]

Anoka-Hennepin School District No. S1 in Minnesota has recieved news coverage, for example, thanks to its policy of curricular "neutrality" regarding sexual orientation: "Teaching about sexual orientation is not a part of the District adopted curriculum; rather, such matters are best addressed within individual family homes, churches, or community organizations. Anoka-Hennepin staff, in the course of their professional duties, shall remain neutral on matters regarding sexual orientation including but not limited to student led discussions."[21] Although this policy did not restrict students from speaking up or organizing, and there are Gay-Straight Alliances in some local high schools, six students nonetheless filed lawsuits in July 2011 charging in part that the curriculum-neutrality policy "fostered oppressive silence and a corrosive stigma."[22] Nine students, many of whom were gay or perceived by others to be gay, had committed suicide in just the previous two years. LGBT-identified students reported being verbally and physically harassed, even urinated on, by other students, with teachers and administrators responding by trying to minimize interactions between the bullies and those being bullied. An adopted son of two gay fathers, for example, was directed to leave classes a few minutes early to avoid harassment in the hallways. One of his fathers plaintively told a newspaper reporter, "We're not asking them to promote anything. But if a kid has gay parents, or is gay or lesbian, why can't the school say, 'You're O.K.?'" In the same newspaper article, Tom Prichard of the Minnesota Family Council counters: "Saying that you should accept two moms as a normal family—that would be advocacy. There should be no tolerance of bullying, but these groups are using the issue to try to press a social agenda."[23]

Silence on the part of the school clearly isn't an answer—but schools may find themselves at sea in strongly contested areas of civic membership. I began this section with the example of undocumented immigrants to underscore in part how difficult it can be for schools to say, "You're okay" to all of their students and families. As a legal matter, these students and families are *not* okay. They are living illegally within U.S. borders. Now, I personally believe that U.S. immigration policy is both inhumane and self-defeating and that the nation must overhaul its immigration laws to offer all residents—including those who are here illegally—a controlled path to citizenship. In this respect, I also support the DREAM Act (Development, Relief and Education for Alien Minors Act), which would enable undocumented children who have been in the country for at least five years to gain legal permanent residency (a first step toward citizenship) through military service or college attendance. But my personal views are irrelevant with respect to the messages that schools can send to students. Schools cannot declare that illegal immigration is itself okay. Similarly, I strongly believe that LGBT rights are human rights. I think that DOMA is a travesty, that all states and the federal government should legalize same-sex marriage, and that discriminating against people for their sexual orientation or gender identity is as reprehensible as discriminating against someone based on the person's race or ethnicity. In many ways, because being LGBT is itself finally fully legal, I feel on much firmer footing to declare that schools should also take clear public stands in favor of LGBT students and families, declaring not only to them in particular, but also to the nation as a whole, "You're okay." But Prichard is right; this is advocacy, not mere neutrality.

Furthermore, advocates of LGBT rights mislead themselves in thinking that sheer enlightenment is the key to resolving such questions or that the eventual extension of LGBT rights nationwide will bring such dilemmas to a close. Charges of moral, behavioral, or social deviance will always be used to justify excluding some people from full (or even partial) civic membership. No matter what one's political ideology, there are limits to the reach of diversity that people accept in a society or state. Currently in Holland, homophobia is diagnosed as deviance. Prospective immigrants to Holland are required to watch a video that shows images of the Dutch way of life, including shots of two men kissing openly in a park. If the viewers express discomfort with the images, they are refused permission to immigrate. (Many observers believe that the real impetus is to discourage Muslims from immigrating to Holland, as opposed to discouraging homophobes per se.) In France, Muslim girls' choice to wear a head scarf is seen as civically deviant; they are refused entry to public schools unless they remove their scarf. In the United States, personal recreational drug use is judged sufficiently socially deviant as to justify denial of access to federal student loans, termination of parental rights, and the risk of lifetime incarceration.

Polygamy provides another interesting case of the contemporary limits of civic diversity in the United States. Many passionate advocates of LGBT rights and other sexual and family structure freedoms draw the line at polygamy, usually on feminist grounds. According to a 2007 Gallup poll, 90 percent of Americans view polygamy as "morally wrong."[24] Nonetheless, there are around a hundred thousand members of "plural," or polygamous, families currently living in the United States. Many of these members are children. The families hail from a variety of faiths; contrary to popular perception, American polygamy is not confined to fundamentalist Mormons. Many Muslims also believe that polygamy is condoned or even encouraged by the Koran—a perspective that accounts for polygamy's legality in most African and Muslim countries worldwide. Because of both religious convictions and sociocultural factors, some black Muslims and immigrant African Muslims in the United States have also embraced plural families.

These Muslim and Mormon families are spread around the country; recent news articles have featured plural families in New York, Philadelphia, Utah, and Texas. Such families almost never reveal their status to state officials, such as public school teachers or administrators. After all, polygamy is illegal nationwide, and even a penchant for polygamy can be considered sufficient justification for denial of an immigration visa. No polygamists are supposed to be admitted to the United States (or many other countries).[25] Children from polygamous families hence pose challenges similar to the aforementioned challenges of undocumented or gay families. They attend public schools, are often invisible and hence unrecognized, and are members of families that are seen in some communities as civically deviant, even criminal. What principles can guide schools' approaches to such students in diverse and civically contested contexts?

To begin with, public schools must embrace their own students, regardless of these students' and families' legal status or membership in civil society. Schools are duty bound as a matter of law and ethics to support each one of their students as the children learn and grow academically, socially, emotionally, and physically. For a stable and democratic state to do anything else would be fundamentally to transgress against children's rights as vulnerable, developing human beings. As a matter of educational practice, this also means that schools need to model and foster—nay, insist on—respect toward all students and families, no matter how diverse. Children cannot be nurtured academically while being pilloried socially and emotionally. Their positive development is not fostered in classrooms that simultaneously make them want to "peel [their] own skin off." As a consequence, schools cannot follow a policy of strict neutrality when students' and families' identities are openly under attack in the civic sphere. Neutrality is a cold accommodation. Students and families should be welcomed with a warm, inclusive embrace, not just by educators and other school officials, but by the school community as a whole.

How can such an approach be squared with concerns—or even opposition—from diverse other students, parents, and community members regarding these students' inclusion in the civic sphere? In part, this can be achieved by insisting on the distinction between the educational sphere of the public school and the civic sphere of the state. State educational institutions are not microcosms of the state itself. To insist that all students and families should be welcomed into the community of the public school, therefore, is not to take a stand on groups' political status or civic membership more broadly. Second, it is important to remind all members of the school community that no one is defined by a single characteristic. We all have multiple identities. An undocumented immigrant may also be a loving father, a skilled craftsman, an upstanding taxpayer, a community translator, and a damn good softball coach. A gay student may also be captain of the debate team and an empathetic peer tutor. When a school models and teaches its members to embrace all children within its fold, therefore, it need not insist that all teachers and students openly embrace the very characteristics they view as morally or civically deviant. Rather, it can emphasize other valued characteristics of diverse students and families—skills, ways of life, and other traits that are valued by the larger community. This is admittedly an imperfect solution—"Mrs. Jones may be oppressed by being a second wife, but she's a great PTA fund-raiser!" is not a model of inclusive respect—but it also may be the best a school community can achieve under the circumstances.

Anoka-Hennepin School District continues to provide an instructive example, as the lawsuits and negative publicity led the school board finally to jettison its Sexual Orientation Curriculum Policy in February 2012. The district's new Respectful Learning Environment Curriculum Policy, adopted the same month, opens with the school board's commitment to "providing an education that respects all students and families." It ends by declaring that "district staff shall affirm the dignity and selfworth of all students" during any discussion of "contentious" issues. No longer singling out sexuality as a problematic topic nor mandating teacher silence, the district instead requires that "curricular discussions of such issues shall be appropriate to the maturity and developmental level of students; be of significance to course content; and be presented in an impartial, balanced and objective manner, allowing respectful exchange of varying points of view. Lessons shall be designed to help students think critically and develop decision-making skills and techniques for examining and understanding differing opinions."[26] Although those advocating for LGBT students and families view it as a significant step forward, the policy faces critics from multiple sides. One school board member denounced the Respectful Learning Environment Curriculum Policy as "caving into the demands of homosexual activists" and promptly resigned. On the other side of the aisle, the Southern Poverty Law Center and the National Center for Lesbian Rights who together filed the lawsuits on behalf of the stigmatized students, released a statement expressing their preference "for the District to have repealed this stigmatizing policy without replacing it." They further cautioned that the repeal is "an important first step, but the District must do much more to create a safe, welcoming, and respectful learning environment for all students."[27] This goal, when applied to students whose very presence is considered anathema by other members of the community, remains a challenge in Anoka-Hennepin and across the nation.

WHEN DIVERSITY FALTERS: SELF-SEGREGATION AS A TOOL FOR CIVIC EDUCATION

Ultimately, it is a mistake to think that every civic difference can be resolved or even accommodated in diverse contexts if people just try hard enough—if they work to understand one another, look past differences and celebrate their commonalities, and try to take the other person's point of view when they feel offended or wronged. At times, therefore, citizens choose to retreat, to hunker down in a community in which they feel at home and understood, where they don't need to prove their civic bona fides by reminding others that they are good craftsmen, peer tutors, or softball coaches, but rather, where just being themselves is good enough. [28] The support found in such communities often also gives members the strength to engage with the wider world, to take civic action with the confidence built on collective solidarity with others. As noted above, social self-segregation of this sort occurs in diverse schools all the time. Students seek solidarity by clustering with others who share their language, culture, ethnoracial designation, religion, politics, or other salient characteristics. Schools with effective civic education programs will dissolve these boundaries by teaching students how to communicate with and learn from a variety of diverse others. But enforced diversity is not the only option, especially when there are massive power and status differentials among groups.

Rather, effective and equalizing civic education is sometimes best achieved in solidaristic groups that seek a temporary sanctuary within diverse settings, creating civic narratives and practices that empower their own members. Probably the most prominent historical example of this approach is the civic education offered by black churches, fraternal organizations, and Freedom Schools. For over a century, these institutions have provided a nurturing and affirming space in which to teach their members about African Americans' ongoing struggle against oppression and injustice, the opportunities this struggle has brought black Americans, and people's obligation to continue the struggle through civic and political engagement. This approach to civic education is culturally specific and solidaristic. It also probably accounts for African Americans' historically high rates of civic and political engagement, which throughout most of the twentieth century were proportionally higher than those of any other ethnoracial group in the United States.[29] Evangelical Christian organizations have been similarly effective over the past thirty years in mobilizing members to become civically and politically engaged through solidaristic affirmation and education. After-school clubs like Christian Fellowship and 100 Black Men have extended this kind of group-oriented civic engagement work to middle and high schools. They are joined by legions of other affinity groups by race and ethnicity, nationality, religion, gender, and other identity markers.

Perhaps the most riveting and contentious contemporary example of solidaristic civic education has been playing out in Tucson, Arizona. The Tucson Unified School District (TUSD) has offered ethnic studies electives in history and a variety of other subjects for over two decades; the electives were developed and bolstered by its district-wide African

American, Mexican American, Native American, and Pan Asian Studies Departments. These departments were created as part of the "unitary status" agreement drawn up to release the district from judicial oversight over its desegregation policies. Ethnic studies courses have explicit goals of increasing students' academic and civic engagement, as well as of promoting social justice and other civic ends. Mexican American Studies (MAS), for example, follows a model of "Critically Compassionate Intellectualism," which "combines curriculum (using counter-hegemonic content), pedagogy, and student-teacher interaction (authentic caring) as a model for increased academic achievement for Latino students."[30]

One such MAS course has been an eleventh-grade humanities block, Chicano Studies/Literature, which students at Tucson High Magnet School could elect in place of American History and Junior English. The course is organized around a "Xikano Paradigm" containing four elements: "*Tezkatlipoka*—self-reflection"; "*Quetzalkoatl*—precious and beautiful knowledge"; "*Huitzilopochtli*—the will to act"; and "*Xipe Totek*—transformation." Within the literature segment of the course, students studied and wrote personal narratives and counternarratives, a social justice research paper, literary analyses, a character analysis, speeches, and rhetorical analyses. Students were expected to complete projects that brought their classroom learning into "the community and focused their efforts to change the world in which they live."[31] Like all MAS courses, Chicano Studies/Literature was a purely elective course and served a disproportionately high but not entirely Latino student body.[32]

In 2007, TUSD's MAS courses came under attack by Tom Horne, then Arizona's superintendent of public instruction and now the state's attorney general. Horne began by writing "An Open Letter to the Citizens of Tucson," in which he called on them to eliminate MAS, or so-called Raza studies, on the grounds that MAS teaches "destructive ethnic chauvinism," Mexican rather than U.S. perspectives on history, and anticivic beliefs that the United States oppresses Chicanos, among other ills. "Those students should be taught that this is the land of opportunity, and that if they work hard they can achieve their goals. They should not be taught that they are oppressed."[33] When the citizens of Tucson failed to take Horne up on his suggestion, he turned to the Arizona legislature, which passed a bill in 2010 prohibiting certain courses and classes in all Arizona public school districts and charter schools:

> A school district or charter school in this state shall not include in its program of instruction any courses or classes that include any of the following:
>
> 1. Promote the overthrow of the United States government.
> 2. Promote resentment toward a race or class of people.
> 3. Are designed primarily for pupils of a particular ethnic group.
> 4. Advocate ethnic solidarity instead of the treatment of pupils as individuals.[34]

Any district found out of compliance loses up to 10 percent of its funding from the state; in TUSD's case, this amounts to well over $1 million per month.

Throughout 2011, TUSD battled with the Arizona Department of Education and the Arizona Attorney General's office over whether Tucson's MAS courses did violate state law. The same day that Horne left the Department of Education to take up his new position as attorney general, John Huppenthal, who had campaigned on a "stop la Raza" platform, took his place as state superintendent of public instruction. Both Horne and Huppenthal immediately declared TUSD in violation of the law, a position that they maintained steadfastly in the months that followed. "Reviewed Mexican American Studies Program materials repeatedly emphasize the importance of building Latino nationalism and unity versus identifying students as individuals," Huppenthal claimed in June.[35] He reached this conclusion despite the concurrently released findings of an independent audit that Huppenthal commissioned, which concluded that the MAS courses have "been proven to treat student[s] as individuals," fully comply with state law, and also enhance students' academic outcomes, including their performance on state standardized tests in reading and writing, and their graduation rates.[36] For instance, students who took MAS courses were 5 to 11 percent more likely to graduate than comparable students who do not enroll in such courses;

juniors who failed the state standardized test as sophomores but then enrolled in MAS courses were also significantly more likely to pass the test than those who did not take MAS classes.[37] Although many MAS advocates initially resisted the audit on the grounds that Huppenthal had hired a corporate tool to support his own agenda, MAS advocates, of course, have now publicized the audit results as evidence that ethnic studies courses are both civically and academically desirable parts of the TUSD curriculum.

In January 2012, TUSD ran out of options to appeal Huppenthal's judgment that MAS courses violated Arizona House Bill 2281. The classes were immediately shut down, with books, curricular materials, and even elementary school students' dioramas about famous Mexican Americans being seized from the classrooms, in some cases in front of students. Curtis Acosta, who taught Chicano Literature, explained that "we have been told that we cannot teach any race, ethnic or oppression themed lessons or units. However, there has been no specific guidance and since our pedagogy is also deemed 'illegal' then we are not sure HOW to teach either. I asked if I could start teaching Shakespeare's The Tempest and was told no, due to the themes that are present and the likelihood of avoiding discussions of colonization, enslavement, and racism were remote."[38] MAS teachers, now assigned to teach non-MAS courses, have been instructed to teach no Chicano, Latin American, or Spanish author. Paolo Freire's Pedagogy of the Oppressed and Sandra Cisneros' House on Mango Street are two of the dozens of books that have been explicitly banned. Teachers have been instructed not to teach about or mention social justice, discrimination, or racism; students' work in former MAS classes is regularly collected and reviewed by the district; and monitors have been placed in front of and within classrooms to ensure that no outlawed concepts are mentioned by teachers or students. "It's a really awkward environment. We're walking on eggshells," one student explained in late February. "We have monitors following us . . . making sure we're not saying bad things, we're not organizing anything. It's not how things should be." Another student explained that it was impossible to ask her former-MAS teachers questions, because "then they'd have to answer" and potentially risk treading on outlawed topics.[39]

There is substantial evidence that MAS' elimination is a consequence of Horne's, Huppenthal's, and their supporters' outsized expression of anti-Chicano racism.[40] To the extent that this is a principled disagreement, however, the dispute seems to come down to whether politically minority perspectives are inherently more divisive or biased than those presented by the political majority or elite. For example, the curriculum audit describes the MAS Department as being "firmly committed to the following" list of goals "with an academic focus":

- Advocating for and providing culturally relevant curriculum for grades K-12.
- Advocating for and providing curriculum that is centered within the pursuit of social justice.
- Advocating for and providing curriculum that is centered within the Mexican American/Chicano cultural and historical experience.
- Working towards the invoking of a critical consciousness within each and every student.
- Providing and promoting teacher education that is centered within Critical Pedagogy, Latino Critical Race Pedagogy, and Authentic Caring.
- Promoting and advocating for social and educational transformation.
- Promoting and advocating for the demonstration of respect, understanding, appreciation, inclusion, and love at every level of service.[41]

These are incontrovertibly non-mainstream goals that promote solidaristic approaches to academic and civic empowerment. But they are also grounded in solid social science research about the positive effects of ethnoracially conscious and solidaristic identities, curricula, and activism on minority students' and adults' academic and civic success.[42] One Latino student recounts his experience when a teacher put an apple in front of the class and asked what they saw: "All the students were saying well, it's an apple. It's red. It's big. And a student of his said, 'I see my family working in the fields all day.' It's empowering. It makes me feel proud that I can come from a background as the class taught me, the culture that I have, and I can actually go on and do something."[43] The MAS Department's goals and outcomes are hence particularly salutary, one might argue, in light of Latino youths' persistent position at or near the bottom of both the academic achievement gap and the civic empowerment gap.[44]

Furthermore, accusations of inappropriate bias hold water only if one considers traditional American history and literature courses totally un-biased, not grounded in other (almost always white) ethnoracial norms. These are implausible claims—equally implausible as Anoka-Hennepin School District's declaration of curricular neutrality over issues of homosexuality. Silence in the face of massive power imbalances and his-toric discrimination is not neutral. When State Superintendent Hup-penthal asserts, "We all have an obligation to make a better society, and not characterize it in racial terms. It's that racial identity that we have a problem with. It's not appropriate. It's not historically accurate,"[45] he seems to be suggesting that it's even possible to teach American history in a way that is independent of students' racial identities. This simply isn't true. Students' (and adults') ethnoracial identities are unavoidably bound up in how they learn, place themselves within, and draw civic lessons from American history.[46] To design an MAS course that is cul-turally relevant, therefore, is simply to make explicit the implicit white cultural relevance of mainstream American history courses. Such ethnic studies courses also enable students to escape the cold accommodation of spurious neutrality by moving into the warm embrace of culturally relevant, transparent, and empowering education. This is positive for all concerned.

Another stumbling block between ethnic studies advocates and op-ponents is their contrasting interpretations of students' political engage-ment over preserving the MAS program. Horne was originally inspired to write his letter to the citizens of Tucson after civil rights icon Dolores Huerta declared in a speech at Tucson High School that "Republicans hate Latinos." Horne arranged for Margaret Dugan, a Latina Republi-can official in the Arizona Department of Education, to rebut Huerta's claims the following week, but during Dugan's speech, some Tucson High students turned their backs to her, taped their mouths shut, or raised their fists in the air (or did all three) to protest Dugan's refusal to take student questions. These students' behavior provoked Horne's letter and then his drafting of the state legislation. Since then, ethnic studies students in Arizona have been arrested while refusing to leave a state school board meeting until they were given leave to speak; held walkouts, sit-ins, and other protests around the state; used YouTube, social media, and a 110-mile run from Tucson to Phoenix in the blazing Arizona heat to organize and publicize their cause; and filed a federal lawsuit in conjunction with some MAS teachers, requesting a stay of the state law. These combined actions have suggested uncivil hordes to some observers, including Horne, who called MAS "racist propaganda . . . fed to young and impressionable students, who swallow them whole, as illustrated by the rude behavior of some students during an address by Margaret Garcia Dugan and subsequent demonstrations. The education they are receiving, to deal with disagreements in an uncivil manner, will be dysfunctional for them as adults."[47] On the other hand, students' passionate civic and political engagement in Save Ethnic Studies, No History Is Illegal, and similar organizations has been seen by others as a welcome broadening of democracy. Students' commitment to standing up for a curriculum they believe challenges, engages, nurtures, and prepares them for success in college and in American society demonstrates exactly the kind of civic engagement that would ideally be displayed by all citizens. In this respect, their mastery of multiple forms of civic action—sit-ins, rallies, public demonstrations, testimonials in public meetings, submission of written and oral testimony to government officials, strategic use of social media, walk-outs, legal action, and even willingness to be arrested and jailed for their peaceful civil disobedience—exemplifies the success of these courses in promoting engaged American citizenship.

CONCLUSION

Diverse public schools represent the public, serve the public, and to a large extent reflect the public. In these respects, they often find themselves grappling with the same civic challenges faced by the public as a whole: namely, how to work in a democratic context with people whose viewpoints, values, and ways of life are so diverse as to be diametrically opposed at times. Public schools do a disservice to their students if they pretend that diversity poses no such civic challenges. On the other hand, schools provide both their students and the polity as a whole a tremendous public service when they do teach students how to work together respectfully, collaboratively, and intentionally across multiple lines of difference. Such civic education is essential for the establishment and maintenance of a just and well-functioning democracy.

At the same time, public schools are not mirrors of the public; even more to the point, they do not restrict their services solely to those deemed full members of the public. This places schools in the politically and pedagogically awkward position of trying to provide inclusive services, including an inclusive civic education, to those who are excluded from literal or symbolic citizenship. In these cases, public schools' obligations are first and foremost the children they serve as opposed to the polity they represent. Furthermore, by emphasizing the respect due to all human beings plus the multiple identities all people inhabit, public school educators can at least in part square the circle of providing a nonpartisan civic education about peaceful coexistence to all students and families, despite their diverse viewpoints. These civic lessons must be inclusive, intentional, and overt. Schools cannot retreat into silence. Silence teaches lessons of its own—lessons that are no more neutral for being implicit rather than explicit. Finally, in achieving a fully inclusive and empowering civic education for all citizens, schools and students may sometimes legitimately decide to establish and seek out settings that promote civic solidarity rather than an all-encompassing diversity. Such settings must ultimately serve democratic civic ends that equip students to work collaboratively in diverse communities. But an emphasis especially on politically minority perspectives may sometimes be necessary for promoting students' equal capacities to engage in diverse democratic settings.

5

HOW TO ENRICH CIVIC EDUCATION AND SUSTAIN DEMOCRACY

James Youniss

On May 12, 2008, Governor John "Chet" Culver of Iowa signed into law a bill prohibiting the disposal of untreated oil filters in waste facilities. Seventh-grade students from West Branch Middle School were invited to the signing ceremony because they had done the key research in a science class guided by their teacher, Hector Ibarra. They found that improperly disposed filters could leach toxic lead, cadmium, and arsenic into the ground to pollute water supplies. They presented their findings to the local landfill director and conservation board, then to a state legislator who responded with concern because, among other things, their modeling estimated that 88 percent of the residual oil in filters was extractable and 351,000 gallons of oil could be recovered annually in Iowa.[1]

This was not the first time Ibarra's students had turned science learning into civic action. A few years earlier, another team of students had mapped the roads in their rural county, plotted the locations of accidents, and prepared a report that convinced the state to insert into the official driver's manual a section on safety for rural roads. Nor is Ibarra the only teacher to have middle school students take science learning into the public policy realm. Students in Debbie Viertel's classes in Lawton Chiles Middle Academy in Polk County, Florida, did research and mounted public awareness campaigns pertaining to the health hazards of improperly disposed medicines and unlabeled mercury levels in personal care cosmetic products. Students made an educational video available to the public and presented their findings at the Wheelabrator Tech USA Symposium on the Environment and Education, demonstrating a productive relationship between science learning in schools, American business, and the public interest.[2]

These cases illustrate what schools can achieve in meeting their civic mission. They can encourage students to apply what they learn to public issues. Schools can cultivate the belief that complex issues such as environmental conservation can be understood by youth. Further, schools need not get caught in a futile debate between the activist ghost of John Dewey and pious reverence for the Constitution. Civic knowledge is not and should not be separated from democratic practices any more than scientific knowledge needs to be separated from application to agriculture or industry. When political matters are integrated with classroom learning, students can develop identities as knowledgeable and capable citizens.

In this essay, I will focus on three effective practices that schools can use to advance citizen education for today: informed, civil discussion and debate of political issues; student government with roles in school management; and service that enriches learning while it connects students to ongoing civic life. Each strategy will be supported by empirical evidence showing that it enhances citizen behavior. Each strategy also comes with a century of endorsement from scholars who believed that healthy democracies encourage the participation of all citizens. And each strategy is pertinent for meeting challenges brought about in this increasingly global, technologically complex, and information-rich, but confusing, world.

The overarching theme behind these strategies is that democratic citizenship is best acquired by taking, rather than reading about, action. This proposition has been voiced by leading scholars who understood democracy to require informed citizens who know how to take action in the rule-bound public sphere. John Stuart Mill compared this task to learning how to ride a horse or to swim, both requiring the formation of habits through exercise.[3] This theme is found also in early-twentieth-century commissions of the fledgling American Political Science Association, which argued that the aim of civics instruction was not to train historians or political scientists, but to prepare youth for active citizenship. To this end, commissioners recommended that youth enter the community to observe and take part in the workings of government.[4]

These three strategies are not the only strategies available to schools. A broad of array of sophisticated print material, digital technology, simulations and games, and classroom protocols can enhance the civics curriculum. The aim is not to restrict selection to a single approach, but to demonstrate what can be accomplished with three strategies for which there are supporting data and which seem especially applicable to the current need for citizen education that prepares youth for the contemporary world.

WHY CIVIC EDUCATION?

Healthy democracies thrive on informed, attentive, and committed citizens.[5] One reason Americans see this theme repeated today is that young adults who are recent graduates of U.S. schools have not been as politically engaged as their predecessors. Evidence of this observation abounds in standard measures such as voting, newspaper readership, and membership in voluntary organizations.[6] Findings also demonstrate that youth who attend college participate at higher rates than do youth with high school degrees or less.[7] Scholars recognize that the gap is inimical to democracy insofar as lack of participation reinforces inequality in access to political power, which, in turn, decreases motivation to participate, perpetuating a vicious negative cycle.[8]

The German civic educator Wolfgang Edelstein, in an analysis that applies to U.S. society as well, provides another rationale by listing disparities between what educators teach students about democracy and how students experience politics. For example, society asks students to be socially responsible, but does so in a cultural context that promotes material consumption in the name of individual satisfaction. Society asks students to be informed, but tells them that policy decisions—say, on energy—are too complex for ordinary people and should be left to experts. Society encourages students to be autonomous thinkers, yet tells them that threats of terrorism demand adherence to opaque protocols while boarding planes or entering government buildings. Americans talk about their nation's history in terms of evolving racial and gender equality, but the economic gap between statuses has grown for decades so that today, ever fewer people command a larger proportion of the wealth.[9]

In listing these contradictions, Edelstein is challenging civic educators to address the larger dimensions of their task. He offers reasons why so many young people distrust and are uninterested in politics, believe they have little to contribute to society, and turn inward for recourse in self-satisfying, nonpolitical activities. The correction, he believes, is for educators to cultivate practices that evoke a sense of social responsibility, awaken a quest to understand policy, and develop a passion for equality.[10]

To those who want to keep political material out of schools, the warnings of historian Walter Laqueur are compelling. Providing a haunting lesson about the fate of youth who remain naive to politics, he recounts the course of the German youth movement (*Wandervogel*) from 1898 to the early 1930s. The movement began as young people reacted against industrialization and capitalism. Youth banded together to shut out the harsh free-market ethos by seeking to restore humanity via a return to nature. The movement grew to include hundreds of thousands of youth who rallied in the countryside for group poetry readings, artistic productions, and the reliving of German romantic history. *Wandervogel* thrived until the National Socialists took power and immediately co-opted and transformed it into Hitler Youth. Laqueur lamented this development: "It has been realized for a considerable time that lack of interest in public affairs is no civic virtue, and that an inability to think in political categories does not prevent people from getting involved in political disaster. [Young people] ought to be educated toward [participation in public affairs] and it is in this respect the Wandervogel . . . completely failed. They did not prepare their members for active citizenship."[11]

CLASSROOM DISCUSSION AND DEBATE

After a stint at a soup kitchen, required for a course on social justice, African American, urban high school juniors were observed discussing their experiences. One student remarked that the day before, a trio of young black males, who were not homeless, came to the kitchen. He noted that the young men had just returned from serving prison sentences and were seeking a free meal. He asked if others thought this was right. Another student said no, and then another said, "I hear they commit crimes so that they can get free food and beds in jail." A girl added, "Yes, and they try to get a degree too." Then another student asked, "Why do they get a degree in jail? Shouldn't they be punished in jail?"

The discussion continued as students focused on the purpose of prison—punishment or rehabilitation. But the dynamic stopped abruptly when a student who had been silent jumped in with a loud voice: "What's wrong with educating prisoners? I mean my brother did that . . . [He] got a degree in jail. I'm saying what's wrong with that?" A couple of students ventured a response, but the boy repeated his question and said, "You're already one step behind everybody else 'cause you got a prison record. How you gonna get a job? You already got a prison record. How else you gonna better yourself?"[12]

This excerpt helps to sketch some of the advantages of students' debate of controversial material. Private thinking enters public space where it meets opposing and reinforcing views. Students experience the dynamics of feedback that broadens perspectives. And students add passion to ideas with narratives and information that might not have been previously considered.

Does such discussion yield benefits to participants' civic education? Consider findings from the 2010 National Assessment of Educational Progress (NAEP). Teachers rated how often "material being studied" was discussed in class. Students whose teachers never or rarely used discussion scored lower than students whose teachers employed discussion monthly or more frequently. Eighth- and twelfth-graders exposed to rare discussion achieved average scores of 125 and 126; students exposed to more discussion achieved average scores of 155 and 152, respectively.

Significant differences also occurred with discussion of "current events." Twelfth-graders with little or no discussion achieved an average of 131, while their peers exposed to discussion scored 152. (For eighth grade, basic level is 134; proficient, 178; advanced, 213. For twelfth grade, basic level is 139; proficient, 174; advanced, 204.)[13]

These data correspond with findings in a wide array of studies of public school classrooms. For example, gains from discussion were reported in a study of fourteen-year-olds in twenty-eight countries.[14] Among several classroom practices, discussion proved the strongest predictor of civic knowledge. The findings, which transcend national differences in educational approaches, indicate that expressing ideas and listening to others' expressions spark a feedback dynamic that enhances cognitive understanding.

Michael McDevitt and Spiro Kiousis reported positive results for a program to promote deliberative discussion. They found that discussion increased students' ability to engage in civil debate with classmates and enhanced student-initiated discussion of political issues at home with parents.[15] Classroom discussion helped students incorporate ideas as possessions that were carried beyond the school walls. This finding supports the well-established observation that discussion of politics at home predicts students' civic knowledge, showing the value of having politics become part of daily life instead of residing in a domain separate from youth's interests.[16]

Diana Hess's decade-long study of twenty-five classes in twenty-one high schools involving 1,100 students offers important data on this topic.[17] She observed strategies for teaching students how to debate controversial issues in the service of what she calls "democratic education," or learning "how to do democracy," versus learning about democracy. Democracy assumes that informed citizens have the right and duty to express views and that diversity within any classroom can be turned into a resource for learning. This logic is pertinent today when divisiveness and polarization cast a pall of silence on public discussion of politics. For example, in one ethnographic study of voluntary groups, Nina Eliasoph observed that the introduction of politically controversial topics often brought sudden stops to ongoing talk among adults.[18] This bodes poorly for democracy because if individuals keep views to themselves, they miss opportunities to learn from others and to reflect critically on their own views.

Hess observed ways that teachers introduced controversial material pertaining to, for example, affirmative action, the Iraq war, free speech, abortion, and amnesty for immigrants. The currency of these topics helps to form a bridge between politics in society and classroom learning. The school becomes a place where students practice democracy by speaking out and learning how to listen to others, respect views different from their own, and grasp that diverse perspectives are part of democracy, not alien to it. Instead of avoiding issues such as abortion or war and letting students' views stultify in individual privacy, teachers encouraged debate, which exposed various takes on issues like women's rights and fathers' input when it comes to abortion, or the role of military conscription, diplomatic negotiation, and international peace movements. Classroom discussion breaks down barriers that artificially separate schools, the family dinner table, television news, and other public forums. In the process, students begin to see classmates as politically interested citizens.

Hess articulates clearly the relation between debate in the classroom and the practice of democracy. Her descriptions of classrooms serve as models of what teachers have done and what others can do. She reinforces the importance of informed citizenship as students are required to prepare for debates by searching out available data and points of view. Her examples illustrate commitment to a form of democracy that accepts a clash of understandings and encourages their public expression in a civil manner. And she shows that classroom debate encourages youth to understand that politics thrives, not just with ideas in one's own head, but with public give-and-take.[19]

Research from developmental and communication sciences supports the efficacy of discussion for learning. Experimental studies spell out processes by which the exchange of ideas leads to deeper understanding of one's own position and the sharing of perspectives.[20] Youth learn from one another, especially through negative feedback, which sharpens knowledge. One person's disagreement is an opportunity for another to gain insight into the limits of his or her own thinking. This applies especially to controversial matters that are steeped in emotion and hard to dislodge. Convinced of one's stance, a person can be shielded from alternatives and can falsely attribute motives to imaginary opponents. By meeting opposing views, students can hone understanding because alternative positions serve as resources for correction, enrichment, and reconsideration.[21]

Observers of actual classrooms have noted that contemporary students and teachers may not appreciate the value of controversy and the role of conflict in democracy.[22] After all, the U.S. Constitution was created through rancorous debate. A case in point is the prolonged deliberation between James Madison, George Mason, and Patrick Henry before the Virginia Assembly. Madison argued for approval of the Constitution's draft without amendments, whereas the others argued for modifications, with both sides trying to persuade members of the assembly to their cause. These three men are considered patriots today, not because they avoided controversy, but because they acceded to the democratic process of expressing differences and persuading others in an open forum.[23]

Teachers today may be cowed by the stilted treatment of politics in the commercial media, which tends to present issues in simplified winner-take-all shouting matches. This portrayal undermines the democratic principle of open debate among equals who hold legitimate but different views. Schools can counter this distortion by requiring informed views and fostering civil discourse. James Gimpel and colleagues' observations across congressional districts between Washington, D.C., and Baltimore add important evidence. Districts with competitive electoral campaigns had more public discussion of politics than did districts where elected officials ran repeatedly without challenge. Importantly, students in the more competitive districts also scored higher on measures of civic knowledge.[24]

Classroom debate may also counter a possible echo-chamber effect of the digital media. If youth choose to attend to politics mostly on the Web—and it remains to be seen how much they do so—they might focus only on supporting opinions and ignore opposing positions. How the new media will contribute to political education as the Millennial generation matures is an open question. Nevertheless, teachers might capitalize on students' interest in the new media and the wealth of information it contains by stressing the importance of information and diversity as students prepare for discussion and debate. As described by Joseph Kahne, Jacqueline Ulman, and Ellen Middaugh in chapter 9, if teachers helped students use digital media to stimulate political engagement, rather than leaving it to chance, they would have done a service of far-reaching educational importance.[25]

A final point pertains to the gap observed for educational level and socioeconomic status on measures of political participation. If adults who ended their schooling at grade twelve or earlier participate at comparatively low rates, say, in voting, then the high school civics curriculum they experience is especially important. The 2010 NAEP scores also suggest that economically disadvantaged students' civic knowledge grows from classroom discussion, a finding that mirrors one discussed earlier for all students. Teachers of eighth-grade and twelfth-grade students who were eligible for free lunch rated the degree to which their classes included discussion of the material being studied. Eighth-grade students in classes with no discussion achieved an average score of 116, whereas eighth graders in classes with almost daily discussion had an average score of 146. The differences were highly significant. A similar differential occurred at grade twelve. Students in classes with no discussion achieved an average score of 112, whereas students with almost daily discussion achieved a significantly higher average score of 138. Schools serving such students tend not to have enriched civics classes, discussion and debate being notable casualties.[26] The data show that these schools are missing out on a proven opportunity to improve civic knowledge.

David Campbell also reported advantages for open classrooms, where students are free to express ideas and encouraged to disagree about political and social issues. Students from open classrooms scored higher on tests of civic knowledge and appreciated conflict more than did students from less-open classrooms. Degree of openness contributed more to these measures than did sheer number of civics courses. And students from lower socioeconomic groups benefited from openness as much as their better-off peers.[27]

SCHOOL GOVERNMENT AND ORGANIZATIONS

If discussion and debate promote knowledge and engagement, student government should also be an effective avenue for enhancing civic education. By design, student government allows young people to build experience with voting, campaigning, forming coalitions, negotiating, and dealing with institutional structure. These elements convey directly to adult citizenship and thus exemplify what Mill and the political science commissioners recommended in the nineteenth and early twentieth centuries.

An impressive study of student government and subsequent citizenship involved sophomores in forty-two high schools and first surveyed the students in 1955. In 1970, fifteen years later, 4,125 members of this sample were surveyed again. These thirty-year-olds indicated whether they voted in the most recent election, whether they were members of voluntary associations and the degree to which they were politically alienated (e.g., "I think most public officials care a great deal about what people like me think"). Assessing several factors, the researchers found that the strongest predictor of current membership in voluntary organizations was participation in high school organizations, including school government. Its potency exceeded both grade point average and parents' educational attainment. In turn, current membership in voluntary organizations was the strongest predictor of present voting and of lack of alienation.[28]

In a more recent study, 2,517 adults were asked about their current voting, demonstrating-protesting activities, membership in voluntary associations, and participation in political campaigns. Analyzing past and present activities, the investigators concluded that "the variables most closely related to [current] participation are those that measure the activity of respondents as a high school student—in particular, involvement in high school government, but also involvement in other clubs and activities—though not activity in high school sports."[29]

Membership in voluntary associations, which distinguishes the United States from other Western democracies, has long been considered an important source of citizenship training.[30] Association membership offers opportunities to acquire democratic habits such as speaking publicly, dealing with scheduled leadership change, and persuading while listening to others. Support for this viewpoint comes from several sources. For example, youth who were active participants in 4-H programs became adults who were three to five times more likely than non-4-H youth to have become members or leaders of voluntary business, civic, charitable, or religious associations.[31]

In a review of contemporary high schools, Daniel McFarland and Carlos Starmanns provide a portrait of the types of student governments found around the United States.[32] Types differ on dimensions such as degree of student voice or administrative supervision and, not surprisingly, correlate with the socioeconomic levels of the students. Schools with high proportions of economically disadvantaged students tended not to have student governments. And if they had governments, students were given little voice in policy. This is a missed opportunity because studies show that economically disadvantaged students are quite capable of exercising responsible citizenship to achieve constructive ends. When such students are given a voice in school policy, they are able to focus on serious problems such as discipline, high-stakes testing, or harassment; to muster collective interest fairly through surveys; and to lobby school administrators effectively.[33] Reed Larson has done sustained research on the development of critical thinking through collective activities. He proposes that the economic and political world that youth are now entering demands strategic skills that are acquired when youth are given tactical challenges to solve and are supplied with adult support.

I conducted an informal survey of student council work for the present essay through an unsystematic review of Web sites that specified purpose, organization structures, and records of yearly achievements of individual high schools. Many Web sites highlighted the goal of developing "leadership," "citizenship," and "participation." Most sites featured the organization of social, athletic, and entertainment events. Many also mentioned sponsorship of charitable activities such as blood donations and food and clothing collections for people in need. Such activities are clearly directed to community needs and parallel volunteerism done through adult civic associations. Other examples that involve politics and policy include efforts to make schools greener and to improve nutrition, starting with the school cafeteria.

There is recognition that student councils ought to play a greater role in educational policy itself, for example, by securing a student voice on district educational boards that decide school policy. For example, a newsletter of a Florida school district proposed that student government ought not to be "a tight little club for the socially elite of a school." Rather, it ought to ensure that "large numbers of students have a real voice in what takes place in their school." The promotion of students' "civic engagement . . . goes beyond blood drives, voter's registration drives, and mock elections. Those and similar service projects are important . . . but more is needed. Budget cuts have begun to cripple Florida's schools and, for the most part, student leaders have remained silent." Thus, the director of the Florida Association of School Administrators concludes, "School board members and legislators need to hear from you. You are the elected voice of your student body."[34]

Perhaps the epitome of policy-oriented student government is found in Hampton, Virginia, where a twenty-year effort has brought students routinely into the making of municipal policy, including schools.[35] Through a series of fortuitous circumstances, the municipal government developed an understanding of youth as co-citizens whose interests deserve to be represented throughout government, from police work through transportation planning. Seeds of like initiatives can be found throughout the country as municipalities include young people in decisions affecting their lives. If early results continue to be borne out, youth who are included in policy making tend to bring responsible ideas to the table and, in turn, earn a newfound respect among adult policy makers.[36] This happens even in contentious cases, such as occurred recently when students from Wilbur Cross High School in New Haven sought school board representation using confrontational tactics. Despite the tactics, Alderman Justin Elicker endorsed the students' efforts: "These kids who 'cause problems' are the ones who actually care. They should have input in their educational system."[37]

SERVICE AND SERVICE LEARNING

A common hypothesis is that service is an avenue to engaged citizenship, although the potential for service to generate political participation on a grand scale has yet to be realized. One study with positive evidence showed that adults who did service in high school between 1990 and 1992 were about 14 percent more likely to vote in 2000 than were their peers who had done no high school service.[38] Still, considerably more evidence suggests that service is unrelated to subsequent political behavior. Scholars who have inspected this issue have drawn a common conclusion. Not just any service stimulates civic engagement. Rather, the kind of service is what counts. Across studies, service is too broadly defined to be predictive of anything. Much of what is called service consists of single acts of doing good, say, by collecting clothes and food for hurricane victims. Such acts are obviously worthwhile and may develop character. Yet they are not in themselves political acts, and there is no logical connection between these acts and political engagement.[39]

An estimated 5 percent of all the service done by college-age students pertains to policy or political issues. The percentage is probably no greater in high school students. Marc Musik and John Wilson suggest that most service may actually help to perpetuate "social inequalities by masking the real power differences on which charitable work on behalf of the 'deserving poor' rests, but the real political damage inflicted by promoting volunteer work as a solution to social problems can be quite severe if it results in neglect of political solutions."[40]

Michael Delli-Carpini echoed this concern about service, which is frequently "defined as the one-to-one experience of working at a soup kitchen, cleaning trash from a river, or tutoring a child once a week . . . Missing is an awareness of the connection between the individual, isolated 'problems' these actions are intended to address, and the larger world of public policy; a sense that the problems might be addressed more systematically and (at times) more effectively through other forms of civic engagement . . . the belief that politics matters."[41]

The amount and frequency of service done by American youth is something of a phenomenon. Two-thirds of high school seniors and about 75 percent of entering college freshmen claim to have done service the previous year.[42] Why such large numbers? A general answer is that volunteerism is built into the American ethos. At various times in the nation's history, service marked an entire generation.[43] One of those moments occurred during the mid-1980s, when presidents of elite universities began a service movement that encouraged students to address society's problems through volunteering. Their effort was, in part, a reaction to the Reagan administration's focus on the problematic status of youth and a purported decline in academic achievement, which made the nation noncompetitive with Japan's and Germany's rising economic power.[44] Whatever the cause, Campus Compact produced an upsurge in service that spread progressively across campuses; today, it claims membership of over 1,100 institutions. This organization views itself as "fulfilling the civic purposes of higher education" as it "promotes service that develops students' citizenship skills."[45]

Campus Compact had far-reaching impact as high school students, administrators, and parents began to perceive service as a desirable activity and as a credential to strengthen students' chances of acceptance at colleges of their choices.[46] As noted previously, student governments commonly sponsor drives for blood donations and organize responses to local needs and natural disasters such as the attacks of September 11 or Hurricane Katrina. During the first decade of this century, many high schools instituted service requirements, further fueling the movement. As with other intended strategies to enrich civic education, however, opportunities for service are less available for students from lower economic rungs than from higher economic levels.[47] In this regard, differential allocation of resources in terms of service opportunities replicates the patterns found for classroom discussion and for student government.

With high rates of service, why aren't more young people engaged in politics as voters, demonstrators, and campaign workers? A plausible answer is seen in the distinction between charitable volunteerism and engagement in policy and politics. Although there is no precise account of what middle and high school students throughout the nation do when they serve, a rough sketch can be drawn from a review of published studies. Common service includes raising money for charitable causes, collecting clothes and food, cleaning parks, visiting or entertaining residents at homes for the elderly, tutoring classmates or students in low-performing schools, coaching or officiating for athletic leagues, helping neighbors, arranging school social events, or working as functionaries for charities.[48]

These activities are not obviously political and do not teach democratic practices directly. They may induce positive social skills, help to develop character, and promote empathy. But to develop habits of citizenship or engagement in policy issues, service would have to be designed explicitly for those purposes. As with the introduction of controversial issues in the classroom, politically oriented service puts schools at risk for criticism and accusations of advocacy. It is one thing to have students serve meals at a soup kitchen but a different matter to focus them on the causes of hunger and homelessness, which, in our own research, led students to question political priorities and policies regarding affordable housing, job training, drug rehabilitation, provision of mental health services, and the like.[49]

How might schools handle this challenge? One answer is found in the broader ecology of service. Instead of starting with the individual student, one can look at where and how services are being offered in most communities. This leads directly to venues sponsored by government agencies, nonprofit associations, and religious institutions. These sites have clear purposes that are often grounded in ideologies of social justice, environmental conservation, civic renewal, and so forth. Workers at the sites express the purpose through their actions, even in ways they administer services to clients.[50] When students volunteer at these sites, they are exposed to the purpose and are trained to deal with clients accordingly.

Because they are purpose-driven, these sites are potential founts of policy and political education. Students exposed to them come in contact with issues they might otherwise not confront. In this way, the act of serving food at a soup kitchen becomes more than handing a hungry person a sandwich when that act symbolizes the sponsoring organization's view of human dignity and social justice. Similarly, while students measure pollutants at a watershed, they are, at the same time, acting as stewards of natural resources. The organizational sponsors of the sites represent America's rich civic, religious, and political traditions. By volunteering at these sites, youth are exposed to, educated about, and become virtual participants in these traditions.

Schools my colleagues and I have studied consciously arranged for their students to be exposed to certain traditions. We observed positive changes in their civic engagement, such as interest in voting or partaking in other political acts.[51] A key to positive change was probably exposure to a sponsor's purpose, which gave the service a civic and political meaning at a time when young people are exploring their civic identities.[52] This hypothesis is in keeping with findings of social psychologists who propose that adults who volunteer, say, by donating blood, come to identify themselves as "blood donors" who are ready to donate again when the occasion rises.[53] In fact, individuals who devote their lives to service typically remark that their actions are unremarkable because what they are doing simply expresses who they have become and now are.[54]

The examples introduced at the start of this essay reinforce this view. These teachers promoted a form of public-interest science. Students entered this tradition as they sought guidance from county extension services, consulted with university professors, and called on other experts. In the process, students met adults who believed in and practiced this public-interest science. Hence, while acquiring rudiments of physics, chemistry, and biology, students participated in this tradition, which became a resource for their developing identities.

Ibarra and Viertel have taught this way, year after year, and thus have built a movement for science in the public interest within their own schools. Each successive class anticipates joining the movement. A similar development occurs in the religious schools, where doing service as social justice becomes a rite of passage. Successive classes have readily taken up new science-in-public-policy projects, for example, promoting safety on rural roads; campaigning to control the disposal of light bulbs with mercury; alerting the community to the dangers of recycling mercury-laden thermostats; addressing improper disposal of over-the-counter medicines; educating the public about mercury in cosmetics; and seeking to reduce water usage by agribusiness strawberry growers. The identity process is probably helped along when students meet political controversy in the public arena. For example, when the bill to recycle oil filters was proposed, lobbyists countered the students' efforts by arguing that "recycling has its place, but right now, it is putting the cart before the horse. We need to protect the competitive market, then the land."[55] Such criticism only heightened young students' resolve to make their case well and to turn their knowledge of science into public policy.

Developmental science asserts that young people find controversy a challenge and are ready to confront it when they join collective efforts for serious moral and political causes. For example, youth played a central role in the civil rights movement during the 1950s and 1960s. They sat in at lunch counters, marched in defiance of police blockades, taught in freedom schools, registered voters, and suffered beatings and repeated imprisonment—all for the sake of equality and justice. Long-term data indicate that twenty-five or so years later, in their midadult years, the civil rights participants were still involved citizens who voted at exceptionally high rates, joined and led voluntary organizations, and were active contributors to their local communities.[56]

Civil rights is not an isolated case showing the long-term power of politically oriented service.[57] Alumni of the Teach For America (TFA) program—in which college graduates commit to teach for two years in low-performing schools—provide another example. This program has gained publicity for its attractiveness to graduates from elite universities. Less well known is that after completing their two-year commitment, TFA alumni manifest many features of democratic citizenship; for example, 87 percent voted in the most recent election, while many strongly endorse statements like "I am willing to go to great lengths to fulfill my obligations to my country." Even ten years later, over 80 percent of the alumni reported doing voluntary service, mostly in the educational sector.[58] These levels of sustained participation far exceed the norms for this age group.

A fair conclusion is that service has potential to enhance civic education, although only some portion of the service that is done through our schools brings that potential to reality. M. Kent Jennings, whose research documents the long-term citizenship benefits of participation in the 1960–1970 antiwar movement, made the following observation: "Unless [service] activities include some form of group involvement or mobilization, it seems problematic that they could produce the kind of sustained high activity levels that stem from early, concrete involvement in the politics of mobilization and collective action, especially over emotionally charged issues." He adds that it is not everyone's lot to be born at a critical moment in history and to be at the right place during that moment. "However, early involvement in proto-collective action such as that represented by school politics and organizational endeavors also leads to heightened levels of future political participation," he notes. "Thus, the challenge is to develop more institutionalized and regularized ways of instilling the habit of participation."[59]

CONCLUSION

The three strategies discussed in this chapter—classroom discussion and debate, school government and other organizations, and service—can enrich civic education for democratic citizenship. The strategies can have both short- and long-term effects on civic knowledge, engagement, and identity. Consequently, schools can make a difference that reaches into communities, government, and the political system.

For two decades, public discourse and educational policy have been focused on raising test scores in math and reading. This commitment involved allocation of public funds, enhanced teacher training, and government monitoring of classroom practices. A similar commitment needs to be made in civic education if reading and math skills are not to be ends in themselves, but integrated into well-functioning citizenship.

A recommitment to civic education would bring the political world into schools through debate on important issues and student government that fosters democratic practices. Simultaneously, schools should connect students to political life through carefully designed service projects in collaboration with civic organizations. In accord with principles of development, these strategies highlight learning and identity—qualities that are founded on the very practice of democratic citizenship. It may be hard to imagine making such a commitment on a broad scale. But consider the effort schools and communities put into athletics with coaches, repeated practice, organized graded leagues, public performances before large audiences, sophisticated equipment, medical support, and more. This nation-wide structure could not have been imagined a century ago. Why can't Americans envision a comparable effort for citizen education? The goal would not be a college scholarship or professional contract, but a contract for America's future.

Behind the beneficial strategies illustrated here was confidence that students would grasp opportunities by taking responsibility in public actions. Hector Ibarra, Debbie Viertel, and Justin Elicker, among others, viewed students as capable and interested. This vision is important for schools serving urban, minority, low-wealth students who lack opportunities with these three practices. Data indicate that such students are as capable as their higher-wealth peers and as ready to take advantage when opportunities and resources are provided. The addition of these practices to the students' schools would create universal opportunities in effective civic education.

Civic education today should not be a matter of left or right partisan preferences. It is in everyone's interest to promote effective educational practices because the future of democracy is at stake. The political scientist Henry Milner summarized well the issue we face in our common dedication to preserving our democratic system:

> Economic globalization and the danger of a widening digital divide add an element of urgency to the choice facing democratic societies. All face the prospect of mirroring a globalized world economy with its minority of "winners" and majority of "losers"—losers not only as a result of economic deprivation but, increasingly, as a result of their inability to take informed action to make their society better for themselves and others. Only high civic-literacy societies institutionally arranged so that a substantial majority of their citizens have meaningful maps to guide them through the complexity of decisions that their community will face, will, potentially, be equipped to meet the challenge.[60]

By strengthening civic education strategically, we initiate youth into the kind of democracy we know, but that only they can sustain as they confront the challenges and vicissitudes with which history will test them.

6

DRY TO DYNAMIC CIVIC EDUCATION CURRICULA

Anna Rosefsky Saavedra

The phrase *civic education* tends to invoke memories of memorization. What are the steps bills pass through before they become law? How is Congress organized? Who elects the president? In this version of civic education, students learn—and often memorize for a short time—facts about U.S. citizenship and federal governance. The focus is rarely on local government or current issues, or on developing the skills necessary to participate civically. Your father may remember his civics class this way. Your daughter might be experiencing a version of this type of civics at school today. This dry characterization of civic education is not surprising, given that the majority of U.S. K–12 students learn about citizenship by reading about it in a textbook, filling in worksheets associated with the textbook, and listening to their teachers lecture about the material covered in the text. This textbook-worksheet-lecture combination, while potentially an effective means through which to convey information *about* citizenship, is not an ideal means through which to answer students' questions about *how* to actually engage as democratic citizens and why they should do it. To gain the skills necessary to engage as citizens, students need to practice those skills. To understand why they should engage, students need to understand the value of doing so.

Though typical renditions of civic education have been and continue to be rather dry, they do not have to be that way. In classrooms, schools, districts, and states throughout the United States, teachers use dynamic, contemporary, and locally relevant curricula through which students not only learn about citizenship, but also practice civic skills and gain firsthand understanding of the individual and social benefits of civic engagement. For example, students learn how to consider different sides of an issue through discussion of current events, how the justice system works through mock trials, how Congress works through proposing and deliberating over policy, and how to vote through simulation voting. They experience firsthand the effects of civic engagement through student government, service learning, and local civic action. Research shows—and common sense suggests as well—that interactive, experiential pedagogies effectively increase students' civic skills, interest in politics, and propensity to vote.[1] These curricula are not partisan and need not be demanding in terms of time, finances, or teacher training. They could and should play a much more prominent role in U.S. students' education.

Civic education practitioners know what flourishing civic education interventions can look like. Further, they know—and can learn from—how much institutional support they have needed to gain traction and remain successful. For example, students from 89 of 122 Chicago Public Schools (CPS) high schools (73 percent) participate in the Mikva Challenge's school governance and direct civic action programs. Through the Policymaking, Activism, and Elections prongs of the Mikva Challenge, students acquire knowledge about civic engagement. To learn how to create and enact policies, students from high schools across the CPS district develop district- and state-wide recommendations relevant to education, teen health, youth safety, and out-of-school time. To learn how to vote as an educated citizen, students meet with local government candidates to ask questions about issues that affect them prior to a mock election.

The Mikva Challenge is successful in CPS, partly because of the quality of its programs, the commitment of its staff, and the influence and leadership of its board of directors and advisory board. But beyond these qualities, the organization is successful because CPS—one of the largest school districts in the United States—has committed to integrating Mikva Challenge activities into the district in a systemized way. This commitment grew for several reasons, one of which is that beginning in 1997, the district's institution of a district-wide service-learning requirement gave civic education organizations greater access to CPS classrooms, providing Mikva with a foothold into the system. Another reason for the success of this partnership is that Mikva "realizes that good teachers make things happen in schools," and so the organization "explicitly targets, recruits and takes care of its teacher base."[2] At the start, both Paul Vallas and Arne Duncan, former CEOs of CPS, "embraced Mikva from the top" and their support "trickled down." Finally, the Mikva leadership believes that civic education initiatives must engage in their own campaigning to negotiate district politics—and so invests in such efforts on a regular basis. The keys to Mikva's success, therefore, have been its capacity to maximize the opportunity afforded by the district requirement, merge grassroots support from teachers with top-down support from policymakers, and invest sufficiently in its own politicking to foster ongoing support from both sides of the spectrum.

There is currently no similar national commitment to prioritizing civics education curricula through which students learn how to be, and why they should be, active democratic citizens. Without a strong combination of district, state, federal government, or community-based organization commitment, these more engaging versions of civic education will not flourish and students will continue to learn about citizenship through textbooks, worksheets, and lectures.

THE STATUS QUO: HOW MOST STUDENTS ARE LEARNING ABOUT CITIZENSHIP

At a first look, it may seem that the civic education status quo is sufficient. State social studies standards enumerate desired civic outcomes, and most states require students' enrollment in the types of courses that can address civic education objectives. Yet a closer look demonstrates that the status quo is deficient in fundamental ways that encompass accountability, assessment, and curriculum and instruction issues.

Graduation Requirements and Standards

States pay some lip service to civic education. Most states require that students enroll in three or more semesters of high-school-level social studies—the most common vehicle for civic education—prior to graduation, and all states require that students take at least one social studies course.[3] With respect to civic education in particular, 71 percent of states require that students take at least one semester of U.S. Government to graduate.[4] Similarly, the education standards in all fifty U.S. states specify civic knowledge and skills that students should learn. Arizona's standards are typical: "The goal of the civics strand is to develop the requisite knowledge and skills for informed, responsible participation in public life . . . Students will understand the foundations, principles and institutional practices of the United States as a representative democracy and constitutional republic."[5] In another representative example, the New York State standards assert that "students will use a variety of intellectual skills to demonstrate their understanding of the necessity for establishing governments; the governmental system of the United States and other nations; the U.S. Constitution; the basic civic values of the American constitutional democracy; and the roles, rights and responsibilities of citizenship, including avenues of participation."[6]

Assessment and Accountability

The vast majority of state education policies, however, do not hold students accountable for learning the material addressed in the standards; nor do the policies hold school systems accountable for addressing the standards. Only thirteen states require that students demonstrate proficiency on a social studies test to graduate; of these states, only seven require that students demonstrate civics-specific proficiency.[7] Further, though all states require that students take at least one social studies course to graduate, only ten states require that students take a civics-specific course to graduate from high school.[8] The vast majority of state policies therefore do not actually require students' exposure to civics-specific material to graduate. Finally, only two states require that schools provide students with specific voting instructions, suggesting that policymakers in forty-eight states assume that students will learn to vote through their own volition.[9] In sum, these statistics indicate that while all fifty states address civic knowledge and skills and two-thirds of students must take a civics-related course to be eligible to graduate from high school, in practice, the standards and graduation requirements have very little real traction.

Given this lack of enforced accountability, to what extent do the state-level graduation requirements and standards actually affect the nature of what takes place in civic education classes at the school level? Nearly six out of every seven elementary and secondary school administrators report that teachers in their schools align their social studies courses to the standards.[10] However, teachers tell a different story at the classroom level, with 75 percent of fourth-grade teachers and 85 percent of eighth-grade teachers reporting that to a large extent, they use local—rather than state—curriculum standards to plan their instruction.[11] This discrepancy suggests that while administrators might encourage teachers to teach civics education according to the state standards and even believe that is what is taking place in classrooms, what happens in classrooms has much more to do with local requirements and pressures than with state-level standards.

The lack of widespread accountability and the corresponding lack of adherence to state civics standards might be a double-edged sword. On the one hand, the lack of systematic accountability provides teachers with considerable freedom to teach civics curricula through experiential, relevant pedagogies that keep students engaged and motivated. On the other hand, as other authors in this book explain in greater detail, the results of recent nationally representative National Assessment in Education Progress (NAEP) Civics Education assessments and statistics about declining participation in the civil sphere indicate that students' civic knowledge, skills, and motivation to engage are very low. These indicators suggest that the lack of accountability also translates into lack of classroom-level prioritization of civic education.[12]

This lack of prioritization suggests the need to develop a means to hold students, teachers, and schools accountable for developing students' civic knowledge, skills and motivation. The first question is what schools should assess. Arguably, they should assess more than just the extent to which students learn *about* citizenship—which might be as simple as requiring that every student pass the U.S. citizenship test to graduate from high school. But schools should also assess the extent to which students learn *how* to participate and *why* they should, outcomes that are admittedly more difficult to assess.

Yet these are not impossible to assess. Other tests in widespread use measure similarly complicated outcomes. For example, the Program for International Student Assessment (PISA) test that the Organization for Economic Cooperation and Development (OECD) administers to fifteen-year-olds of the principal industrialized countries every three years addresses whether students "are well prepared for future challenges . . . can analyze, reason and communicate effectively . . . [and] have the capacity to continue learning throughout life."[13] The Tailored Adaptive Personality Assessment System (TAPAS) measures potential military recruits' adaptability, commitment, discipline, ability to work as part of a team, problem-solving skills, and capacity for continuous learning.[14] There is no reason that it would be more difficult to assess students' understanding of the how and why of civil participation than it is to assess "twenty-first-century" and "noncognitive" skills like those assessed though PISA and TAPAS.

What is required, however, is a strong dedication to developing measures that reliably and accurately measure the how and why and that are proven to predict future civic engagement. Schools could then assess the how and why as well as the what through sophisticated yet traditional paper or online tests, or they could harness new technologies like virtual civic environments as means of assessment. Schools would then need to build accountability systems around the new assessment system, such that, for example, all students would be required to score above a certain threshold to graduate from high school, or even to pass fourth grade or eighth grade. Skilled practitioners, researchers, and technical experts could build this system. What is required is political will and funding for the necessary research and development.

What Students Say They Are Learning, and What Teachers Say They Are Teaching

According to several nationally representative surveys of U.S. high school students, in their civics classes most students learn about how the U.S. government works. According to the 2006 Civic and Political Health of the Nation Survey (CPHS), 41 percent of students aged fifteen to twenty-five reported that that the civics curricula they had experienced emphasized the Constitution and how the U.S. government works, and 30 percent reported that their civics curricula emphasized great American heroes and the virtues of the U.S. governmental system.[15] This topical focus is in contrast, for example, to a focus on personal responsibility or social justice, which are two of many other conceivable focuses of civic education.[16] Only 11 percent of students reported that their civics education curricula emphasized racism, other forms of injustice, or other problems facing the nation today—which are all likely to be forms of civic education for social justice.

Teachers seem to concur with students' characterization of focus of the content of civic education courses. For example, of the eighth-grade social studies teachers surveyed as part of the 2010 NAEP civics assessment, nearly 80 percent reported placing a heavy or moderate emphasis on the foundations of the U.S. political system, politics and government, the roles of citizens in a democracy, and the U.S. Constitution. Similarly, over 80 percent of high school administrators reported that teachers in their schools heavily or moderately emphasized the same topics.

Most students learn about how the U.S. government works through a traditional, pedagogical combination of textbook, lecture, and worksheets. Of the NAEP eighth-grade teachers, 86 percent use textbooks at least once a week, with 53 percent of them reporting daily use of textbooks. Thirty percent lecture almost every day, and an additional 53 percent lecture at least once a week. Over 70 percent require that students fill in a worksheet at least once a week. Twelfth-grade students report similar trends, with 65 percent of 9,900 nationally representative twelfth-grade students reporting on the 2010 NAEP that they read from their civics or social studies textbooks at least once a week.[17]

A Closer Look at Civics Textbooks: Learning "About" Citizenship

Given that most students learn about citizenship through textbooks, what are key features of civics textbooks? Textbooks convey facts. They provide students with long and detailed explanations of how the U.S. federal government works and its historical precedents. They also place a heavy emphasis on explanations of U.S. economics and consumerism. They focus as well—albeit to a lesser extent—on facts about state and local government and U.S. foreign relations. In a nutshell, textbooks are chock-full of information *about* citizenship.

While it is important that students learn the factual knowledge included in textbooks, textbook-based civics education on its own is not sufficient. Given the inherently static nature of hard-copy print, textbooks are not well equipped to help students practice their civic skills or to help them understand the value of civic participation in a meaningful way. Nor is textbook-based civic education an ideal way for students to learn to contextualize factual information about citizenship in current or local settings. Further, textbook-based civics education is the status quo, and current measurements of students' levels of civic knowledge and engagement indicate that the status quo has resulted in less-than-satisfactory civic outputs among U.S. youth.

To demonstrate what textbooks do and do not do, I refer to examples from three representative civics education textbooks, each of which is published by a for-profit company and is appropriate for middle school and high school students. They are (in alphabetical order) the 2005 edition of *American Civics*, published by Holt, Rhinehart and Winston; the 2005 edition of *Civics Today: Citizenship, Economics and You*, published by McGraw Hill; and the 2005 edition of *Civics: Government and Economics in Action*, published by Prentice Hall.[18]

Right off the bat, each of the three textbooks positions itself as a tool with which to communicate knowledge about civics. The introductory statement to *American Civics*, for example, reads: "In your study of civics, you will learn a great deal about U.S. government. Your study will also include many other topics that concern most U.S. citizens."[19] The paragraph goes on to list a number of topics about which students will learn. It does not indicate that students will also learn and practice civic skills or that a purpose of the text will be to motivate students to engage as citizens. Similarly, the first section of *Civics* explains to students that the purpose of the study of civics is to answer questions like "What does it mean to be an American? What do we believe about our country and government? How do we know what to expect from our government? How do we know what is expected of us?"[20] The most natural answers to these questions are lists of facts about U.S. government and the rights and responsibilities of citizens. Notably absent from this list are questions like "How do Americans engage as citizens? Why should we civically engage? How can we affect how our government functions?" In a comparable introductory section to *Civics Today*, the authors suggest that learning about citizenship and economics will naturally extend to civic engagement and to responsible consumerism: "Understanding how the government operates and how you can participate in it will help you become a responsible and informed citizen. Understanding the basic economic principles of the American market system will help you learn how to make wise economic decisions."[21] The assumption is that with their newfound knowledge about citizenship and economics, students will be able to transfer what they have learned about citizenship and consumerism to action. This assumption minimizes the well-documented challenge that people—and especially adolescents—generally find it extremely difficult to transfer learning from theoretical to practical settings.[22]

Each of these three introductory statements indicates that the purpose of all three texts is to teach students about citizenship. They accomplish that purpose by providing students with hundreds of pages of facts and arguments about a rather consistent set of topics. Each of the texts begins with a unit about what it means to be a citizen and the roots of democracy. The following unit typically includes information about the Constitution and Bill of Rights. Other units address the federal government's purpose and structures, as well as units on state and local government. All three texts also include units on economic principles and citizens' economic rights and responsibilities. Textbooks are a reasonable means with which to convey to students vast amounts of information about citizenship in a reference-book format.

To actually engage as citizens, students need to learn not only *about* citizenship, but also *how* to engage as citizens. That is, they need to learn and practice the skills necessary for citizenship. Textbook authors attempt to address this need by including lists of skills that effective citizens use and even suggest ways to practice these skills. *American Civics*, for example, claims to address the following skills:

Using the internet, learning from pictures, reading flowcharts, reading bar graphs, interpreting political cartoons, reading organizational charts, writing to your legislator, reading newspaper articles, registering to vote, understanding polls, reading pie graphs, using television as a resource, distinguishing fact from opinion, working in groups, conducting library research, understanding warranties, reading labels, writing checks, reading line graphs, creating a database, reading help-wanted ads, reading tables, using primary sources, comparing points of view, reading maps.[23]

Civics Today contains a shorter list of similar skills, including "taking notes, reading an election map, interpreting a political cartoon, analyzing news media, using library resources, making decisions, problem solving, reading a time zone map."[24] These are all skills that citizens need to participate effectively.

There are, however, two fundamental problems with these lists. First, they omit other critical skills that are very difficult to address in a static book format, including effective oral (and written, if teachers assign worksheets in place of essays) communication, deliberative skills, and teamwork. Second, to effectively engage as citizens, students would almost always need to integrate the skills, not just to practice them individually. For example, to successfully ask the city to put a new crosswalk in a highly trafficked area near a school, students would at least need to synthesize their abilities to use the Internet; read charts, tables, graphs, and maps; and analyze news media and communicate effectively through written and oral means. And they would need to transfer these individual textbook skills to the local-government context. While it is one thing to learn and practice each of those skills on an individual basis, it is quite another to practice integrating a set of skills within the context of an actual civic project.

Civics addresses the concern of synthesizing skills in a more effective way than do the other two textbooks. This text includes a page dedicated to each of twelve citizenship "skills," including "how to volunteer" (page 9); "how to interview for a job" (68); "how to analyze public documents" (119); "how to conduct a survey" (248); "how to write a letter to the editor" (304); "how to analyze an editorial" (362); "how to be a wise consumer" (408); "how to write a letter to a public official" (468); "how to analyze television news programs" (517); "how to analyze news articles" (568); "how to conduct an interview" (630); and "how to express your views" (678).[25]

Each of these individual "skills" can be understood as *civic actions*, most of which students will need to engage effectively in democracy. To successfully execute each of the civic actions listed above and expounded upon in *Civics*, students must integrate many of the individual skill components listed in the other two textbooks. To successfully analyze public documents, for example, students will probably need to learn to use the Internet, learn from pictures, read flowcharts and bar graphs, read organizational charts, read newspaper articles, and use at least nine other skills listed individually in *American Civics*. To synthesize a host of separate civic skills and transfer them to a particular civic context requires sophisticated integration of basic civic skills.

The challenge is that the nature of the overpacked, reference-book format of the textbook makes it impossible to dedicate the necessary amount of attention to building civic skills that young people actually require. *Civics* allocates one page to each of the twelve skills. Each page includes a brief overview of the skill (or action), a fictional example of how a student practiced that skill, and the steps required to first learn the skill, then practice the skill, and finally apply the skill. For example, the "how to express your views" page begins with an example of a student who "was upset with her city's plan to tear down her school and build a new one."[26] Below, the text recommends that to express their views, students first need to identify a local issue of importance about which they could become involved. Next they should learn which are the relevant governmental departments and the roles of individuals with potential impact within those departments. Finally, students should determine the most effective means through which to express their opinion. For example, the text recommends that students could write a letter to the most appropriate person or attend a city council meeting or speak with neighbors, or do some combination of these. Finally, to actually apply the skill, the text suggests that students prepare a short summary of the topic they researched and deliver the speech to the class.

While the instructions seem specific enough, on the ground, students will usually need far more guidance to successfully undertake a given civic action. Identifying a local issue that interests the student and about which he or she could become involved requires much more unpacking than the brief instructions would suggest. Understanding the organizational and power structures of local governmental departments requires even more. While the above example is theoretically an excellent way for students to learn to express their opinions, in reality, to successfully implement the task, teachers will need to dedicate preparation and classroom time. If a teacher's main objective, however, is to "cover" the vast amount of textual subject matter, he or she may either speed through the skill-building exercise in a superficial way or skip it entirely. As Meira Levinson recounts in *No Citizen Left Behind*: "Given standardized curriculum and especially standardized testing mandates, teachers have no incentive—actually, a negative incentive—to use these textbook resources . . . When I taught eighth grade, therefore, I skipped over almost every one of the sidebars, insets, and pages emphasizing active citizenship because they did not fit into my curriculum calendar. It is hard to see how and why other teachers might be led to make a different choice."[27] Though it is impossible to assert with complete certainty, it seems unlikely that many teachers currently use textbook-based skill-building exercises to effectively develop students' civic skills.

WHAT SHOULD BE THE STATUS QUO: LEARNING HOW TO ENGAGE CIVICALLY AND THE REASONS FOR ENGAGEMENT

A grasp of American history, government, and economics covered by textbooks is critical to understanding the hows and whys of engagement as citizens. But while this knowledge foundation is necessary, it is not sufficient. Textbooks are not well equipped to help students to practice their civic skills or to develop a meaningful, effective understanding of the value of civic participation.

Fortunately, many ways of teaching civics do not seem to suffer the challenges faced by textbook-based learning about citizenship. These methods are appropriate for students and teachers of all political persuasions and are not expensive. Teachers can incorporate all three types of civic education into classroom learning, or they can offer these programs as extracurricular activities. It seems likely that if districts and states supported these nontextbook civic education methods to the extent to which they support textbooks, teachers would readily incorporate them into their classrooms. The programs that are most successful in terms of their reach and sustainability work in partnership with schools, districts, states, and community organizations rather than on a one-off basis with individual teachers and schools.

Discussion of Current Events

As several authors in this book point out and some studies demonstrate, through discussion of current issues, students can learn to consider different sides of an issue, to engage in reasoned debate, to give adequate attention to issues of public importance, and, more generally, to understand educated discourse in a healthy democracy.[28] The best practices shared by teachers who effectively incorporate discussion of current events into their civics courses include selecting relevant topics, defining clear discussion protocols, using background materials that teach students about various perspectives, and recognizing the importance of whether or not to share their own position on an issue.[29]

Following these best practices can be challenging for teachers who may have little personal knowledge or understanding of a given current issue or who do not have experience guiding structured discussions, especially of potentially controversial topics. To address this need, several organizations have created guides to current-event topical content and best practices for teachers. For example, to stimulate classroom-based discussion of historical and current political events, the Close Up

Foundation annually publishes *Current Issues*, which provides teachers with tools to moderate discussions of themes with which they might be unfamiliar or of which they have only limited personal understanding. Among other topics, the 2011–2012 edition of *Current Issues* helps teachers to discuss events that were the focus of the national policy agenda in 2011, including the debates over health care, the national debt ceiling, airport screening, the war on terror, and trade with Latin America.[30] For each topic, *Current Issues* first outlines the issue, citing sources with a range of political affiliations. The guides also include speculative statements about the issue's potential future policy directions, lists of debate questions, and links to further readings.

Founded in 1971, Close Up has published *Current Issues* for the past thirty-five years and has a current circulation of approximately ten thousand. Since its inception, Close Up has also organized trips to government institutions in Washington, D.C., for approximately seven hundred thousand students from throughout the United States. The members of its board of directors and advisers are influential people, and the program itself has persisted in part because of the quality of its curriculum. Yet what differentiates Close Up from other providers of effective civic education curriculum are its funders and partners, who include the U.S. Congress, the U.S. Department of Education, the U.S. Department of the Interior, C-SPAN, and Bank of America. This level of institutional support has permitted Close Up to offer *Current Issues* at one-half to one-third the cost of textbooks. Close Up therefore is an example of an organization, like the Mikva Challenge, that is successful not just because of the quality of its programs but also because of systemic support.

Tools like *Current Issues* and other similar resources (e.g., the Speak Out program provided through the Leonore Annenberg Institute for Civics and Deliberating in a Democracy, sponsored by the Constitutional Rights Foundation and Street Law, Inc.) could, at a cost that is a fraction of that spent on textbooks every year, improve the nature of existing classroom discussions of current events. These resources could also increase the prevalence of discussions among the nearly half of fourth-grade teachers and the quarter of eighth-grade teachers who report that they incorporate discussion of current events into their civics and social studies classes less than once a week.[31] These materials are relatively cheap and easy to use and provide teachers and students essential knowledge about a range of issues.

Teachers will not universally use them, however, unless their schools, districts, and state support—even require—that students regularly discuss current events. Without institutional support from above, teachers understandably focus their teaching on what is required—for example, the steps a bill goes through to become law—rather than on what is not required, for example, the most recent status of the U.S.-Afghanistan war. And they understandably rely on conventional resources like the textbooks that are already in their classrooms, rather than on resources like *Current Issues*, which they might need to expend time and energy to obtain.

Simulations

Through a type of experiential education knows as simulation, students contextualize their civic knowledge and practice civic skills in realistic imitations of civic activities such as trials, voting, and congressional deliberation. Simulation-based learning is not new. For example, students simulated League of Nations proceedings beginning in the 1920s and continue today to learn about global issues by role-playing international representatives during Model United Nations simulations of UN proceedings. Yet despite simulations' long-standing use, recommended status, and evidence of positive correlations between simulations and students' civic engagement, less than half of U.S. students report ever participating in simulations in their social studies or civics classes.[32]

MOCK TRIAL

In one example of a simulation program, students learn about the justice system by preparing for and participating in mock trials. To successfully take part in the mock trial process, students must learn information about the structure and functioning of the justice system. They must also understand abstractly that to take part in the legal system, they need to follow stated procedures, thoroughly collect and examine evidence, consider multiple perspectives, develop organized and coherent arguments, and communicate clearly and persuasively in oral and written forms. Short of participating in a real trial, there is no other way for students to understand as tangibly the value of trying a case in front of a jury. Through mock trials, therefore, students do not just learn about the justice system. They also learn how to take part in the system and why people do so. In a lesson that is especially valuable for youth, they learn firsthand that the justice system—and by extension, the government—is theirs.

Most mock-trial programs usually take place at the middle school, high school, college, and postgraduate levels. Court cases become increasingly complex as students get older and develop more experience with the law. Depending on the complexity of the case, students may spend anywhere from several weeks to most of an academic year preparing to try the case. For example, through the duration of the ten-week mock-trial program of Discovering Justice (DJ), a Boston-based, non-profit civic education provider that works primarily with underserved communities, middle school students meet once a week with volunteer lawyers who help them to prepare for the culminating trial. During the first few weeks of the program, students are supported by the lawyer and work in real law offices, learning the details of the case. They interview witnesses, determine which witnesses to include in the trial, and piece together facts. As a united group, they sort through the facts and figure out which testimony belongs on each side. Midway through the ten-week program, in consultation with DJ staff and the students' teacher, the guiding lawyer divides the students into the two sides and assigns students to specific roles. Students then organize the presentation of their evidence, prepare their opening and closing statements, and plan for their examinations and cross-examinations of witnesses. The entire preparation process requires a substantial amount of analysis and organization on the parts of students, teachers, lawyers, and the DJ staff. During the trial itself—which takes place in local courtrooms in front of real judges—student prosecutors and defendants give opening statements, examine and cross-examine witnesses, and give closing arguments and rebuttals.[33]

Through mock trial curricula, students learn how the U.S. justice system works by actually trying legal cases in a courtroom in front of a judge and jury. They also practice the mechanical skills that lawyers use to try cases and gain exposure to the career options and opportunities that are available through the justice system.[34] From a theoretical perspective, students also learn that the U.S. system is designed to resolve conflicts fairly and peacefully and that people cannot base their arguments on emotions. Rather, they learn that winning arguments must be reasoned, ordered, structured, and formal.[35] Learning firsthand how the justice system works can be a compelling way to believe in the benefits of the U.S. justice system and to draw students into the civic system.

Like other successful civic education programs, DJ works in partnership with schools, districts, other community partners, and funders. By 2011, across its four programs (of which the mock trial DJ program is one), DJ currently works with over fifty Massachusetts schools across seven districts, including over half of Boston Public Schools and all of Lowell Public Schools. DJ also works with, among others, law firms, the City of Boston Legal Department, the Boys & Girls Clubs of Boston, and Citizen Schools.[36] According to DJ's executive director, Elisabeth J. Medvedow, the primary reason DJ has the traction it does for its four programs in Massachusetts is because of superintendent support, support of the judiciary, law firms, and legal agencies, as well as school-level support and community partnerships.[37] This high-level support has facilitated DJ's ability, for example, to share its Children Discovering Justice program with principals, who in turn pass along program materials to teachers and otherwise manifest their support. Another key contributor to DJ's success in Massachusetts is that funding from private foundations, corporations, and individuals enables DJ to subsidize the costs of running its simulation programs. And finally, presence in the Massachusetts legal and business communities legitimizes DJ's credibility in schools and districts throughout the state.

SIMULATION VOTING

Through textbooks, students can learn the characteristics of a representative democracy and how representation compares and contrasts with direct democracy. They can learn the historical precedents behind the electoral college system, campaign finance rules, and election procedures. They can even learn the steps necessary to vote (how) and why every vote counts. By taking part in a voting simulation program or working at a poll, however, students practice the skills associated with educated voting and feel the value of casting their vote.

Several organizations offer curricula that are specifically intended to teach students why they should vote and how to do it, through simulation. In one example, the Kids Voting USA (KVUSA) program, students register for elections and then vote for their candidate as part of a school-wide simulation election, either online or via paper ballots at official polling sites alongside adults. The KVUSA organization personalizes its voting platform for individual schools, by school name, grade, and candidate. The elections can be a motivating way for students to understand how to vote and why people vote.[38] As a fifth-grader from Ohio explained, "When I first heard about us doing the polling place I was very excited. I knew it was going to teach us a lot about what voting is like and why we vote in the first place."[39]

In addition to organizing the technical side of the voting simulation, KVUSA offers lessons on the importance of voting, the responsibilities of the positions the candidates are running for, and the candidates themselves. The organization also helps schools to facilitate students' participation as volunteer poll workers. Based on her KVUSA experience volunteering as a poll worker, a high-school participant explains that "it is through voting that all the 500 or so people who came into that church to vote were able to have their voices heard . . . Voting is what shows politicians that even though we may not be in charge, we do have a voice and more than anything, voting forces politicians to listen."[40] Through KVUSA, students learn that the process of registering to vote is quick and efficient. They feel the excitement of casting their vote and waiting for the results to come in.[41] They learn what it feels like when their candidate wins or loses. Especially in close races, they gain a firsthand experience of why every vote counts.

KVUSA, founded in 1988, currently partners with schools and election officials in nineteen states. Each of these nineteen states has a state-, county-, or district-wide executive director who coordinates KVUSA activities, disseminates materials to participating schools, manages tasks like aligning the KVUSA curriculum to state social studies or civics standards, and shares innovations, both within the local network and externally with other networks nationwide. For example, the KVUSA Tampa affiliate built the original version of the online voting system, which is now used by KVUSA at the national level. Regional associations also fund-raise to pay their KVUSA "affiliation fee," so that participating schools do not have to pay for KVUSA program materials and training.[42] Its regional association-based organizational structure has been an effective way for KVUSA to gain traction outside its local headquarters area and to extend its program to a national audience.

Civic Action

Civic action curricula, including student government and service learning, go a step beyond simulations, providing students with opportunities to learn the hows and whys of engaging in the political process by actually participating in it. They can learn how to contextualize their knowledge and practice their skills through engaging in local civic action. They can learn why people value civic action though firsthand experience. As James Youniss argues in chapter 5, "by design, student government allows young people to build experience with voting, campaigning, forming coalitions, negotiating, and dealing with institutional structure." Youniss also demonstrates that students who take part in service learning that is designed explicitly to develop their civic engagement in policy issues do in fact increase their propensity to engage in political acts.

STUDENT GOVERNMENT

Through participation in student government, students learn how to address relevant issues through a governmental structure that aligns rather closely to that of local government. Their experience in every step of the student government process—from campaigning, to assuming a given position, to fulfilling the responsibilities of that position, to addressing issues of importance to constituents (namely, other students), to proposing and enacting new policies—prepares students to later take on actual governmental roles. Through student government, students learn and practice the skills necessary for effective citizenship in a context that can have real and lasting impacts on their local school communities.

In an example of a district-wide student government (see other examples in chapter 5), through the Chicago-based Mikva Challenge's Youth Council program, students from high schools across the Chicago Public Schools district develop district-wide recommendations relevant to education, teen health, youth safety, and out-of-school time. In 2010, the Education Council wrote a report recommending ways to use new technologies to make district pedagogy and curricula more relevant and rigorous. The Teen Health Council recommended strategies to increase students' access to healthy food and exercise—recommendations that have led to improvements in the quality of school lunch food. The Youth Safety Council recommended ways for district security officers to more effectively contribute to reducing violence in district schools. Their recommendations contributed to CPS's adoption of a program that matches students with a person who accompanies and protects them as they walk to and from school. The Out-of-School Time Council works with city government to increase students' access to after-school and summer employment; their efforts contributed to the passing of a statewide out-of-school bill in the spring of 2010.[43]

To develop and communicate these policy recommendations, the Youth Council students must learn and synthesize virtually all of the skills listed in the three textbooks discussed earlier in this chapter. They practice civic skills in an organized forum through which they have sufficient support. Throughout the policy creation and recommendation process, students "have access to city decision makers" and they are able to communicate their findings to a receptive audience. Participating students also feel that they gain an increased understanding of politics and policy making, gain confidence that what they have to say matters, expand their network beyond their home school, mature, develop their oral and written communication skills, and feel encouraged to persist in school.[44]

SERVICE LEARNING

According to Learn and Serve America, a program of the federally administered Corporation for National and Community Service, service learning "engages students in the educational process, using what they learn in the classroom to solve real-life problems. Students not only learn about democracy and citizenship, they become actively contributing citizens and community members through the service they perform.'[45] Service learning projects have clearly defined academic and civic objectives, which typically include the goal of developing students' sense of responsibility to their community. For example, through learning about the science and economics of waste management best practices, students can then create and execute a recycling plan for their school.

Service learning rates vary quite dramatically between states; for example, 51 percent of students aged sixteen to eighteen volunteered in Utah, compared with 16 percent in the District of Columbia. Maryland is the only state that requires that all students fulfill a community service obligation to graduate from high school.[46] Since 1993, the state has mandated that each of the state's twenty-four districts require that students complete a service-learning requirement to graduate from high school. Students must either complete seventy-five hours of service learning that includes planning, action, and reflection phases or complete an individually designed program that is approved by the state superintendent.[47] The state also provides schools and teachers with service-learning training, curriculum, and evaluation means. Maryland contrasts starkly with other states, in which currently less than 50 percent of schools implement a service-learning requirement and in which 80 percent of fourth- and eighth-grade students never participate in community projects.[48]

Most service-learning programs follow roughly the same steps, which require students to identify problems in their communities, learn different perspectives about the problem and who the key stakeholders are, create a plan that addresses the problem, implement the plan, and then reflect upon the whole experience. While most K–12 teachers create their own context-specific service-learning curriculum, several organizations provide packaged service-learning curricula, including the Center for Civic Education, the Constitutional Rights Foundation, Earth Force, the Kids Consortium, Learn and Serve America, and Street Law.

Curricula that promote engagement with local and state government as a means of addressing local problems are a less common form of service learning. Yet as Youniss explains, this type of service learning arguably increases students' civic engagement more effectively than do more conventional service projects that do not require governmental interaction. For example, students who participate in the Project Citizen program, which is run by the Center for Civic Education, learn how local and state governments function. They do this by choosing a local problem, researching how the problem affects their community, and proposing a public policy that will address the problem. The curriculum clearly outlines each of the steps necessary to successfully address a local problem through working with local government, so that teachers understand how to guide their students, who subsequently understand how to proceed from one task to the next.

The initial steps of the Project Citizen curriculum are for students to identify several problems in their community and to choose one that they will study in depth. Using Project Citizen, students have successfully driven policy initiatives to widen the road in front of a school; create a local recreation center; change voter registration rules; reinitiate a school music program; and require bike helmets. During the identification stage, teachers lead discussions about the extent to which students are already aware of local challenges and the extent to which they need to learn more from members of their community and local or state government representatives. The next step is for students to research the problem, by first identifying sources of information, including local or state government, and then gathering the information as part of research teams. The final steps are for students to synthesize their research findings and then propose a public policy that addresses their summary of the problem. Students present their public policy recommendations to their peers and others in their school and then can also present their recommendations to a panel of local citizens organized by the Project Citizen staff. The entire project typically takes anywhere from a few weeks to several months to complete.

Until 2011, the U.S. Department of Education funded the Center for Civic Education, which had offered Project Citizen and the We the People simulation program though a national network that includes all fifty states and 435 congressional districts. State and district coordinators provided Project Citizen and We the People materials and training to schools and organized panels of local citizens with whom students share their policy recommendations. Funding was cut abruptly in mid-2011, reducing the Center for Civic Education's staff of seventy-four down to twelve. Without Department of Education support, it is not clear whether the Project Citizen and We the People programs and network will continue.

CONCLUSION

The problem is not a general lack of civic education curricula. Nor is it a lack of innovative, experiential, motivational, nonpartisan, and inexpensive civic education curricula. The problem is that the majority of U.S. students currently do not benefit from the resources that exist. Only a minority of eighth-grade students report that their civics classes include curricula other than the textbook or discussion of current events. Fifty-nine percent of fourth-grade students, 53 percent of eighth-grade students, and 56 percent of twelfth-grade students report that they never participate in simulations or mock trials.[49] Nearly 70 percent of students never write letters to newspapers or otherwise express their opinions in a public way. Only 30 percent of fourth- or eighth-grade teachers report that their students engage in some form of student government. Less than 20 percent of fourth- or eighth-grade teachers organize visits from members of the community or report that their students participate in community projects.

If dynamic civic education curricula exist, why do less than half of students experience them? At the base of the system is an American public who gives lip service to the premise that civic education is fundamental to the purpose of public education but that does not back up that lip service with demand and support for classroom-level emphasis on civic education. The widespread lack of high-level adoption and of student- and school-level accountability for developing or demonstrating civic competencies demonstrates this lack of demand.

Without systemic support starting at the state level and working its way to the district level, teachers encounter time challenges that hinder their ability to teach civic education. Currently, most teachers must scramble to cover the material that will be tested—material that rarely includes civic knowledge and almost never includes civic skills or attitudes. This coverage pressure leaves teachers with insufficient classroom time to use the excellent civic education resources that they could integrate, at little financial cost, into their course plans. Structural support for dynamic civic education strategies is necessary if teachers are to overcome the coverage challenge. This focus will require multipronged, top-down efforts from district, state, and federal policymakers and bottom-up efforts from teachers, administrators, parents, funding sources, and community organizations. It also requires that civic education providers, like those that I spotlight in this chapter, continue to take it upon themselves to persist in building the sorts of political alliances that will strengthen their footholds in communities and schools.

A necessary element of the strategy is accountability. Without some assessment and accountability system, civic education takes the backseat to subjects for which schools, teachers, and students are held accountable. This is not to say that the answer is to use a traditional bubble-test format assessment to test students' knowledge. I have argued throughout this chapter that learning facts about citizenship is not a sufficient way to prepare students to participate in and strengthen our democracy. Rather, we should develop, research, and use measures of the civic and political knowledge, skills, and inclination to engage that students gain through dynamic curricula.

Finally, from a research perspective, there is much more to be done beyond the critical step of developing and researching an assessment system. Most of the existing research on civic education is based on observational data, permitting only correlational conclusions, and is small in scale, limiting generalizability.[50] The U.S. educational system needs research that permits causal inference, is applicable to broader settings, and can be used by policymakers to address the problem of students' low civic knowledge and participation in the civic sphere. Educators should learn why some districts and states like Chicago Public Schools and Maryland have been able to enact and sustain policies that promote schools' implementation of active civics programs. Stories of success can teach a lot. Similarly, educators should study the impacts on student outcomes of dynamic programs that enjoy strong local, district, state, or federal support and how those programs have built and maintained that level of support. U.S. education should also better understand the contexts and motivations of administrators and teachers who are able to prioritize nontextbook civic education curricula, including in settings that benefit from less structural support of civic education. This agenda is robust and needs much higher levels of financial and political support than it currently receives. Yet to build and institutionalize a dynamic, nationwide civic education system based on strong evidence of what works and knowledge of how to measure its impact on student learning, it is an agenda Americans must address.

7

EXPANDING PRESERVICE TEACHERS' IMAGES OF SELF, STUDENTS, AND DEMOCRACY

Keith C. Barton

Public schools in the United States should play an important role in preparing students to participate in democratic life, for schools are places in which they can deliberate issues of public concern, engage with people whose backgrounds differ from their own, and develop the knowledge and skills needed to reason deeply about public affairs. Schools serve other functions as well, and they are not the only sites for encouraging democratic participation; nonetheless, the link between education and democracy is deeply rooted in the nation's history, and it is difficult to imagine a democratic future that does not depend on an educated public. Promoting civic participation is a central purpose of schools, and so it is central to the work of teachers.

Yet, too often, schools fall short of this goal. In particular, they frequently fail to develop young people who understand how knowledge is constructed, who engage with diverse perspectives, and who reason carefully about difficult issues. Instead, students may receive a steady diet of superficial and uncontroversial content, with few opportunities to examine authentic issues critically or to consider alternative view-points. They are especially unlikely to learn about controversial public problems; schools sometimes prohibit such topics from even being mentioned. If they never encounter the issues that animate public life, however, students will be ill equipped for their own roles as informed decision-makers. Minority students and those from lower socioeconomic backgrounds are particularly unlikely to experience the kind of schooling that will prepare them for democratic civic participation.[1]

There is no shortage of blame for the ills of schooling. Fault is variously attributed to the restrictions of the standards and accountability movement, or a lack of standards and accountability; to shortcomings of traditional teacher education programs, or weaknesses of alternative routes to teaching; to a tenure system that protects incompetent teachers, or inadequate protection for those who take risks; to an oppressive system of social hierarchy that sorts students into anticipated future roles, or an entrenched liberal bureaucracy that focuses on self-esteem instead of academic learning. However much truth (or how little) there may be in these explanations, it is teachers themselves who deserve special attention in thinking about how to develop schools that are more democratic. Whatever institutional and societal constraints direct their work, teachers nonetheless make decisions about how to educate students. All teachers have at least some latitude—and sometimes a great deal of it—in choosing materials, developing instructional activities, and selecting topics for study. Teachers can use this latitude to encourage democratic participation or hinder it.

In recent years, a large body of literature has developed that places teachers and teacher education—rather than the organizational forces of schooling—at the center of attention. This work emphasizes the importance of developing teachers who understand subject matter deeply and who know how to teach it, who have experience reflecting on instructional practices, and who can modify their teaching according to evidence of effectiveness. Such efforts are indispensable for meaningful civic education, and teacher educators have long been involved in developing, implementing, and refining procedures that would enhance teachers' capacities in these areas, particularly in the preparation of social studies teachers.[2] Yet helping new teachers learn *how* to teach will never be enough. A teacher education program must do more than provide its students with pedagogical skills and knowledge; it must also help them develop a commitment to actually implement these when they have a chance. Not only must teachers know how to teach for democracy, but they must also *want* to do so.

To help teachers learn both how to teach democracy and why it is critical to do so, teacher education programs must devote systematic and sustained attention to the aims of education, including the relationship between democracy and schooling, the role of teachers, and the views of youth. Teachers begin their preparation programs with admirable perspectives and motives, but their images of themselves, their future students, and democracy itself often are limited, and these limited visions place important obstacles in the way of promoting democratic participation. This means that teacher education can never be a purely instrumental endeavor. It must also be devoted to expanding teachers' visions, for only a commitment to the democratic purposes of schooling will lead to lasting changes in practice. Expanding teachers' visions, though, requires more than presenting them with new ideas or perspectives; it requires democratic engagement with these ideas, and deliberation over the ideas' implications for teaching and learning. University-based teacher education programs can fulfill this responsibility in a way that other settings and institutions cannot.

DEVELOPING IMAGES OF EDUCATION FOR DEMOCRACY

Walter Parker argues that educators are "the primary stewards of democracy" because "they must do what no one else in society has to do: intentionally specify the democratic ideal sufficiently to make it a reasonably distinct curriculum target, one that will justify selecting from the universe of possibilities a manageable set of subject matters, materials, instructional methods, modes of classroom interactions, and school experiences."[3] This is asking a lot of teachers, but Parker's description highlights how in U.S. society, Americans explicitly and intentionally charge schools with preparing students for democracy. Many other groups and individuals—from courts to politicians to civic organizations to fellow citizens on the street—have an *interest* in such preparation, but no one else has such direct responsibility for turning democratic ideals into educational experiences. Teachers must engage students in pursuing what Parker calls "the central citizenship question of our time," namely, "how can we live together justly, in ways that are mutually satisfying, and which leave our differences, both individual and group, intact and our multiple identities recognized?"[4]

Helping young people tackle this question is a responsibility of all teachers in public schools. Although issues of democracy are ever present in social studies lessons, preparation for civic participation also occurs throughout the school day—not only during academic study but also in corridors, playgrounds, clubs, and other public spaces. Elementary teachers, for example, direct students' experiences during at least half of the children's years in school, and this is the time when children first learn what it means to be part of a public beyond their homes and families. At these grade levels, students not only learn about the nature of government and society but also learn how to get along with others, how to make themselves heard, and how to reason carefully about matters of joint concern. In middle and secondary schools, meanwhile, students need to apply democratic ideals in a variety of subjects and settings. This includes not only such obvious procedures as developing classroom rules but all the many elements of democratic life: considering multiple viewpoints, basing conclusions on evidence, communicating clearly and respectfully, and so on. Teachers have to think about how these principles apply to their subject matter, and they must also consider how to deal with daily civic dilemmas—how to respond to a racist comment, when to include controversial topics, how to promote self-direction without ignoring the curriculum, and so on.[5] All of this requires that teachers have a sophisticated image of democracy, because otherwise, they won't easily recognize which materials, activities, and interactions are best suited to its pursuit.

Yet teachers rarely enter their programs with such images. Most teachers have a positive image of democracy and believe that it deserves promotion, but they generally have not thought much about its complexities, its relationship to schooling, or their own lives as democratic citizens.[6] Sometimes they even recoil at the mention of the word *democracy*, or they suggest that developing a commitment to democratic life is something that belongs at home, not school.[7] When asked to discuss the characteristics of democracy, meanwhile, they quickly identify voting as its essential element, but they have trouble going much further. Secondary teachers in fields such as math, science, or art may see little reason even to discuss democracy, while social studies teachers often limit themselves to talk about basic features of the U.S. political system (especially the three branches of government or how a bill becomes law). Even teachers who have specifically chosen to teach students about civics usually have little to say about the variety of individual, collective, and institutional aspects of democratic societies.[8] Most beginning teachers are not deeply conversant with such fundamental democratic ideas and procedures as justice, human rights, civil society, or public deliberation.

Teachers usually find the term *citizenship* more familiar them *democracy*, but here, too, their ideas are thin ones. Most preservice teachers identify the characteristics of good citizenship as behaviors that involve being personally responsible, following laws and being loyal to the nation, and getting along with and helping others (including nonpolitical community engagement).[9] They value the contribution of education to society and even identify this as one of their reasons for becoming a teacher, but the lessons in citizenship that they hope to impart are often those of obedience and compliance. They want students to learn the difference between right and wrong, to respect authority, and to recognize the importance of private property.[10] Good citizens should certainly demonstrate these behaviors (although their meaning is complicated and contested), but such characteristics are not unique to *democratic* citizens. After all, subjects of authoritarian and totalitarian regimes are also expected to be responsible, to follow laws, to be loyal to the nation, and to get along with and help others.[11]

To fulfill their role as stewards of democracy, teachers need to move from these initial ideas toward more complete and complicated ideas about the nature of democracy. They need to think about multiple forms of political participation, the relationship between public policy and the common good, the need for deliberation and reasoned judgment, the productive tension between unity and diversity, the necessary (but difficult) task of hearing multiple perspectives, and all the ways that democratic citizens depend on and are responsible for each other. In particular, teachers need to consider the implications of democratic ideals for schooling. They need to grapple with sometimes competing ideas about the purpose of education; how schools have succeeded or failed in contributing to democracy; the relationship between public and private aims of education and the responsibilities that schools have toward each; and what kinds of education best prepare students for civic participation. These are highly authentic issues, ones that consistently animate local, state, and federal debates about educational policy. And importantly, they are open and contested questions, ones for which no single right answer exists. There are multiple perspectives, for example, on how best to serve democratic ends (should schools promote unity or emphasize diversity?) and how far the public purposes of schooling should reach (should schools require public service? should they teach sex education?). When teachers discuss these issues, then, not only are they learning *about* the role of education in a democracy, but they are also practicing democracy themselves.

This is not an argument, however, for transforming teacher education programs into courses in political philosophy. Teachers' coursework cannot be limited to abstract, theoretical considerations, although abstract ideas certainly have their place as a foundation for reasoning. Nor should students consider only public policy that takes place at the organizational level, such as governmental decisions about curricula or school structure. Rather, discussion of educational aims should be part of subject- and grade-specific preparation of specialized courses as well as general ones. Teachers need to evaluate the democratic implications not only of broad educational policies, but also of the day-to-day practices of schooling. They need to consider how resources, assignments, instructional objectives, lesson activities, classroom organization, management procedures, and interpersonal relations promote or hinder students' civic participation. Only if preservice teachers have examined such questions thoughtfully and systematically are they likely to teach in ways that reflect a principled understanding of the relationship between teachers, students, and democracy. That should be the core of teacher preparation: considering the consequences of pedagogical practices for the life of a democratic society.

EXPANDING TEACHERS' IMAGES OF THEMSELVES

My own students, future social studies teachers from cities and towns speckled across the Midwest, have admirable reasons for wanting to teach—from developing children's potential, to making them feel valued, to providing role models. But there is one thing they never say, at least not at the beginning of their program: no one wants to become a teacher to improve democracy. They are not alone. The reasons people have for becoming teachers are remarkably consistent, and while most of those reasons are commendable, they are not necessarily relevant to preparing students for democratic participation. In some cases, their motivations even make such preparation more difficult. As a result, even if teachers develop more complicated notions of the relationship between democracy and education, teachers may still not see a role for themselves in the equation because they have entered the profession for other reasons altogether.

Most people become teachers because they want to work with young people.[12] There's nothing wrong with that, and in fact, it's an indispensable requirement for a career in teaching. But teachers' ideas about what it means to work with young people are influenced by their own previous experiences, and these ideas can be constraining. In elementary schools, many teachers conflate their role with that of mothers; after all, teaching has long been equated with "women's work." As a result, many elementary teachers see their jobs in terms of caring for and protecting children. (Secondary teachers may be more likely to think of themselves as coaches or role models.) But as Jennifer Hauver James points out, this blurs the distinction between the public space of classrooms and the private space where mothering typically occurs, and as a result, teachers often withhold experiences that would prepare students for democratic life.[13]

For example, James notes that elementary teachers resist engaging students in activities that involve historical interpretation, such as looking at multiple perspectives or drawing conclusions from evidence. Both these procedures are indispensable for the kind of historical understanding necessary in a democratic society, and both are well within the capacity of young children. Yet these activities are rarely found in elementary schools, particularly in the primary grades. Teachers explain their avoidance of historical interpretation by pointing out that it is both "developmentally" and morally inappropriate. Exposing students to multiple viewpoints, they suggest, is too difficult and confusing for young children; letting them know that Columbus and other explorers mistreated Indians, meanwhile, would be too upsetting.[14] Even at the secondary level, teachers often avoid controversial topics out of fear that students will encounter upsetting perspectives, or that class members will make comments that offend each other's beliefs. Confronting students with information, interactions, or tasks that are difficult, confusing, or upsetting violates teachers' image of themselves as protectors of young people.

Another of the most common reasons for entering the profession is a love of schooling—or, especially at the secondary level, a love of subject matter.[15] Prospective teachers often hope to inspire a similar passion in their students. This too is an admirable goal, for civic participation depends on far-reaching knowledge of the human and natural worlds and an ability to acquire and evaluate information. But too often, the kinds of subject matter that teachers love, and the kinds of schooling they are fond of, may not be those that will contribute most to the needs of a democratic society. It is a commonplace that most of us who have become teachers were "good" students ourselves—not necessarily the most academically advanced ones, but the ones most likely to accept the norms and constraints of educational institutions. We were, by and large, the students who strove for good grades, who sought our teachers' approval, and who rarely got into trouble. We were the hall monitors, not the wasters. It is also commonplace that beginning teachers imagine that their future students will be just like they themselves were. Shocked when they discover that many students are motivated by neither grades nor teachers' approval, the natural response of these adults is to convince students to be more like the teachers themselves. Instead of expanding their image of themselves as teachers, they hope to change the environment so that it matches their image. This does a disservice to the many students who want and need something very different from schools and from teachers.

Subject matter, meanwhile, is the particular love of secondary teachers, yet they usually have not thought about the contribution of their subjects to civic life. Even social studies teachers, whose field most directly relates to democratic citizenship, have not usually considered content in these terms. Many of them, for example, "love history," but as a colleague once said to me, that doesn't mean they love analyzing evidence or understanding long-term social changes (much less guiding students in such undertakings). Instead, it often simply means that they like telling stories about Civil War battles. Stephanie van Hover puts it this way:

> When asked to write about why they want to become a teacher, almost every applicant to our program describes a favorite teacher, the knowledgeable and charismatic teacher who sparked interest in the study of history or politics through humorous and fabulous lectures. And the applicants want to be that person—in most cases, if you push them to describe their vision of a great teacher, they will go back to this default teacher, the one who knows everything and tells great stories and is charismatic and funny. My preservice teachers think about teacher-student interactions, not about becoming or being the person who promotes meaningful student-student interactions. In fact, they almost never use the word "student" in their essays.[16]

Who doesn't love funny and charismatic teachers? They certainly make it easier to get through fifty-minute classes, and they may leave students with some affection for their subjects. But if classrooms are meant to replicate the civic life of a democracy, then holding up charismatic individuals as ideal teachers is problematic. Beginning teachers enter teacher education with an admirable appreciation for subject matter, but they have not previously thought about how particular topics, methods, or approaches within a subject are related to the civic goals of schooling.

To prepare students for democratic participation, teachers need to expand their own self-images to include practices that may not fit these initial motivations so clearly. Most preparation programs focus on the crucial importance of teacher decision making, which has been a central feature of recent scholarship in the area. But too often, preservice teachers are simply asked to consider a rationale or "personal philosophy" as a basis for decision making, rather than to think about the consequences of their practices for the future of democracy. Political deliberation does not principally involve making decisions about private moral or ethical issues; important as such decisions are, they often belong in another realm of reasoning, particularly since they may be intensely private. Yet when preservice teachers are required to reflect on their goals and motivations, they are asked to share precisely this kind of personal reasoning. No wonder they often resist this attempt, and no wonder they have trouble articulating what they feel.[17] Worse, such requirements may degenerate into uncritical sharing of opinions, with no basis for judgment or evaluation, as neither faculty nor peers have any basis on which to question anyone else's private motivations.

Rather than talking about personal philosophies, teachers would be better served by being asked to reflect on their *public* responsibilities. Drawing from their deliberations on the role of education in a democracy, teachers should begin to see that as employees of the state, their practical, day-to-day work with students is itself an implementation of public policy. The decisions teachers make—about curriculum materials, instructional strategies, and interactions with students—are profoundly public choices, and teachers have to consider the consequences of those choices for society. Once decisions move from the personal to the public, they become appropriate for deliberation; when teachers share reasons for choosing some practices rather than others, it opens up space for critical feedback from faculty and peers. Although there may be no single, agreed-upon answer to issues of instructional practice, standards do exist for distinguishing better arguments from weaker ones—standards such as using logic, marshalling evidence, considering short- and long-term consequences, and applying the law. These criteria are not appropriate for private educational philosophies, but they are indispensible for public policy deliberation.

Nonetheless, moving teachers beyond their initial images of themselves is one of the trickiest elements of teacher preparation, because it touches on their very identities—not an easy object for reflection or transformation. Moreover, teachers' love of children, of schooling, and of subject matter is itself admirable; people without those characteristics probably shouldn't become teachers. Rather than giving up these images of themselves, teachers must begin to see how they might be fulfilled by attending to larger democratic purposes. Democracy, for example, is often difficult, confusing, and upsetting, and in the long-run, withholding such experiences from students may be neither nurturing nor protective. Teachers might consider how they can express their care for students by providing planned and systematic exposure to the messiness of democracy rather than isolating children from it. Similarly, teachers can consider how they can share their love of schooling by engaging with students' diverse needs, motivations, and personalities, rather than hoping that everyone will become a teacher pleaser. And those secondary social studies teachers can reflect on whether they might better inspire long-lasting appreciation of history by supplementing battlefield stories with student-led deliberations over Lincoln's suspension of habeas corpus. Educators at all levels must meet students where they are, and if teacher education programs help students make these connections, the result may be an enlarged understanding of their role as teachers in—and for—democracy.

EXPANDING TEACHERS' IMAGES OF STUDENTS

Preservice teachers' images of students mirror teachers' images of self. If they see their own future as caring for, protecting, and inspiring students, then they think of their students as needing care, protection, and inspiration. One unfortunate result of this is that teachers often devalue students' knowledge, abilities, and backgrounds. This is one of the most important challenges facing teacher educators—helping preservice teachers recognize the value and importance of young people's perspectives. Democracy fundamentally depends on equality, and if teachers do not understand or accept that their students have ideas, opinions, and experiences that are as worthy of respect as the adults', then teachers will fail to provide experiences that prepare young people for democratic participation.

Seeing oneself as a mother or role model for young people, for example, implies that there is something missing or inadequate in their backgrounds; if their parents had been doing their jobs, after all, children wouldn't need so much nurturance from teachers. In fact, teachers are often very explicit about what they see as the failures of students' homes lives, particularly when students come from poor or minority backgrounds. And as James notes, when teachers see themselves as mothers, they often assume that they intuitively know what students need, without any reason to listen to students or try to understand children's actual experiences.[18] This is perhaps why teachers so often aim not to help students develop values but to *impart* lessons or moral values to them.[19] As a result, the knowledge and values that students have developed in their homes and communities can easily go unrecognized, and the impact of this inattention is doubly debilitating for civic education. On the one hand, it means that schools will miss opportunities to connect the curriculum to students' backgrounds. Making such connections is one of the most well-established principles of effective teaching, and when students fail to see links between school and their own lives, they have trouble comprehending the information they are expected to learn.[20]

But just as important, ignoring students' backgrounds sends a strong message about what counts as legitimate knowledge. If teachers make little effort to understand or build on students' own ideas and experiences, then they signal that those are unimportant. And when students see teachers devaluating their perspectives, along with those of their families and communities, they have two choices. Some students may internalize the perception that people like themselves are unworthy of full respect and participation in the public sphere; this is unlikely to lead to any future political participation or sense of political efficacy. Other students take a more antagonistic stance: secure in their own backgrounds, they conclude that the education they encounter at school is at best irrelevant to their lives—or perhaps that it literally stands in opposition to their needs. These students respond to the rejection of their ideas by rejecting those they encounter in schools, and this results in a self-perpetuating cycle of dismissal that undermines the conditions for democratic participation.

Teachers often dismiss not only students' experiences and perspectives but also their intellectual abilities. By assuming that students—of whatever ethnic or economic backgrounds—are not cognitively able to participate in higher-order intellectual tasks, teachers thus refrain from engaging students in the kinds of challenging activities necessary for civic learning, such as interpreting historical sources or discussing controversial issues. At the elementary level, as noted earlier, teachers often claim that such tasks are not developmentally appropriate—a claim directly contradicted by empirical research into children's thinking—and thus resist confronting students with activities that they might find too difficult or confusing.[21] Such challenges, they maintain, are best left for later grades.

Unfortunately, when students enter middle school, they are still unlikely to take part in lessons that require higher-order thinking. Teachers at this level also hold low expectations for young adolescents' intellectual potential, in part because of a belief that students' "raging hormones" control their thinking. As Hilary G. Conklin and her colleagues put it, "the prevailing wisdom among many teachers—and indeed among the general populace—seems to be that young adolescents' immaturity should simply be managed as well as possible and teachers should do their best to provide middle school students with essential factual information so that they can do more challenging work when they get to high school."[22]

It doesn't always get better in high school. Preservice teachers are often shocked at the lack of factual knowledge displayed by high schoolers and sometimes conclude that since students obviously don't know anything, it is the teacher's duty to cover massive amounts of material. The emphasis on coverage crowds out attempts to engage students in activities that demand higher-order thinking. Teachers are afraid that if students don't know enough facts about history, then young people won't have enough contextual knowledge to interpret primary sources; if they don't know how the government works, they won't be able to discuss issues of public policy. And some teachers fear that without enough factual knowledge, students might actually reach the wrong conclusions.

As with their images of both democracy and their roles as educators, teachers' images of students are not so much inaccurate as they are limiting. Preparation programs, though, can provide opportunities to expand these ideas, not only by investigating the perspectives and abilities of young people but by setting these within the context of educational purposes. When elementary teachers interview students about their understanding of history, for example, often they are amazed to discover that even young children know more and can reason in much more sophisticated ways than expected, even though they may not know specific dates or many facts about the legal and political history of the United States.[23] Older students, meanwhile, may have learned historical narratives that contrast with those that are sanctioned in schools.[24] This provides a chance to discuss the nature and purpose of history teaching: how can teachers capitalize on the knowledge students develop outside school? Should schools honor alternative perspectives students find in their families and communities? Should the curriculum emphasize remembering facts or drawing conclusions from evidence? Similarly, adolescents may know little about the governmental mechanisms covered in high school civics, but they do have ideas about civic participation grounded in their own experiences.[25] These too can provide a rich basis for discussing the purpose of civic education and its relationship to students' lives. By expanding preservice teachers' understanding of students' knowledge and abilities—from a recognition of what students *don't* know to an appreciation of what they *do* know and can do—teacher preparation programs can help these new educators become more effective teachers of content while also enriching their understanding of the very nature of curriculum.

Similarly, teachers are correct to note that students' values are in need of development. This is not, however, because young people have none, or because their parents have failed them. Rather, the values that students develop outside school generally are private values—values that influence their behavior with their friends and families. Talking with adolescents will quickly show how loyal they are to the people they care about, and how protective they are of those people's interests (including the teachers whom they like and respect). But families do not necessarily teach students to extend these values to others outside their own affective circle; after all, taking care of the rest of the world isn't the primary concern of family life. The values students may still need to develop, then, are public ones: the extension of their concern for people they know to those outside the family—classmates, citizens on the street, people on the other side of the world. Listening to students also makes it clear that what may initially appear to be an absence of some values (such as a regard for formal education) may actually indicate differing values (such as an emphasis on family or tradition) or may reflect students' realistic assessment of their economic opportunities.

Such conversations raise another series of important questions. What values are necessary for a democratic society? What is the relationship between private and public values? To what extent are schools justified in encouraging students to develop values that differ from those of their families? And just how can values be encouraged—by "imparting" moral lessons, or by means that are more public and deliberative? Again, by focusing on the perspectives that students *do* have, preservice teachers may reach more richly grounded conclusions about the democratic purposes of schooling and their own responsibilities as educators.

THE DEMOCRATIC IDEAL IN TEACHER EDUCATION

To prepare students for their lives as participants in a democratic society, teachers must have a deep understanding of the nature of education in a democracy, the role of public school teachers within such a system, and the ideas and perspectives of young people. Yet preservice teachers begin their programs with incomplete and limiting images of themselves as teachers, of their students as thinkers, and of democracy as a form of social and political participation. Clearly, the gap between novices and experts is wide, and given the inadequate state of civic education in the United States, something must be done to improve the education of teachers. Two popular proposals for reforming teacher preparation, however, are unlikely to achieve such results.

One fashionable recommendation is to be more selective in admissions. Programs held up as models of effective teacher preparation (though not specifically in civic education) typically are small ones that admit only students with outstanding records of academic achievement and high levels of commitment.[26] Similarly, alternative routes to teaching, such as those that recruit recent graduates from programs outside teacher education, also rely on careful selection of candidates. Both these attempts are based on the reasonable notion that teachers should be highly knowledgeable about their fields and should care enough about students that they will work hard at teaching. And certainly, many teacher education programs would benefit from higher admission standards. But small, selective programs will never be responsible for preparing the majority of teachers; nor will most teachers ever come from the ranks of the academic elite—particularly given the relatively low salaries and high job demands of the profession. Most teachers will continue to be educated the way they are now: in programs whose admission requirements are designed to ensure large and stable numbers of students, not to guarantee a capable and committed cohort of outstanding candidates. This is the way teacher education has operated for over a century, and there is no reason to think that it will change anytime soon.

A second approach is to do away with schools of education altogether and to situate teacher preparation within a combination of university subject-matter departments and K–12 schools. This would allow university graduates to work directly in schools, with their academic backgrounds supplemented by on-the-job training or school-based professional development. Implementing this proposal would, more than anything else, utterly devastate the possibility of education for democratic participation. Subject-matter departments at universities rarely devote systematic attention to the civic purposes of schooling. Even political science departments focus primarily on the analysis of political behavior or the nature of government and international relations, not on democratic participation. Future teachers prepared in history, chemistry, or mathematics departments would be even less likely to encounter attention to democratic principles, and it is unlikely that any of them would have a chance to systematically consider the relationship between education and democracy.

Nor would these discussions usually occur when new teachers entered schools, because teachers typically are encouraged to teach quietly and think quietly. Although teachers in some settings regularly discuss the purpose of schooling and the possibility of reform, most schools are conservative institutions—not necessarily in a political sense, but in terms of the expectation that no one should rock the boat. The basic practices of schooling in the United States have endured relatively unchanged for over a century, and mavericks are not usually welcomed. One way of perpetuating this conformity is by discouraging newcomers from exploring the implications of curricular content or instructional practices. In their field experiences, preservice teaches are often told to forget everything they have learned at the university—not because the content is objectionable but because the very idea that they should question underlying assumptions is misguided. They usually hear one clear message in schools: "This is the way it's done. Accept it."

For most prospective or beginning teachers, university-based schools of education are the one setting in which they are likely to experience discussions of educational purpose. The task for such programs is to ensure that students have a chance to develop and expand their images of themselves, of students, and of democracy itself. Prospective teachers need to discuss competing ideas about democracy and the implications of those ideas for education; they need to think about how an enlarged understanding of their role can help them better fulfill their motivations for becoming teachers; they need to listen to young people's ideas and perspectives and to consider the implications of these for schooling. Such activities and discussions are not going to take place in subject-matter departments and are relatively uncommon in schools. Schools of education, however, have long placed these activities at the core of their efforts. The civic responsibility of teachers is a central component of nearly all teacher education programs. But if such activities are central to teacher preparation, why isn't civic education in better shape? Why haven't programs produced the teachers they claim to be developing? At least two shortcomings of teacher education may account for the gap between rhetoric and reality.

The first is the tempting but counterproductive strategy of overemphasizing instrumental techniques for teaching. Teacher educators have long recognized the difficulty of changing their students' ideas about the profession, and many programs respond to this difficulty by trying to perfect preservice teachers' delivery of the knowledge and skills necessary for effective teaching. Most recent scholarship on the preparation of preservice teachers stresses the importance of clear and consistent messages about teaching, communicated throughout a program: field experiences that give preservice teachers a chance to see and try out teaching methods that differ from those they may be accustomed to, consistent attention to evidence of students' learning, and reflection on the effectiveness of teaching. Only with such in-depth, practical experience and reflection are teachers likely to overcome what may be deeply ingrained ways of thinking that stand in the way of effective instruction.[27]

This body of work holds great promise for preparing professionals who know how to help students understand the content of the curriculum, including the knowledge and skills of civic education. Yet such efforts are not enough. Knowing how to prepare students for democratic participation, and having the skills to do so, does not ensure that teachers will actually implement these procedures in the classroom. Greater knowledge does not necessarily lead to greater commitment, as research on civic education with high school students shows.[28] Ironically, research on the preparation of social studies teachers has shown that what they learn has a limited effect on their actual teaching practices. Learning about such topics as the nature of the discipline of history or the cognitive abilities of middle school students does little to change what teachers intend to do in their classrooms.[29] Even combining university-based coursework with high-quality field experiences, in which preservice teaches have a chance to observe and try out sophisticated forms of civic education, is no guarantee that they will carry their knowledge and skills into their own classrooms. This is particularly true for the most difficult topics, ones that might call into question current societal arrangements, that allow for criticism of the United States, or that touch on issues that are intensely controversial in the wider society. Even teachers who have learned effective means for engaging students in deliberation of controversial issues are not always willing to tackle such topics, particularly if they think anyone will object to the topics—as people sometimes do.[30]

Preservice teachers' images of themselves, their students, and democracy are not simply instances of inadequate knowledge or skills; nor will the images be transformed solely by better field experiences. Such ideas fall less under the domain of *knowledge* and more under *belief*—that is, they serve as the means by which teachers *define* their work, rather than mechanisms for pursuing that work.[31] Pedagogical knowledge and skills are indispensible for realizing teachers' goals, but cannot determine those goals in the first place. Responding to a racist, sexist, or homophobic comment, for example, is a matter not just of technique but of purpose—it depends on ideas about whether schools should promote civic values, which of those should be prioritized, and how such values develop.

Most teacher education programs do not focus solely on pedagogical knowledge and skills, although such techniques often receive priority, particularly during subject-specific preparation. Most programs include some attention—often a great deal—to the aims of education, particularly with regard to issues such as multiculturalism or social justice. Programs accredited by the National Council for Teacher Education (NCATE), in fact, evaluate not only the knowledge and skills of candidates but also their "dispositions"—which usually includes values related to the civic purposes of education. Yet this is where there is a second shortcoming of many institutions, which too often simply try to impose the proper values on teachers without systematic reflection or deliberation. Telling education students what they are supposed to believe about the purpose of schooling, though, is notoriously ineffective; preservice teachers are adept at parroting values and beliefs promoted in university coursework, but most do not internalize these in any meaningful or long-lasting way, and often they resist discussion of educational aims.[32] This is hardly surprising. Telling beginning teachers that they have the wrong values is unlikely to lead them to change; if anything, it may lead them to cling more tightly to their prior views. Deeply held beliefs are not so easily amenable to tampering.

In addition, the idea that teacher education programs can require students to adhere to a given set of beliefs about such highly contested issues as the nature of democracy is fraught with political problems. Students sometimes perceive that they are expected to mimic the ideologically driven positions of their instructors, whom they may see as more interested in pushing their own agendas than considering multiple viewpoints. And when commitment to specific values is a requirement for graduation, students may recoil at what they see as unwarranted attempts to modify their political beliefs. When an instructor asks students how they will teach for social justice or promote multiculturalism, for example, he or she may marginalize those who consider such terms to be code for left-wing social and political ideologies.[33] Politically conservative students, in fact, often perceive teacher education programs as hostile territory—hardly an environment that will make them feel safe in reflecting on or sharing their ideas, much less in opening themselves up for change.[34] Such conflicts are inevitable when programs identify a set of "correct" values that students are expected to acquire.

If teacher education programs hope to prepare teachers who will teach for democratic civic participation, there's no point trying to impose beliefs on them, looking for different students, or hoping that better field experiences will work some magic on them. Teacher educators must look elsewhere for inspiration, and the only place to look is democracy itself. Form never follows function, and if a goal of education is democratic life, then preservice teachers must experience that life themselves. Undemocratic methods of teacher education can only lead to undemocratic teachers, and if students see their own ideas being rejected, they surely will reject the new ones. They need to have the validity of their understanding recognized at the same time that they are exposed to alternative views. Their ideas will change, develop, and become more elaborate when they have a chance to talk with each other, with university faculty, with practicing teachers, and with other citizens. This is precisely what teacher education programs have to offer, and it can't be accomplished elsewhere: the chance to talk about educational purposes. Rather than capitulating to the view that university-based coursework is impractical, teacher education programs must embrace their unique role in preparing teachers, that is, to engage them in the deliberation of educational aims.[35] This is where preservice teachers have a chance to talk about themselves, their students, and democracy in a way that they are unlikely to find elsewhere. If deliberation is a democratic ideal, then it must also be a pervasive part of teacher education.

Deliberation does not mean directionless chatter in which preservice teachers exchange uninformed opinions about their "educational philosophy." Teachers are understandably disdainful of such discussion. Deliberation requires high-quality talk—in other words, discussions that encourage many people to talk, to feel comfortable expressing ideas, to thoroughly and critically examine multiple viewpoints, and to spend the time needed for ideas and arguments to develop and flourish.[36] This kind of talk depends on careful preparation, not the offhand circulation of casual ideas. Preservice teachers need to follow contemporary educational policy debates, read the work of democratic theorists, interview practicing educators (and others), and watch classrooms in action. The purpose of deliberation, after all, is to extend and refine ideas, and this requires meaningful talk that involves mutually exploring ideas and evidence. Without preparation, discussion of educational aims may simply confirm and entrench ideas that students start with—a result that serves no civic or academic purpose. There is some research, however, that shows that when preservice teachers are asked to respond to their peers' ideas about democracy, their own concepts become more elaborate.[37] Asking them to make arguments based on an even wider range of considerations—theoretical writings, empirical evidence, public debate—would lead to the kind of thoughtful and rigorous reasoning that is appropriate for university education, but that often is missing from coursework in teacher education.

Deliberation also requires acknowledging and capitalizing on the ideological diversity found within teacher education programs. In a democratic society, it's perfectly reasonable to begin with the assumption that education should promote democracy and even that teachers should encourage specific democratic values such as tolerance or equality. The specific application of these ideals, though, is always contested, and this is the foundation for good discussion. Fortunately, no matter how homogeneous preservice teachers appear to be, they invariably represent a range of social and political perspectives. Unfortunately, this does not always lead to open discussion of contested ideas, in part because the culture of teacher education is one of polite conformity. Students at either end of the ideological spectrum keep their ideas to themselves, to the detriment of meaningful deliberation. Attempts to discuss educational purposes, therefore, often are plagued by silent students, silent perspectives, and silent assumptions. Teacher education programs need to acknowledge, respect, and capitalize on the multiplicity of student voices and to regard this diversity as an important deliberative asset.[38]

Schools, too, are sources of diversity. Many teachers have thought deeply about how their practices prepare students for democracy and have reached differing conclusions about it. Teacher education programs need to give beginners a chance to engage with those teachers as well—if not by being placed in their classes, then by hearing them as guest speakers or talking with them individually. Such experienced teachers can provide insight into how to navigate the conflicting demands of teaching (e.g., the requirements of state standards versus a focus on higher-order thinking); how to broach sensitive topics without attracting public acrimony; how to work with colleagues and students whose goals and values differ from one's own; and how to be a good teacher without going home exhausted every night. Not only can these teachers supply practical advice, but they can also provide hope that lofty goals can be realized even in the complex and messy world of real schools. Just as teacher educators need to make the ideological diversity within their classrooms clear, they need to highlight the diverse perspectives found within schools, so that beginners recognize that democratic ideals are not as irrelevant as they are sometimes told.

CONCLUSION

Prospective teachers enter their programs with valid yet underdeveloped images of themselves as teachers, of their students as learners, and of democracy as a social and political ideal. These images usually are grounded in admirable beliefs and motivations, but they are incomplete, and sometimes they stand in the way of teaching democratically. Teacher education programs have to do a better job of expanding these images. Providing teachers with greater pedagogical knowledge and skills will not be enough, though, and trying to impose proper values on teachers is both pedagogically and politically suspect. A commitment to preparing students for democracy cannot be imposed on, instilled in, or transmitted to teachers; teachers can only develop it themselves. And to become committed to democracy, preservice teachers have to see democracy, hear democracy, talk democracy, live and breathe democracy until they want democracy so badly that they can no longer imagine a classroom that doesn't promote democracy.

8

PROFESSIONAL DEVELOPMENT AS A TOOL FOR IMPROVING CIVIC EDUCATION

Diana Hess and John Zola

Imagine three programs for teachers designed to improve civic education. First, a group of teachers sitting in a circle and deeply engaged in the nuances and implications of a significant Supreme Court decision regarding student free speech rights in schools. The conversation is fluid, the sharpening of understanding evident, the raising of additional questions frequent. Second, a different group of teachers working with local experts to better understand a problem facing the community. Engaging in exactly the same process they will soon share with their students, the teachers become more knowledgeable about both the content and the processes of how public policy can be crafted to address problems. And third, a group of teachers from across the country is meeting in Washington, D.C., to learn about the Supreme Court from lawyers, journalists and justices. While in Washington, these teachers become immersed in learning about several cases on the Court's docket and ultimately have an opportunity to hear decisions delivered from the bench.

These examples are authentic. Thousands of teachers in the United States have participated in the programs to good effect. While quite different in content and design, they share some central characteristics of high-quality professional development. In this chapter, we elaborate on these characteristics. Ultimately, we argue that wise and timely investments in teacher learning are needed if this nation is to improve the quality of civic education in the United States.

Our argument is based on a central claim: one of the most important roles of schools is to prepare young people to participate effectively in political life. To that end, students need to become informed about the events and issues currently facing their communities and nation, build an understanding of the processes used to create and enforce political decisions, and gain the knowledge, skills, and dispositions to influence those decisions. Moreover, youth in the United States need to learn how to discuss issues with those who disagree with them.

Teachers are central to this process. The most transformative civic learning programs are teacher-driven and teacher-dependent, as "models of wisdom" and descriptions of high-quality civic education demonstrate.[1] The quality of teaching is the most powerful determinant of students' access to a meaningful civic education. However, to effectively support teachers, the American education system must provide high-quality professional development that enables them to prepare all students for participation in civic and political life. Currently, few teachers have the opportunity to observe or be mentored by strong civic educators when they are entering the profession. Nor are most able to access high-quality civic learning opportunities once they are in the classroom. Fewer than 50 percent of teachers rate their professional development experiences as "useful," and a similar number have little or no control over the types of professional development they receive.[2]

Exemplars of high-quality professional development for civic education do exist, but the quality and quantity of this professional development must improve dramatically and quickly if schools are to fulfill an important mission: making sure that the nation's unique experiment in self-government does not falter on the shoals of ignorance, apathy, or inequality.[3]

CASE STUDIES OF HIGH-QUALITY PROFESSIONAL DEVELOPMENT

We illustrate high-quality professional development for civic educators in the following three case studies. The first program we describe teaches K–12 educators how to conduct Socratic seminars, a form of classroom discussion that revolves around important "texts" to meet civic education goals. The second focuses on Project Citizen, a national policy-based service-learning program for fifth- through twelfth-grade classes that teaches young people how to analyze problems in their communities and to investigate and propose potential solutions to policymakers. The third professional development program combines up-to-date content about the U.S. Supreme Court and the U.S. Constitution with challenging classroom activities that help students learn important concepts such as federalism, the rule of law, free speech, and equal protection.

Case One: Learning to Teach with Socratic Seminars

It is the first day of a three-day Socratic seminar training, and two dozen civics and social studies teachers sit at desks arranged in a circle. In front of each participant perches a name tent and a carefully read and annotated copy of the Supreme Court's decision in *Tinker v. Des Moines* (1969), the text for today's Socratic seminar. In this case, the Court faced the issue of whether a student could be suspended for wearing a black armband at school in silent protest against the Vietnam War. The leader of the seminar begins: "Does the Court's opinion in *Tinker v. Des Moines* adequately protect student rights to free speech at school?" After a moment's pause, a tentative participant says, "I think so . . . The Court seems to be saying that school officials can't just decide to ban things like arm bands willy-nilly." From the other side of the circle, another teacher tries out an idea: "But it seems that if there is a disturbance, then maybe Mary Beth and her friends shouldn't have worn their arm bands . . . and their speech is not protected." The leader asks the participant, "Is there somewhere in the text that gives you that notion?" Pages flip furiously, and one participant suggests looking at page 509 of the decision. Once everyone finds that page, that person begins to read from the text.

So begins a Socratic seminar on a landmark First Amendment Supreme Court case. For almost one hour, conversation—sometimes slow-paced, sometimes lively—ensues about the Court's decision and reasoning, as well as an exploration of Justice Hugo Black's scathing dissent. The conversation's direction is determined by the participants themselves, with the leader asking clarifying questions and urging participants to use textual evidence. The seminar ends as time demands, although the leader expresses the hope that the participants will continue to puzzle over the meaning of the text.

The discussion is effective for a number of reasons. As civic educators discuss the text, they deepen their understanding of the issues, ideas, and values in the Supreme Court decision. They engage in skills at the heart of productive classroom interactions and civic discourse: close reading, critical thinking, listening, oral expression, and deliberation. As meanings are respectfully constructed, the text's ambiguities become more apparent, sometimes causing frustration. Those ambiguities are tested by the participants' and leader's examples. For instance, one teacher asks during the seminar, "What about the 'I (heart) Boobies' T-shirts that middle school students want to wear in support of breast cancer awareness?" Another wonders, "I had a student on the day after the Columbine High School shootings wear a black trench coat to school to protest the bans on such coats because of an alleged connection to the two shooters. Would that be protected?" Participants wrestle with each example and do so in a civil manner, despite the emotions related to both the struggle against breast cancer and the vulnerability of being a teacher at the time of the Columbine shootings. It soon becomes apparent that issues like these don't have clearly right or wrong answers. The conversations help participants think about how they might engage their own students in exploring similarly complex civic questions. Participants come to realize that in the Socratic seminar, interpretations are shared, challenged, and deepened with steady reference to the text and to other participants' ideas.

During the three days, participants debrief the experience of participating in Socratic seminars and work to determine how to incorporate this strategy into their own classrooms and make student-centered dialogue a priority. Setting aside one's classroom and content agenda is difficult for teachers, yet their experiences in the workshop reinforce the notion that productive discourse can arise from the ideas and meaningful work of the group. In this vein, the Socratic seminar models what citizens should do in society as they face ambiguous "texts" such as "Who would make the best president?" or "What is society's responsibility to the poor?"

The training also develops the teachers' discussion skills. During the program, participants practice asking open-ended questions as a means of generating conversation. This, in turn, sharpens participants' listening skills. A common insight is that "the conversations are much richer when I actually build my questions on the comments of the participants and allow them to explore their ideas more deeply." Participants engage in *leader groups*, where they plan and prepare to lead micro-seminars in small groups of four or five. Leader group conversations are rich explorations of texts such as excerpts from *Letter from a Birmingham Jail* or *Federalist Number 10*, where participants explore issues, ideas, and values in the text and consider ideas for opening questions. In the culminating training activity, participants conduct micro-seminars and then offer peer critiques of the leader's performance. As participants move between being a discussion leader and participant, they gain a better understanding of what is needed to effectively scaffold the activity for their students.

Finally, to encourage implementation of, and experimentation with, seminars, participants schedule follow-up meetings during the school year. When participants gather and report on their implementation of the seminars, they often share amazement at the ideas generated by students, the evolution of student ownership in classroom conversation, and students' desire to have more seminars. At these gatherings, participants make plans to extend coaching and text-sharing opportunities.

THE FIVE CORE ELEMENTS OF EFFECTIVE PROFESSIONAL DEVELOPMENT

Five characteristics help make the Socratic seminar training professional development a powerful, even transformative, experience for teachers.

They include a focus on important and challenging content; modeling and providing practice with classroom strategies that have been proven to work well with students; a collaboration-centered design so teachers can learn from and teach one another; encouragement of ongoing collaboration with participants; and sensitivity and responsiveness to the context in which individual teachers work. Research indicates that professional development that changes teacher practice and, ultimately, student learning has these five core characteristics. To better understand them, we return to the Socratic seminar training case study.

The first characteristic of high-quality professional development is that it be *content focused*. Skillful teaching of content is central to promoting effective civic education. While a central focus of the Socratic seminar training is on the processes associated with productive classroom and civic discourse, the conversations are intentionally centered on important civic content. Here, teachers are developing a deeper understanding of the Court's reasoning about student rights at school in *Tinker vs. Des Moines*. A subsequent adult seminar might use *West Virginia State Board of Education, et al. v. Barnette, et al.* (1943) to discuss the related issue of imposed speech on student rights at school. Anecdotal and other evidence indicates that civics teachers are hungry to discuss the content that brought them to this discipline in the first place. High-quality professional development in civic education provides teachers with up-to-date information about recent political issues and trends, as well as specific judicial, legislative, and executive actions.

Moreover, the content teachers learn in professional development programs should be ideologically wide-ranging to ensure that teachers are able to construct lessons that provide a balanced and rigorous analysis of the multiple and competing views on the political issues they bring into the classroom. The seminar described above intentionally spends time exploring the reasoning found both in the opinion of the Court and in Justice Black's dissent. The experience allows teachers to try on divergent perspectives and models how this can be done without rancor in their own classrooms. This practice is especially important for teachers who live in ideologically homogenous communities, where students are at great risk of being marinated in like-mindedness. Discussing controversial political issues in schools is nothing new, but the need for such discussions has a new urgency, because adults in the United States have been migrating to ideologically homogeneous communities (a phenomenon that has been labeled the "big sort").[4] As a result, the nation's residents increasingly talk primarily with people who already share their views, access media that reinforces what they already believe, and generally live in an echo chamber of like-mindedness.

While schools cannot fix the "big sort" on their own, they can be part of the solution, because schools are exceptionally good venues for discussing controversial political issues. In fact, in some ways, they are better than locations outside school: not only do schools have courses in which controversial issues fit naturally (e.g., civics and history), but students come from a range of political, religious, and social class backgrounds. Students are more likely to encounter diversity in school than out, and this is why schools are such critical sites for preparing them to engage with viewpoints that differ from their own.

A second characteristic of high-quality professional development for civic education is that it *models and provides practice with classroom strategies that have been proven to work well with students*. Socratic seminars are an example of one of these strategies. The most effective way to move experiences from the workshop setting to the classroom is for teachers to actually experience the instructional strategy and then have multiple opportunities to unpack that experience and adapt it to fit their own school and classroom realities. In the Socratic seminar training discussed above, participants experience a seminar, work in groups to develop their own seminars, and then practice being a discussion leader in front of their peers. In other words, teachers move recursively from experience to reflection to implementation and back to experience.

Research indicates that the third characteristic of high-quality professional development, *teacher collaboration*, whether in planning teams or in larger collegial groupings, results in more effectively implemented strategies.[5] Collaboration is closely linked to the fourth characteristic of high-quality professional development: its *ongoing* nature. These two qualities feature prominently in the Socratic seminar discussed above. Planning and practice in the Socratic seminar training is explicitly collaborative with the goal of modeling the effectiveness of working with others on text selection and in leader groups. In the workshop setting, peer coaching is ongoing in both small and large group settings. Teachers of similar grade levels or content meet to exchange ideas for potential seminar texts. Participants in the training are encouraged to meet in small teams to facilitate collaboration when back at the school site. The use of follow-up meetings to share implementation experiences, as well as online and in-person coaching and support, are all key to successfully implementing Socratic seminars in the classroom.

At its best, ongoing collaboration between teachers takes place at the building level, but increasingly, it is being successfully facilitated via online technologies. Given this development, it's no wonder that teachers report frustration and disappointment with one-shot professional development experiences, which offer little opportunity for long-term follow-up or support. High-quality professional development provides structures that make learning experiences durable and sustainable. Examples might range from informal and ongoing mentoring, to periodic and more formal meetings to discuss the participants' progress as teachers and what their students are learning, to explicit supervision and coaching by experts or other colleagues. Changing one's practice takes time, and it is easy to slip back into old habits. Teachers need the support of colleagues so that they can overcome the challenges they face and continually develop toward better practice.

The United States is a nation of diverse ethnicities, socioeconomic classes, genders, and cultures. Professional development, especially for civic educators, must reflect this reality by being *context sensitive*—the fifth characteristic of high-quality professional development. The civic realities facing students in a generally homogenous, upper-middle-class community are different from the civic realities in a school or district where poverty and linguistic and racial diversity are the norms. Effective professional development situates its work in the participants' communities and classrooms; it attempts to address the pedagogical concerns of teachers as they experience them with their students and recognizes that there is no one-size-fits-all approach. In the Socratic seminar training, these issues find their most robust expression in discussions about text selection and working with linguistically diverse students. Adult training seminars explicitly use texts from diverse sources to model expanding the canon and include, for example, texts that would be appropriate for students with limited English proficiency. Discussions also take place about the pedagogical prowess of Socratic seminars as an instructional strategy and how this "high-status" and empowering pedagogy is frequently unavailable to students outside the upper-tracked classes.

Appendix A, at the end of this chapter, summarizes the requirements for each of the five characteristics of successful professional development programs. Studies of professional development efforts have found that few programs include all of these five characteristics. Moreover, even when there are elements of each of the characteristics, their use will probably be uneven. For example, in the case of the Socratic seminar program, there was much more attention given to helping teachers understand the strategy than there was to ensuring that teachers received ongoing support when they sought to use it in their classrooms.

The challenge of ensuring that professional development programs incorporate all of the essential characteristics cuts across all subject areas, not just civic education. But civic education professional development programs are typically funded on a shoestring, and the most effective programs are, by definition, those that require significant resources. Despite these challenges, the following two case studies showcase the careful attention that some professional development experts are giving to crafting programs that are high quality.

Case Two: Learning to Teach with Project Citizen

It is clear that young people must build important content knowledge to effectively engage as citizens. But knowledge alone, even when coupled with strong academic skills, cannot ensure effective, sustained engagement. After all, Americans don't just want citizens to *know* about the political system and their role in it; Americans want them to *act*. Toward that end, many civic educators believe that it is critical to teach students how to engage politically. One curricular approach is to provide students with structured opportunities to identify a problem in the community, teach them how to investigate the problem, consider options for solving it, and then decide as a class what they think the best solution is. Ideally, the policy recommendation is then communicated to relevant policymakers. Often labeled *policy-based service-learning*, this form of civic education has many permutations, such as Project Citizen, a federally funded program of the Center for Civic Education, and Active Citizen Today, a privately funded project of the Constitutional Rights Foundation of Los Angeles.

Given the strong evidence that this authentic form of civic education has powerful and lasting effects on student learning, it would seem logical that service-learning would be widely used in schools. Evidence suggests, however, that very few young people are taught how to engage politically by working on a real (and not simulated) problem that they help to select. Numerous reasons account for why this form of civic education is so unusual, but topping the list is how exceptionally demanding Project Citizen is as a form of teaching. To pull off policy-based service-learning, teachers need extensive knowledge about their local community (which, in many cases, is not the community they live in). Teachers also must understand what public policy is and how it is structured, have access to local policymakers and policy experts who can help their students learn about a problem and its possible solutions, and have the pedagogical skills to guide often large and diverse classes of students through a complex process that barely resembles traditional school.

Service-learning is clearly a challenging form of civic education, but can be implemented well if teachers receive the necessary professional development. As a case in point, let's examine one professional development program that supports Project Citizen: the summer institute and follow-up support offered by the Center for Education in Law and Democracy (CELD), a Denver-based nonprofit organization.[6] For many years, CELD has been funded by the Center for Civic Education to provide professional development about Project Citizen for fifth- through twelfth-grade teachers. Most of the participating teachers are from Colorado, but for the past several years, teachers from throughout the nation also have attended.

Before teachers come to the week-long intensive institute, they are surveyed about policy issues that matter personally to them and their students so that the CELD staff can target the content of the institute to the teachers' interests. This reflects a core principle: for authentic learning to happen, the learner needs to identify a real problem that is worthy of study. Because any local problem can be used as a means to teach the Project Citizen approach, developing a small list of problems in advance enables the staff to invite content experts who can provide explicit instruction to the teachers as they investigate the problem and potential solutions.

The institute begins by asking teachers to identify student outcomes for civic (and often literacy) education: what do teachers want their students to know, be able to do, and be disposed to do as a result of their course? Beginning the intensive program with what teachers think is important for students to learn is not done simply to engage the teachers (although the teachers almost universally report that they find these discussions eye-opening); it also illuminates for teachers the close connections between the context in which they are working, the students they are teaching, and what they think their students need to learn. For example, teachers from schools with many students who are undocumented immigrants report different objectives and identify very different problems than do teachers from well-funded suburban schools. Additionally, while on the surface these opening discussions are about student outcomes, they inevitably involve exploring much larger questions, such as, "What do citizens in our communities need to know and be able to do to participate effectively?" And based on that foundation of knowledge and skills, "What can and should schools do to help shape these kinds of citizens?" After comparing, contrasting, clarifying, justifying, and questioning outcomes with other teachers, participants pick just two or three that are most important to them.

Starting the program by focusing on what teachers know and believe sends a clear message about how CELD views teachers. The staff recognizes that teachers come to the institute with content expertise, often years of experience, and deep knowledge about their students and how they learn. The teachers are not empty vessels to be filled, but professionals who are being asked to learn new techniques, relate them to their contexts, and make judgments about how and why this form of civic education could work in those contexts. Moreover, CELD staff members recognize that teachers come with widely varying levels of experience and expertise, and so there is no one-size-fits-all approach.

Next, teachers carefully analyze a collection of middle and high school students' Project Citizen portfolios, listen to the students explain the content, and ask the students questions about their work. This is a replication of what students participating in Project Citizen do—create elaborate portfolios that capture their work and then engage in a dialogue with the adults attending the Project Citizen showcase. Exhibiting students' work confirms that students are indeed capable of engaging successfully in the Project Citizen process (although teachers may require more tangible evidence of achievement). Importantly, teachers are asked to look for evidence in the students' work (and presentations) that the outcomes the teachers value were achieved by the students who created the portfolios. Teachers invariably find that at least some of the outcomes they value are taught through Project Citizen, and it is not uncommon for the student work to actually *raise* teachers' expectations about what students can and should be expected to learn.

Throughout the rest of the week, teachers work in small groups doing Project Citizen while being coached by mentor teachers who have had success using the program with their students. The CELD staff crafts a mentor cadre composed of teachers with expertise working with differently situated students. For example, there are mentors who teach in low-resourced urban schools, and those who teach in rural communities. With the mentors' help, each group of teachers selects a problem (from a list based on pre-institute surveys), talks with experts about the nature of the problem and possible solutions, selects the public policy solution that they think will best address the problem, and, finally, creates portfolios that showcase all of their work. Their portfolios are then explained to the other teachers and experts brought in to ask questions during the capstone showcase.

In addition to learning the Project Citizen process by actually doing it, the teachers engage in many other activities designed to enhance their content knowledge—especially with respect to public policy. For example, participants take a field trip to the National Conference of State Legislators (a nonpartisan think tank based in Denver), where they learn the nuances of social policy from analysts and other issue experts. For some teachers, this is the first time they have received any kind of formal instruction about public policy, especially if their focus in college was history and not political science.

Mentor teachers also lead sessions on topics such as how to use new technologies with Project Citizen, how to assess and evaluate students' work, and how to manage the inevitable challenges that arise with any form of teaching that is this complex. What should a teacher do when some students are not doing their part in the small groups? What if the students decide to work on a problem that is so controversial that it will create more heat than light? What happens when the experts in their local community don't treat their students with respect or are simply so busy that they can't take the time to teach students about how the problem manifests in their local community? How can Project Citizen fit into an already-packed curriculum? While there are no pat answers to these questions, the mentor teachers have undoubtedly encountered them in their own practice and can often offer useful guidance on dealing with these challenges.

If we want teachers to learn how to engage their students in some of the most complex forms of what it means to be a citizen, then it is critical that teachers are provided access to the very kind of high-quality and challenging professional development that institutes like those organized by CELD provide. Very few school districts have the in-house expertise to create and teach such high-quality professional development about civic education. Unfortunately, many school districts no longer provide financial support for teachers to attend off-site institutes, the districts' rationale being that all professional development should be ongoing and site-specific. Nevertheless, without ongoing support, much of what is learned at an institute will most likely not be implemented on a long-term basis. For this reason, CELD wisely provides a range of follow-up assistance to the institute's participants. For teachers living in the Denver area, CELD organizes the annual Project Citizen Showcase, where literally hundreds of students present their work to adults who have content expertise on the problems the students have selected. CELD staff frequently visit classes and provide teachers on-site coaching; using their vast network of experts, CELD staff also help teachers find content specialists to interact with their students. At their annual civic education conference, the mentor teachers teach sessions about Project Citizen, and teachers have opportunities to network and get advice from peers. Teachers outside of CELD's immediate service area are linked to other organizations working with Project Citizen.

Project Citizen is widely used in Colorado. It is taught extensively in the Denver Public Schools (where it has been promoted as a unique approach to both literacy and civic education). This widespread use is particularly laudable, given the challenges of providing high-quality civic education in urban school districts. In some Colorado school districts and in many schools, all of the students do Project Citizen. We believe that the quality and reach of Project Citizen in Colorado is largely due to the high-quality professional development offered by CELD. The institutes and follow-up assistance are content-rich and intellectually demanding; teachers are encouraged to relate to their teaching what they are learning in professional development sessions; and the focus throughout is on the kinds of high-leverage teaching practices that research shows produce meaningful learning.

Case Three: Professional Development to Improve Teaching About the Supreme Court

Socratic seminars focus on teaching young people how to use a particular form of discussion that builds important civic knowledge and skills. Project Citizen has as its primary goal involving young people in analyzing and proposing public policy solutions to problems in their community. Our third case study, the Supreme Court Summer Institute for Teachers, is designed to help teachers become better prepared to teach challenging content about the Supreme Court, its landmark and contemporary cases, and, more broadly, the Constitution by using domain-specific pedagogies that have proven successful in the classroom. By marrying content and pedagogy, the institute aims to help teachers both know more and do more with what they know.

While it is clear that teachers' mastery of the content knowledge *alone* does not guarantee high-quality teaching in any subject, the adage "you cannot teach what you do not know" is true. If society is concerned about ensuring that what students learn in civic education is accurate, reflects the right tension between depth and breadth, and is relevant to the contemporary world, then content knowledge not only should matter, but also must be studied by teachers throughout their careers. This ongoing professional development for teachers is important, because so much of the most worthwhile knowledge in civic education changes over time, even though many of the controversies that students should wrestle with are perennial.

As a case in point, consider the concept of free speech, specifically the constitutional question of the circumstances under which the government is justified in limiting a person's speech rights. Teachers need to know quite a bit to teach this issue well: the historical context of the First Amendment, current free speech jurisprudence, the changing definition of speech, the line of cases that established the categories of protected and unprotected speech, the tensions between speech rights and societal standards, and current speech issues relevant to young people. Moreover, there are some very high-quality curriculum materials that have been developed to help students learn this content; teachers need to know where to find these materials and how to use them with their students.[7] Even if civic educators graduate from higher education with a solid grounding in this kind of content (which is unlikely, given that few have taken political science or law courses that focus explicitly or intensively on these topics), the field and its attendant conversations are continually evolving; as a result, ongoing professional development is a necessity.

If you truly cannot teach what you do not know, it follows that you cannot teach if *all* you have is content knowledge. In teacher preparation programs, most teachers did not learn, or at least did not have adequate time to master, the kinds of high-leverage pedagogies that are so critical to quality civic education.

To illustrate how a professional development program can focus on both content and pedagogy, we turn to our final case study, the Supreme Court Summer Institute for Teachers, a six-day program taught in each summer in Washington, D.C. The program is designed to enhance teachers' understanding of rich, important, and up-to-date content while simultaneously demonstrating the type of pedagogies that can be used to teach this content to middle and high school students.

Developed by Street Law, Inc., a nonprofit civic education organization, with financial support from the Supreme Court Historical Society, this program has several unique, coherent, and well-structured features that mark it as an exemplar of civic education professional development.[8]

The institute, not surprisingly, takes full advantage of the Washington, D.C., legal community, which includes many people with significant expertise about the Supreme Court, to assist with content development and teaching. Relevant content and replicable teaching strategies drive development of the institute's agenda each year. Street Law staff track the Supreme Court's annual docket and work with legal experts to select four to six cases that will form the core content for the institute. Cases selected for inclusion in the institute curriculum are those that might wind up in the school curriculum in the future (such as *D.C. v. Heller* [2008]), or that can be used to teach vital components of the Constitution or civic principles, even if they are not blockbuster cases per se (such as *Snyder v. Phelps* [2010]). Sometimes a case is selected because it may be of particular interest to many young people, such as cases involving students' rights in school, the juvenile justice system, or technologies that many young people use.[9]

Street Law staff write classroom-ready materials on the cases and key operational concepts of the Supreme Court like the certiorari and judicial nominations processes. These materials are reviewed by legal experts and range from relatively straightforward case summaries to elaborate multiday lessons, written at multiple reading levels. Throughout the institute, teachers learn the cases and concepts by using the same materials and engaging in the same pedagogical practices that they are being encouraged to use in their own classrooms. Most sessions include an outside resource person, and the institute staff counsels teachers on how to effectively use resource experts in the classroom.

As in the other professional development cases, teachers are not lectured to about how to engage their students in discussion of the cases; instead, they experience the pedagogy itself, in this case by preparing for and participating in discussions that are carefully facilitated. They are not told to use moot court simulations, but are taught how to do so by participating in one and then analyzing what they would need to do so that the same simulation could work with their students. All strategies are thoroughly debriefed, and this analytic work is collaborative, focused on practical transfers to the classroom, and typically led by the teachers, often in groups formed around grade level and course content so that the conversation can be as relevant to the teachers' practice as possible. Even though attention is paid throughout the institute on how to use, and the reasons for using, particular teaching practices in classrooms, the institute employs these high-leverage pedagogies not just to model their classroom applications for teachers, but also because the teachers will learn more from engaging with complex intellectual tasks that the pedagogies demand.

The institute's focus goes beyond contemporary cases and their important historical antecedents. The teachers also study how the Supreme Court works literally and within the context of the U.S. political system. They are in the courtroom in the Supreme Court building when decisions are handed down, they tour the building, and they meet one of the sitting justices at a reception. They also participate in roundtable discussions with former Supreme Court clerks, journalists who cover the Court, and scholars who research and write about the third branch.

Supreme Court decisions often spark a lot of controversy that is embraced and reflected in the institute agenda, but the role and practices of the Court itself can be controversial. For example, teachers have learned about and deliberated over such controversies as whether the Court should be deciding more cases each term (its docket is now about half the size it was thirty years ago), whether the Court is granting certiorari to cases that should properly be decided in the political branches, whether the nomination and confirmation process for federal judges and justices works well or should be changed, and whether interest groups exert too much influence over the Court. By specifically including these and other controversies about the Court, Street Law staff seek to demonstrate that while understanding how political and legal systems work is important, the goal should not be educating toward blind acceptance of current practices. Engaging in deliberation about both the content of controversial decisions and the practices that produce them is not unpatriotic or partisan, but democracy-enhancing.

As noted, one problem with off-site teacher institutes is that they can have a harder time providing the ongoing assistance necessary to help teachers improve their practice. Street Law tries to make up for this shortcoming to some extent by providing up-to-date curriculum materials that make it easier for teachers to help students understand complex content. Teachers frequently tell us that they check Street Law's Web site each August, when the new case materials are posted.[10] The sheer number of hits on the Street Law Web site to access these materials shows that they have particular value to teachers—in large part because the materials provide timely, student-friendly content that goes well beyond what is found in textbooks. Although the focus on pedagogy at the institute and the annual development of free, Web-based materials provide important support that can affect teaching practice, they are clearly inadequate if the goal is to help teachers improve their practice. Consequently, in recent years, Street Law has developed a social network for institute attendees to support each another and has created phone-in study groups to provide teachers with access to an intellectual community that shares their interest in particular content and pedagogical practices. In some large metro areas where there are many teachers who have attended the institutes over the years, study groups have formed to analyze students' work, assess evidence of student learning, and discuss what teachers can do to improve their teaching.

Similar to the professional development programs of Socratic seminars and Project Citizen, the Supreme Court Summer Institute offers a rich professional development activity that is content-based and focused on learning about and using high-leverage teaching practices. The three approaches share other benefits as well: teachers learn collaboratively and have multiple opportunities to discuss how to improve their practice in the classroom to better meet their students' needs. But the three approaches also share some drawbacks: they all lack the degree of intensive, classroom-based, context-specific, and local follow-up that research shows is needed, although innovations with the use of new technologies in professional development suggest that there may be emerging solutions to this problem.

Despite this limitation, the three cases just described help teachers create learning experiences that meaningfully prepare students to engage in democratic processes and the tasks associated with being an active citizen. These examples of professional development include classroom activities that are based on rich content and build the civic skills for democratic discourse: exchanging ideas, listening to opposing viewpoints, finding common ground, reaching compromise, exploring controversial topics, working with those who may have meaningfully different values and perspectives, and engaging in processes that develop understanding of how public policy is made and how to influence those processes. If not in the classroom, where are these skills to be taught, practiced, and nurtured?

Robust professional development for civic educators has at its core the understanding that as citizens in a democracy, students must be adept at engaging in conversations about the issues and controversies of the day. Meaningful civic discourse is, at best, based on content knowledge that meets standards of veracity, is up to date, and is grounded in understanding of history and other disciplines. In a society that has increasing comfort with ideas like "truthiness" and notions that "I have my facts and you have yours," there can be little doubt that civic educators and citizens need rich content. But civic discourse alone, even when grounded in strong content, is insufficient in a functioning democracy: effective citizens know that citizens both live with and try to influence public policy, understand the role of policy in civic life and, as appropriate, attempt to influence policymakers through a variety of actions. Policy is where government most commonly meets its citizens and where citizens most likely confront their government. These commitments to civic competencies within a democracy are at the center of professional development for civic educators.

CHALLENGES TO PROFESSIONAL DEVELOPMENT IN CIVIC EDUCATION

The three case studies just described are examples of high-quality professional development in civic education. But even these strong examples do not meet all the qualities of what is needed if professional development is going to have the impact it must have on classroom practice. The first and most important challenge, then, is to develop and make widely available more comprehensive forms of professional development, especially those that build on existing high-quality exemplars.

Specifically, what is needed are hybrid approaches to professional development. Such approaches would combine effective off-site professional development with a wide variety of follow-up and support, including district and school-based coaching. In this way, teachers would receive ongoing, local support while they implement what they have learned. A hybrid approach is not conceptually or even practically all that challenging, but it will take resources (investments in human capital so there are enough educators at the local, state, and national levels with appropriate expertise in civic education professional development) and support for teachers to participate in these programs.

Unfortunately, funding for programs that include professional development for civic education teachers has suffered from huge cuts in the federal budget as of late; we are especially concerned that there is no movement in the states or in local school districts to fill the resource hole these cuts will create. Clearly, one reason why civic education is given such low priority is that to many policymakers, its importance pales in comparison to literacy and numeracy. Consequently, most state and federal policies that directly or indirectly influence how much professional development emphasis is placed on various school subjects or outcomes give short shrift to civic education. Given the lack of emphasis placed on civic education and the current budget woes of government at all levels, it is unlikely that a public investment in professional development for civic education will happen in the near future—although a case can easily be made for why this is just the kind of investment that is needed now more than ever, and we certainly support continuing to make the case for government funding of professional development in civic education. However, private funders (individuals and foundations) need to be persuaded to fill this critical need.

It is also crucial to support high-quality, independent, and rigorous research on the effectiveness of these programs so the field has a better understanding of what works and why. Design-experiments, of the type developed by Walter Parker and his colleagues at the University of Washington, are the gold standard. They have developed a new curriculum and are researching its effects on the Advanced Placement American Government course.[11] This design-based research project takes seriously the need to focus on the deep learning of a relatively wide array of content by engaging students in a series of "looping" collaborative inquiries (such as a simulation to design a government, a moot court on a landmark U.S. Supreme Court case, and a legislative simulation). Building on scholarship that shows the importance of the nature of instruction on students' complex understanding of important ideas, this new curriculum takes aim at the misguided and simply erroneous assumption that teacher lectures and rigorous learning go hand-in-hand. The University of Washington team has developed a new curriculum, has designed professional development so that teachers can learn how to implement it, and is assessing what the curriculum looks like in practice—and, notably, its effect on what students learn.

But studies that look at existing approaches to professional development in civic education are also needed. Given the dearth of research about professional development in civic education, it would be wise for the civic education research community to develop a voluntary national research agenda. This would make it more likely that future studies about professional development will be directed toward the most critical questions and done in a wide array of communities that represent the diversity of programs and students in the United States. Studies should be designed to carefully build on one another, and accumulated findings that come from a train of research instead of a single study could be disseminated in ways that make it more likely to inform the quality of professional development in the future. Education research has been able to extrapolate the characteristics of high-quality professional development in civic education from research conducted in other disciplines (most notably, from the math community) and from the few studies that focus specifically on civic education. But an understanding of what teachers need to learn to improve their practice, and more importantly, how these programs should be structured, is still in a very developmental stage. The education community simply doesn't know enough yet to feel fully confident that the professional development programs in the field will have the full impact desired.

To conclude, the quality of teaching is what matters most in civic education. While we advocate for the intense content preparation of new teachers prior to entry into teacher education, and rigorous and in-depth teacher education, we recognize that effective civic education teachers must be learning throughout their careers—which is why professional development is so important. There are powerful examples of professional development programs in the United States now, such as the three described in this chapter. These three approaches go a long way toward helping teachers know and do what is necessary to produce powerful civic outcomes for their students. Because these programs often lack the local follow-up that research says is critical, we advocate providing more follow-up and other support to add these components; we also advocate designing new approaches to professional development and carefully researching whether, how, and why they work, especially if such studies are part of a coordinated national research agenda. If implemented, these recommendations likely will promote the one goal that matters the most—improving the quality of civic education for all students.

APPENDIX A

CHECKLIST FOR HIGH-QUALITY PROFESSIONAL DEVELOPMENT FOR CIVIC EDUCATORS

CONTENT-FOCUSED

- The content that teachers learn is rigorous, accurate, and balanced
- Teachers are improving their understanding of content that is closely aligned to what they will be teaching
- Content presented authentically represents historical and contemporary controversies that are at the heart of civic education (such as multiple perspectives on important policy issues)
- Content presented values depth of understanding of important concepts rather than more superficial coverage of purely factual information

CONNECTED TO DAILY WORK VIA HIGH-LEVERAGE PRACTICES

- Learning activities are modeled and thoroughly debriefed and critiqued so participants can experience the learning process and better implement activities in their own classrooms
- Practices reflect and model state-of-the-art research, such as that from the Civic Mission of Schools project
- Time is provided for participants to reflect on their experiences and to plan for adapting and implementing new practices in their own schools and classrooms

COLLABORATIVE

- In the workshop setting, participants have opportunities to work and plan together

- Participants are encouraged to attend trainings in collaborative groupings of fellow teachers or administrators, or both
- Time and support are provided to create structures for peer coaching or mentoring back at the school site

ONGOING

- Goals include explicit expectations and support regarding implementation in the school and classroom
- Structures exist for regular or periodic opportunities for participants to share and analyze implementation successes and challenges
- Professional development leaders or mentors are available for periodic on-site consultation, mentoring, and coaching
- Structures are in place for administrative support and reinforcement for outcomes from professional development experience

CONTEXT-SENSITIVE

- Diversity in the school and community (e.g., race, ethnicity, socioeconomic status, political and religious perspectives) is reflected in the goals, materials, and learning experiences of the professional development program
- Training is sensitive to local resources and conditions such as aging computers or limited access to online technology
- Community and school demographics are represented in the workshop presenters and ongoing support personnel

9

DIGITAL OPPORTUNITIES
FOR CIVIC EDUCATION

Joseph Kahne, Jacqueline Ullman, and Ellen Middaugh

I'm 16 and I thought that you'd be mine.

I used to tweet you and text you and call you and hit you on Facebook all the time.

Can't believe that you did me wrong.

We were on iChat all night long.

—Justin Bieber, "Baby"

Every generation needs a new revolution.

—Thomas Jefferson

Picture a university lecture hall, filled with first-year college students. In walks the philosophy professor who, unfortunately, has not had the chance to prepare for her Introduction to Philosophy class. However, she has a solution—she will pose a provocative question and then facilitate the conversation. She asks, "Which is worse: apathy or ignorance?" The class is silent for a moment before a young man in the front row sleepily replies, "I don't know. And I don't care."

To some, this situation summarizes what's wrong with American democracy and, especially, why educators need to get much more involved: there is simply too much apathy and too much ignorance. On one level, these concerns seem warranted. The youngest generations participate the least in civic life, with a full 55 percent of those under thirty recently judged as civically and politically "disengaged," in a report by the National Conference on Citizenship.[1] Close to two-thirds (64 percent) of young adults aged eighteen to twenty-nine say that they are "not at all" interested in campaign news. And while the 2008 presidential election generated a great deal of press because of higher-than-average youth participation, numbers from the recent 2010 midterm election do not reflect that continued upswing.[2] Judged by traditional measures, current levels of youth civic knowledge and participation are problematic.

In this chapter, we argue that civic educators' ability to address this situation productively requires increased attention to the civic and political dimensions of digital media. We say this for two reasons. First, civic and political life has moved online. If youth are to participate, educators must help youth learn to employ these online forms of activity. Second, there are many ways educators can take advantage of youth engagement with digital media to foster youth civic and political engagement and development.

In addition to discussing the two preceding points, this chapter summarizes several studies that the authors of this chapter wrote with co-authors Namjin Lee, Jessica Timpany Feezell, and Chris Evans. These studies quantify the relationship between youth, digital media, and civic engagement. We conclude with a discussion of ways policymakers can support these educational efforts.

CIVIC AND POLITICAL LIFE HAS MOVED ONLINE

Online activity has become the norm for many people, if not for nearly all young people. As a result, many practices that are central to civic and political life now occur online. For example, youth gain information, share perspectives, learn participatory skills and norms and raise funds in the digital realm. Mobilization of youth and by youth also occurs online.

Gaining Political Information

Half (50 percent) of 18- to 29-year-old consumers of Internet news say their voting decisions are influenced by what they learn online, and 37 percent of those aged 18 to 24 obtained 2008 campaign information from social networking sites, compared with only 4 percent of 30- to 39-year-olds.[3] Online sites are regarded by American youth as convenient places to get information. Three out of five (61 percent) voters aged 18 to 29 who get their election news from the Internet reported going online because it is more convenient than other methods of accessing political information.[4]

Sharing Perspectives

Seventy-five percent of American young people are active participants in social networking via Facebook.[5] Networked spaces allow for conversation, debate, and information sharing in an unprecedented way. Further, in terms of personal expression, 64 percent of teens report creating online digital content, and 28 percent have written and designed an online journal or blog.[6] At their best, online communities serve as the town square of yesteryear for young people, allowing them to grapple with their fears and hopes and providing a significant space for political commentary.

Learning Participatory Skills and Norms

Youth are increasingly engaged in informal online communities that define themselves around shared interests and that often center around expressive activities, such as the sharing of fan fiction, collaboration around a video game, or the production of YouTube videos. These online activities may function similarly to offline, extracurricular activities, which have been found to provide youth with opportunities to develop both civic skills—such as how to plan collective undertakings or mobilize others—and productive norms of behavior within social networks and organizations.[7]

Fund-Raising and Mobilizing

Just as online spaces provide a convenient way for young people to learn about global issues or disasters, these sites also allow concerned individuals to rally to a cause and contribute both opinions and financial assistance with great ease. Indeed, Americans under the age of forty were just as likely to donate to the 2011 Japan tsunami relief efforts through electronic means (online, through text messaging, and through e-mail solicitations) as through more traditional means, such as by phone or mail.[8] Similarly, given the ease of sending mass e-mail solicitations or including a call to action as part of a Web site's home page, online spaces are increasingly used for recruitment. Recent survey findings suggest that youth under twenty-five are more often recruited for civic or political activities online than through other methods and when compared with their older counterparts.[9] Young people can also be rallied through their mobile phone applications and alerts. As youth digital media saturation evolves, this shift toward computer-based and smartphone-based recruitment will also probably show exponential increases.

Risks as Well as Opportunities

While many aspects of civic and political life increasingly occur online, these changes create risks and challenges as well as opportunities. For example, it is often difficult to judge the quality of information found online; individuals may choose primarily to read viewpoints of, and engage with, those whose views align with their own; the distribution of media access and participatory habits may exacerbate inequalities in civic and political voice; and online communities may, at times, be characterized by a disturbing lack of civility. Thus, in addition to recognizing the many ways civic and political life rely on digital media, it is important for civic educators to think about risks and challenges as they consider ways to engage with the digital dimensions of civic education.

USING DIGITAL MEDIA TO FOSTER CIVIC AND POLITICAL ENGAGEMENT AND DEVELOPMENT

While youth participation with many dimensions of civic and political life *is* low, youth engagement with digital media is high. Ninety-five percent of teenagers aged 14 to 17 and 93 percent of young adults aged 18 to 29 use the Internet, and almost a quarter of the smartphone market is held by teenagers and young adults, aged 13 to 24.[10]

Civic educators can foster youth civic and political engagement by meeting youth where they are: in online and digital spaces. As we will discuss, bridges to civic and political issues arise in these contexts, and the participatory nature of much online activity often parallels the demands and dynamics of civic and political life. By tapping the power of video games and the compelling nature of social networks and online interest-driven communities, civic educators may well be able to foster desired forms of youth civic and political activity and development.

Charting a Strategy

This new territory does not come with a road map. There is still much to learn both about how online opportunities are influencing the quality, quantity, and equality (across different demographic groups) of civic and political participation and about ways civic educators can leverage the appeal of these media to promote desired outcomes. In the following section, we present four studies we've conducted that provide directions for educators. Some of our findings may be surprising—calling into question what for many has become conventional wisdom. In particular, we share findings related to the civic impact and potential of online participatory communities, ways digital media may foster or constrain exposure to diverse perspectives, needs related to digital media literacy, and opportunities associated with video game play. Drawing on this discussion, we conclude by highlighting several steps policymakers can take to support digital dimensions of civic education.

RESEARCH ON DIGITAL MEDIA AND CIVIC AND POLITICAL ENGAGEMENT

Between 2006 and 2010, we conducted a series of studies to examine whether either media literacy efforts or different forms of participation with digital media might influence youth civic and political development and activity. [11] The first three studies drew on surveys conducted with a diverse group of roughly 5,000 California high school students from more than twenty-one school districts from across the state. We followed a subgroup of 435 youth for up to 3½ years as they progressed into early adulthood, and we have follow-up data from this group.[12] Drawing on a framework developed by Mizuko Ito and colleagues, we also examined differing ways youth participated while online.[13] We examined how often youth participated in politically driven online activity (getting or sharing political information and perspectives), interest-driven online activity (participation in online communities tied to hobbies, sports, or other interests), and friendship-driven activity (socializing via e-mail and on social networks), as well as their exposure to media literacy education. Data from the fourth study, executed in partnership with the Pew Internet and American Life project and drawn from its 2008 Teens, Video Games, and Civics Survey, consisted of a random, nationwide sample of just over one 1,100 young people, aged 12 to 17.

These four studies provide an early look at the ways online participation and media literacy education may influence both online and offline civic activity and development. We discuss findings from each of these studies and highlight examples of strategies educators are using to tap the potential of youth engagement with digital media.

Online Participatory Communities and Civic Engagement

Conventional wisdom says that online communities distract youth from real-world issues. In a cartoon depicting the evolution of good Samaritanism in the digital age, a man walks by a homeless person lying on the street and does nothing. In the next frame, he is at his

THE EVOLUTION OF GOOD SAMARITANISM

Source: Cartoon by Cam Cardow and used with permission from Cagle Cartoons, Inc.

computer—"What's this?!! Sally needs a bag of fertilizer for her Farmville farm? I better get right on it!"

Many are struck by how many people participate in online communities. There are, for example, thirty million virtual farms in *Farmville*. (There are, by the way, two million real farms in the United States.) Such statistics lead some to wonder if the vast engagement with virtual worlds distracts from real-world issues. Often, we believe, the opposite is true.[14] Participation in online communities often functions much like offline, extracurricular activities, which have been found to foster later civic engagement by teaching skills, by developing a sense of agency and productive group norms, and by fostering an appreciation of the potential of collective action. Moreover, in the context of a social group with shared interests, civic activity often takes place.

Consider, for example, Gaia Interactive, an online site where fans of avatars and virtual worlds come together, not only to connect in Gaia's virtual space—playing online games and sharing artwork, writing, and avatar creation—but also to discuss their specific interests in a wide variety of online forums. Of the monthly 1.4 million American visitors, the vast majority are teens and young adults, and many of the interest-based chat forums reflect stereotypical interests of this younger demographic.[15] Alongside forums on body piercing and celebrity gossip are Gaia Community Projects, where participants rally their fellow users to get behind a social cause such as breast cancer or autism awareness. For the month of April 2011, for example, Gaians were encouraged to equip their avatar with a daffodil to support cancer awareness as a form of on-site engagement. Further, off-site engagement was also part of the drive, with teams (e.g., Team Melanoma, Team Leukemia) creating YouTube videos to promote awareness and making donations directly to charities supporting cancer research. The site also contains guilds, or groups of users associated with a particular cause. More than two hundred such guilds can be categorized as political in focus.

In our study, we did not assess the impact of a particular Web site, but rather looked at participation in interest-driven communities more generally.[16] Overall, we found that young persons' nonpolitical, interest-driven participation was a strong predictor of their civic participation. Indeed, even controlling for their prior level of engagement with civic life, when youth were highly involved in interest-driven, online participatory communities, they became more likely to volunteer in their community, raise money for a charitable cause, or work together with other individuals to solve a problem in the community where they live.

In explaining why such a relationship might exist, Henry Jenkins and colleagues note that interest-driven communities are often characterized by a participatory culture—one in which peer-to-peer exchange and mentorship is common.[17] These cultures enable voice, respond to an impulse for expression and social relationships, and tie to what participants find valuable—all features that align well with dynamics of civic engagement. They also create or expand an individual's networks that would potentially strengthen the likelihood of recruitment into civic or political activity. In short, these results challenge the conventional notion that immersion in online communities is distracting or socially isolating and, instead, highlight the potential civic benefits of nonpolitical participation in online communities.

The civic value of nonpolitical, interest-driven activity within a participatory culture has interesting implications for educators, parents, and others who work with youth. First, helping to guide youth toward interest-driven online communities may well make sense. Indeed, in that same way that many extol the value of offline extracurricular (and generally interest-driven) activities, it makes sense to find ways to promote youth engagement with online interest-driven activities.

In addition, educators should develop ways to create participatory cultures around aspects of the academic experience. One early experiment with these possibilities is InterroBang, a problem-solving social network game that engages youth in missions to enhance the study of science, history, art, and culture.[18] Students and teachers select missions according to interest and curricular requirements and post their work online, where it can be viewed and commented on by other youth as well as by game moderators and teachers. More than eight thousand students in seventy-two countries have submitted missions on a variety of topics linked to civic and social engagement. One student created a photo essay and reflection statement comparing produce from the local grocery store chain to produce from a nearby farmers' market. Another painted a mural encompassing students' dreams as motivated by Martin Luther King Jr.'s "I Have a Dream" speech. Drawing on the affordances of social networks, youth can view and comment on the work of others and can create missions for other youth to do. The platform provides an authentic audience and community for student work, enables youth to pursue their interests and to interact with those who share their interests, and engages youth in activities that develop both media literacy and civic skills associated with production.[19]

Youth Exposure to Diverse Perspectives Through Online Activity

Conventional wisdom also says that the Internet functions as an echo chamber for youth, surrounding them with only those perspectives that match their own. Political theorists have long extolled exposure to a wide range of perspectives as an essential support for a free and democratic society.[20] To an increasing extent, individuals using the Internet can select which sites to visit and for how long, which home page should be launched by the browser, which news features to look at, and which e-mail updates to receive. The Internet enables users to control what news and perspectives they see, causing some to worry that the Internet will lead many to enter echo chambers—isolated enclaves of like-minded individuals.[21] In addition, platforms are increasingly designed to focus users on information and contacts consistent with preferences revealed by prior behaviors. For example, while Facebook users once controlled their home page content by promoting or demoting, Facebook now determines this based on use patterns. Users have to seek out the updates of those they do not normally interact with. Similarly, as iPads and iPhones gain popularity, companies steer users toward the use of apps (applications)—stand-alone sites dedicated to that company's services. Where once users might have begun with a Web site dedicated to one topic and followed the links to different places, the increasing trend toward using apps may discourage this sort of intellectual roaming. Little is currently known about whether these developments change the likelihood that youth encounter diverse information and viewpoints. As Eli Pariser warns, this tendency toward customization may lead people into "filter bubbles" in which they are decreasingly exposed to information that challenges their worldviews.[22]

To consider this possibility, we examined whether youth exposure to divergent views and to political views with which they agree was linked to (a) politically driven online activity, (b) nonpolitical, interest-driven activities, and (c) to friendship-driven activities.[23] In contrast to conventional wisdom regarding Internet echo chambers, our findings revealed that few young people, 5 percent, report interacting only with those whose views align with their own. Most youth, 57 percent, who report exposure to views that align with their own also report exposure to individuals who hold divergent views. In line with a good bit of political theory, we view this dual exposure as desirable.[24] Engagement with those who share one's perspectives often makes civic and political engagement more likely and can help deepen and clarify one's perspective. Further, exposure to divergent perspectives has been found to foster an individual's perspective-taking ability, knowledge of rationales put forth by those who disagree, and political tolerance for those with differing perspectives.[25]

We also found that young people's politically driven online activities were strongly and positively related to their exposure to diverse perspectives and that friendship-driven socializing had no impact one way or the other. Perhaps more interesting was the finding that online nonpolitical, interest-driven participation was related to increased exposure to diverse perspectives on civic and political issues, even after controlling for young people's politically driven activities and for prior levels of reported exposure to diverse perspectives. It appears that these nonpolitical, online interest-driven communities provide a setting for youth to engage with civic and political issues, affording a valuable form of social capital where diverse perspectives are considered. Indeed, the discussions that occur in nonpolitical online contexts may be particularly important because they can reach those who lack strong civic and political interests and can provide more ideologically diverse environments.

This finding is consistent with results from a study of adults by Magdalena Wojcieszak and Diana Mutz, who found that 53 percent of those engaged in online groups where discussions concern sports, entertainment, hobbies, and other interests end up exchanging perspectives on political issues.[26] In fact, participants in interest-driven groups were the most likely to be exposed to cross-cutting political discussions. These findings do not mean that exposure to highly partisan blogs or Web sites may not be occurring or that such exposure may not be of concern. Rather, it reminds us that the networked nature of interest-driven, online participation may often expose youth to diverse viewpoints.

At the same time, a substantial number of youth (34 percent) in our study disagreed when asked if they were exposed to any perspectives or information on societal issues. Thus, while few youth reported exposure to echo chambers, it appears that many youth are in "empty chambers," where they are not exposed to any perspectives on societal issues. This should be an area of great concern. Indeed, this finding suggests a broader and well-recognized phenomenon—many youth are largely disengaged from civic and political life. Such realities underscore the need for civic education and, especially, for civic education efforts that are universal (like compulsory high school civics courses) so that the efforts reach students who might otherwise never engage with these issues. In addition, the relationship between nonpolitical, interest-driven activities and exposure to diverse political perspectives indicates that nonpolitical, interest-driven participation might be used to create a gateway to civic and political engagement.

YouMedia, headquartered in Chicago and currently being expanded to thirty cities, provides an interesting model. In partnership with the Digital Youth Network, YouMedia includes both a physical space—a library and a complete media repository with computers, studio equipment, video and digital cameras, and much more—as well as an online youth network. Both the network and the physical space provide youth with opportunities to develop media literacy skills and to express themselves through projects that often integrate music, art, books, personal interests, and other issues in their lives and in the broader society. Online and offline, YouMedia provides participants with both an audience and a space for discussion, collaboration, and debate. The physical space provides an after-school and weekend hub, and the Digital Youth Network provides a way for youth to participate anywhere and anytime. Their reach is expanded through partnerships with public schools in Chicago. One interesting initiative is the Change Society—a subgroup of older teens in the YouMedia fold who work with one of the organization's mentors to create media pieces (music, poetry, video) with a focus on civic engagement. They use both literature and current events as inspiration for dialogue. More generally, while YouMedia does not focus primarily on civic or political engagement, its rich array of activities such as poetry slams, book discussions, digital art, music, and video projects often inspires the sharing of diverse perspectives on civic and political issues.

Digital Media Literacy and Online Civic Participation

In March 2010, *The New Yorker* published a cartoon popular with "techies'" and teachers alike. Set in a hospital nursery, the cartoon features an infant holding up a cell phone and texting, "OMG! I just got born!"

Source: Cartoon by Mick Stevens and used with permission from the Cartoon Bank/Condé Nast Publications Inc.

Conventional wisdom holds that when it comes to digital media, youth are digital natives who learn on their own what they need to know and that adults have little to offer.

Research indicates that this view is mistaken. If the ability to text or tweet was all that youth needed to tap the civic potential of digital media, this observation might be true. However, accessing online content with any depth takes a certain level of media literacy, which research has demonstrated is not evenly distributed among all youth.[27] For example, those from privileged backgrounds demonstrate higher-level know-how—Internet search skills, the ability to download or send files, an understanding of Internet vocabulary—than those from lower socio-economic status.[28] All youth must learn to judge the credibility of digital media content in order to navigate almost limitless options regarding both content and technology and to become competent, civil, critical online participants.

Taking an early look at the impact of digital media literacy instruction on online behaviors for young people, we investigated digital media learning opportunities for high school and university students.[29] To remove the confounding effects of other digital media use on skill development, we controlled for various forms of digital media engagement, including communication (e-mail, text messaging, online chat), blogging or social networking, online video game activity, and overall time spent online.

Our results indicated that digital media literacy instruction is fairly widespread, at least within our California sample. More than 80 percent of high school students in our sample reported opportunities to assess the trustworthiness of online information, and close to 90 percent were required to use the Internet to find both information and differing viewpoints on political and social issues. Participants were less likely to report creating original online content as part of a school assignment, with approximately 65 percent of both high school and college students reporting "never" being given such an assignment.

These media literacy learning opportunities appeared to have a positive impact on civic engagement, even with controls for political interest and prior levels of online activity. Youth who had media literacy opportunities were more likely to both engage online politically and report being exposed to diverse perspectives during their discretionary time. This supports the idea that as youth have opportunities to learn *how* to engage online, they become more likely to do so.

Unfortunately, few studies have examined the civic impacts of particular media literacy programs in school settings.[30] At the same time, this work, along with work by media literacy educators, clearly highlights the potential of such efforts. One example is Project Look Sharp. Its lesson guides, media documents, and staff development aim to help teachers engage students in critical analysis of current political and societal issues and the ways those issues are portrayed in the media. For instance, lessons on criminal justice expose youth to news articles and other media that make varied arguments. Youth are then asked to critically analyze both arguments and associated imagery within the news report (the cover of a magazine article, for example) or the ways in which statistics are used to make an argument more convincing.

In addition, those focused on media literacy are increasingly attending to youth as producers as well as consumers of media. For example, the Civic Action Project is a curriculum for high school students in civics and government created by the Constitutional Rights Foundation. Students identify a problem, a policy, or an issue and design an action project with a tangible civic goal. Engagement with digital media is woven into this curriculum. Students create project blogs, learn how to use multimedia sources to persuade and inform others, and gain the necessary skills to navigate online sources of information about their chosen topic. Further, students learn about the importance of the media in setting the public agenda.

The Civic Potential of Video Games

While conventional wisdom has it that video games are largely a waste of time, distracting youth from other, far more meaningful pursuits, some educators and developers view video games as powerful learning tools. We collaborated with the Pew Internet and American Life Project to investigate the relationship between video game play and civic and political engagement in young adults.[31]

We found that 97 percent of teens reported playing video games, but that overall, playing video games was not related to engagement, one way or another. We also examined youth who played video games that incorporated the same opportunities found in high-quality civic education such as opportunities to help others, to be a leader of a city or nation, or to encounter controversial societal issues.[32] We found that many games provided youth with such civic learning experiences and that youth who played games that provided these opportunities were far more likely to seek online sources of political information, to give money to a charity, to be interested in politics, to protest or demonstrate, and to say that they had persuaded someone to vote in a particular way. No doubt, some of this relationship exists because youth who like politics also like playing games that provide these experiences. But given positive findings from studies of the impact of such simulated and school-based civic learning opportunities, we also suspect that civic gaming experiences can enhance the likelihood that youth will be active when offline. What's more, in contrast to school-based civic learning opportunities, civic gaming experiences were equally distributed by race, ethnicity, and family income.[33] Although research has shown that white, high-achieving students from higher socioeconomic levels receive more civic learning opportunities, the situation is different with video game play. With gaming, youth decide what they themselves want to do, and it turns out that all demographic groups of youth are equally likely to pursue civic content.

Interested stakeholders from political, government, and educational organizations have already begun to develop ways to foster civic outcomes through video games. *Quest Atlantis*, a popular, educational, virtual-reality game played by more than ten thousand young people on five continents, opens by telling tweens that they *have* "to help save Atlantis!" Kids are presented with a compelling narrative surrounding the social and environmental problems of the mythical world Atlantis and are entreated to help solve these problems with the help of other "questers." Game challenges are structured around seven social commitments, several of which are distinctly civic in nature, including "social responsibility" and "healthy communities." Recent research has found that the game promotes civic outcomes such as ecological stewardship, an understanding and appreciation of community action, and social responsibility.[34]

There are many other such initiatives, including *Real Lives*, a simulation game where youth in a class can each be assigned an identity that is modeled on the world census.[35] Students then must live their life (get an education, find a job, stay healthy, etc.) making decisions and being affected by different events; the probability of any given event's affecting a given player is tied to actual data regarding the likelihood. The game provides youth with insight into the ways different political, economic, and cultural realities, as well as chance, influence both decisions and life courses of individuals in different parts of the world.

The growing number of independently designed, socially conscious video games has inspired the work of the Games for Change organization, which supports the creation of video games with a social impact and curates online lists of relevant games, organizing them by appropriate age range and game focus, including areas such as human rights, politics, global conflict, and public policy.[36]

THE VIRTUAL WORLD CAN BE GOOD FOR THE REAL ONE: IMPLICATIONS FOR POLICY

The research and broader trends in digital media highlight some potentially valuable directions for policy and practice. We found that both politically driven and interest-driven engagement in online communities can promote civic and political engagement. Friendship-driven online socializing appeared to make little difference one way or the other. Our studies also indicated that media literacy instruction about ways to engage with issues civically and politically promotes engagement during young people's discretionary time. In addition, politically driven and interest-driven online participation as well as media literacy efforts all appear able to bolster the degree to which youth are exposed to diverse opinions. Finally, while the total volume of video game play is not related to overall levels of engagement with civic or political life, when the video games provide civic learning opportunities by focusing on societal issues or placing the player in the role of a political leader, playing video games is strongly associated with offline civic and political activity and commitments.

As discussed, these findings represent initial investigations into a fast-changing field. Much more research is needed to fully understand when and why varied kinds of online experiences influence particular outcomes. Nevertheless, these early findings, along with those of other researchers, provide helpful guidance for policymakers and educators who must act now. For this reason, we conclude with five recommendations.

Promote Media Literacy

Despite multiple strong rationales for media literacy, it is still often on the margins of school curricula and school reform efforts. Within the United States, it has rarely been a sizable focus of curriculum standards or district or state policy. Indeed, there has not been a single national survey that details how often this goal is attended to by teachers. Still, the momentum may be shifting.[37] A number of policy statements and efforts to bolster attention to media literacy are emerging. For example, media literacy receives significant attention in the Common Core State Standards.[38] It makes sense for policymakers and educators to amplify such efforts and to be sure that the civic dimensions of media literacy (learning how to critically assess media, to produce compelling and informed media tied to societal issues, and to engage in dialogues in a respectful manner, for example) are included in these efforts. Our data indicate that when youth are given structured opportunities to gain political information online during school time, they become more likely to use these tools during their discretionary time. In addition, media literacy opportunities are needed to expand the number of youth who can judge credibility and assess bias in online information, can produce and share work that is compelling and informed, can engage with others respectfully, and know what to share and what to keep private. Media literacy is also far preferable to relatively hopeless efforts to prevent youth from engaging with digital media. As the leaders of Common Sense Media explain, "We believe in teaching our kids to be savvy, respectful and responsible media interpreters, creators, and communicators. We can't cover their eyes but we can teach them to see."[39]

Close the Digital Divide and the Participation Gap

Currently, data regarding the inequitable nature of civic participation and influence are troubling. Low-income and less educated citizens, as well as recent immigrants and those less proficient in English, have far less voice in the political process.[40] Given the increasingly digital nature of civic and political life, it is fundamentally important that the nation enact policies that close both the digital divide and the participation gap.

By the digital divide, we refer to unequal levels in access to technology. For example, 95 percent of households with incomes over $100,000 had broadband in 2009, compared with 38 percent of those with incomes under $25,000.[41] At the same time, youth of different races are equally likely to own cell phones, and recent research shows that black, Hispanic, and Asian American youth are the heaviest consumers of digital media content (games, music, videos) using that device.[42] When deciding which aspects of the digital divide on which to focus, it is very important to know more about how different kinds of technology are related to desired forms of participation.

Indeed, many now argue that rather than focusing solely on the digital divide, policymakers should also focus on the participation gap—on differences in how youth participate when online.[43] For example, it may be more important for youth to have affordable access to smartphones than for them to have computers at home with broadband. In addition, closing the participation gap may depend as much on ensuring equal support for media literacy education and for opportunities that support the desired use of digital technology for civic and political purposes as on equalizing access to technology. In other words, at the same time that policies advance the cause of access, other policies should both assess whether in-school and after-school support for media literacy and desired forms of participation via digital media are equitably distributed and respond to disparities once they are identified. Such policies can strengthen U.S. democracy by helping to ensure that all individuals can and do voice their perspectives.

Promote Out-of-School Opportunities Along with In-School Ones

Often, civic educators focus only on schools. When it comes to leveraging the power of digital media to support civic and political development, we believe this stance would be a sizable mistake. After-school and extracurricular opportunities as well as young people's discretionary time have the potential to be quite valuable for fostering desired civic and political outcomes. Indeed, while schools can support this agenda in many ways, it is often easier for those outside of schools to support youth engagement in actual political and civic activity both because these organizations are often community based and because schools are often hesitant to engage youth in activities that might be considered politically partisan or controversial. Thus, it makes sense to look for ways youth can engage civically and politically in out-of-school contexts and at ways media literacy can be developed in these settings.

For example, the Philadelphia Student Union (PSU) is a youth-led, community-based organization in which youth learn organizing strategies to address issues of educational quality and access.[44] As part of their activities, youth engage in political education and action but also in new-media literacy and new-media strategy. Video, Web radio, digital photography, blogging, and a dynamic Web presence are embedded in PSU's organizing efforts, and recent research with PSU alumni has detailed the substantial influence the organization has had on both their traditional and nontraditional forms of civic and political involvement.[45] Recognizing the value of digital literacy as a skill and as a social justice issue, PSU has recently launched the Young People's Computer Center to provide a space where youth can learn together and "bridge the digital divide."

Fund the Development of Digital Civic Infrastructure

The need for increased attention to digital infrastructure is enormous. When we speak of the need for digital civic infrastructure, we are referring less to digital technology and more to the need for digital resources that can foster desired civic and political engagement. Some outstanding models already exist.

Puget SoundOff, with offices in Seattle, is an online hub where teens can do all the usual fun stuff—blog, share and comment on photos and videos, connect with friends in a self-contained social networking space—while simultaneously learning about, generating original Web content on, and mobilizing around regional political, environmental, and social issues. The site provides a space for teens to learn about what's happening in their area, for them to share their perspectives, and for peer-to-peer encouragement to get involved, as well as room for discussion and reflection. Educators in both school and out-of-school contexts are invited to use the site as a way for youth to learn about issues and to develop media literacy while the integrated social network provides a valuable and sizable audience for youth productions. Such online platforms are relatively easy to replicate in other regions and to tailor to local conditions. Civic educators and designers are only just beginning to develop this kind of infrastructure; it will be key to supporting high-quality civic opportunities for youth in school and out.

Conduct Relevant Assessments

Assessments, rightly understood, are essential. They provide a meaningful way for individuals and groups to receive feedback on the quality of their work and for educators and policymakers to assess the impact of varied efforts. There may well be ways that digital media and the networked nature of digital media can provide important support for quality assessment.

Imagine, for example, if every high school student had a digital civics portfolio. Throughout his or her time in high school, each student might post writings, videos of activities, and other artifacts of the student's civic and political analysis and action. These portfolios might also be placed within a network so that teachers and students could see and comment on each other's work. There would be many details to work out, of course, but such portfolios might enable more authentic characterizations of student engagement and of their analytic and expressive capacities than a survey or test. By having the portfolios span several years, it would hopefully also be possible to see how students' thinking and levels of engagement develop.

Digital badges might be tied to these portfolios to provide an additional support for this kind of assessment. Badges call attention to the skills youth are using and the experiences they are having during their digital activities. These electronic badges are earned when an individual accomplishes a given task or demonstrates a particular skill. They can be used to motivate accomplishments and to provide clear indicators of varied capacities and experiences. One could imagine earning badges for engaging in a service activity, for sharing an informed perspective on a societal issue with a large audience, or for seeking out diverse perspectives on a controversial topic. In addition, the networked nature of badges mean that those pursuing badges might receive feedback and enter into dialogues with a range of individuals, spurring reflection and engagement. While the use of badges as part of assessment structures is just beginning to take shape, badges are especially appropriate as a way of characterizing civic learning, skills, and levels of engagement. They can focus on a wide range of priorities, on both individual and group accomplishments, and on what individuals have done and can do.[46]

CONCLUSION

Educators and policymakers should look for ways to leverage the civic potential of online activity. Unfortunately, they often do not. Lumping all activities together, educational policymakers often focus on this question: how much time do kids spend with media? The answer is shocking—something close to 7½ hours a day if you include television—but it's the wrong question. Society needs to focus both on what youth are doing when they engage with media and on the impact of different practices. Answers to these questions can help Americans highlight ways that educators, policymakers, and others can leverage youth engagement with these media to foster young people's productive engagement in society.

In short, the virtual world can be good for the real one. There are forms of online participatory activity that can give youth civic and political engagement a much-needed boost. It is vitally important that educators and policymakers in both school and out-of-school settings seize these opportunities to more fully tap this potential.

10

CIVIC EDUCATION IN TRADITIONAL PUBLIC, CHARTER, AND PRIVATE SCHOOLS

Moving from Comparison to Explanation

David E. Campbell

A small but convincing literature has demonstrated, empirically, that America's private schools do at least as well as—and in some cases surpass—traditional public schools when it comes to providing civic education. Likewise, a smaller body of empirical research has also provided evidence that some charter schools also excel in some aspects of civic education. Such findings fly in the face of what has long been conventional wisdom among education theorists: whatever their other faults, traditional public schools are in a class of their own when it comes to producing democratic citizens. While this chapter details the evidence regarding civic education in different types of schools, my objective is *not* to convince you that one type provides a superior form of civic education. Rather, the objective is to convince you that asking whether traditional public, charter, or private schools do civics better is the wrong question. The right question is to ask what makes for a successful civic education, regardless of the type of school. Given that we know relatively little about what makes a successful civic education, careful study of schools in different sectors is a rich vein to mine. What can traditional public schools learn from the successes of their charter and private counterparts? Likewise, what can choice schools learn from traditional public schools?

This chapter begins with the premise that over roughly the last twenty years, elementary and secondary education has undergone a revolution. It, regrettably, has not been a revolution of dramatically rising academic achievement. American education problems have not been solved. However—and this *is* the revolutionary part—the American public knows a lot more about its schools and the students within them than it did a generation ago. Americans have experienced a revolution of information. Information in the form of international exams (Program for International Student Assessment [PISA] and Trends in International Mathematics and Science Study [TIMMS]) spurs education reform nationwide. Within states, educators can compare the performance of students on state-administered exams. In turn, comparing those state tests to National Assessment in Education Progress (NAEP) reveals when the two diverge. And this information revolution is not limited to test scores. Scholars, policymakers, and parents alike can learn about myriad aspects of U.S. schools. Often, this information is readily available online.

A cynic might suggest that all of this information has not done any good, as America has hardly undergone a renaissance of rising academic performance. I disagree. Collectively, scholars, policymakers, and parents are learning more and more about effective schools. Parents especially can use this information to make informed decisions about their children's education. As a society, Americans will never reach consensus on the most effective education policies and practices. But as people debate what makes for good schools, are they not better off traveling down a path illuminated with data than stumbling in the dark?

There is, however, a glaring omission—or near omission—in these reams of information. For all that scholars, policymakers, and the public know about performance in reading, math, and science; for all that they have learned about graduation rates, college acceptance, average SAT scores, Advanced Placement courses; and for all that they know about class and racial disparities in all these indicators, people know very little about the civic dimension of K–12 education. Indeed, there is not even consensus on what a civic education entails (more on that below). Yet what concerned citizens do know only reinforces how much they have yet to learn. In a nutshell, people know that some types of schools—particularly some private schools—do well in providing a sound civic education. Scholars have hypotheses as to why, but the jury is still out. Most importantly, the education system does not know what, if anything, about these civically successful schools can be replicated in other types of schools.

The chapter proceeds as follows. First, it will detail what is known about differences in civic education across school sectors—traditional public, private (in its many forms), and charter. Then, it will highlight what is not known, and provide an explanation for why more is not known. Finally, it will make a case for why Americans' collective ignorance should motivate researchers, policy makers, and parents alike to learn more—in the service of enhancing civic education for all.

WHAT IS CIVIC EDUCATION?

Step one in evaluating the effectiveness of civic education is, of course, to define the very term. As should be clear from the other chapters in this volume, civic education is a lot like obscenity—in the oft-quoted words of Justice Potter Stewart, we know it when we see it. It is indicative of America's polarized political climate that the essentials of a civic education are contested, often along ideological lines. As long as the discussion stays at a high level of abstraction, everyone can agree on the importance of civic education. *Civic* is a usefully vague term with a positive, even aspirational, connotation. Yet get into specifics, and conservatives and liberals begin to disagree, often vehemently, on what a civic education should entail. To a conservative, a civic education should prioritize instruction on the constitutional limits on federal power. To a liberal, to be civically educated means learning about the civil rights protections of the Fourteenth Amendment. Conservatives are more likely to emphasize responsibilities and negative liberty. Liberals are inclined to stress rights and positive liberty. And so on.

Perhaps I am naive, but I believe that it is possible to find common ground on the criteria for a civic education. A personal anecdote illustrates the reason for my optimism. A few years ago, I participated in a roundtable on civic education. One of the other participants was a recently retired Republican member of the U.S. House of Representatives. In my remarks, I mentioned political tolerance as one objective of a civic education. In his subsequent remarks, this former member of Congress criticized the reification of tolerance, suggesting that instead, civic education should focus on understanding the application of the U.S. Constitution in Americans' lives. Specifically, he was concerned about the apparently rampant lack of civics knowledge among Americans, young people especially.[1] Fortunately, I had the opportunity to respond, as I pointed out that he and I agreed on more than we disagreed. As I read out the questions that are typically used to gauge tolerance—essentially, whether unpopular groups should enjoy freedom of speech—I noted that they perfectly reflect his stated objective of providing real-world applications of constitutional principles. Testing the application of First Amendment protections *is* a test of civics knowledge; it might even be the best test of all. In other words, once he got past his preconceived notion of what tolerance entails, this former congressman found that our notions of civic education were not so far apart after all.

The point is not that I have some idiosyncratic definition of tolerance that met with approval from an equally idiosyncratic former politician. Rather, it is that the general definition of political tolerance as studied by social scientists for decades aligns with a school of thought that is suspicious of the term *tolerance* from its use in other contexts. My broader point is even more important: this moment of consensus building gives me hope that the various parties involved in studying civic education can find consensus on other issues as well.

This anecdote notwithstanding, I do not mean to suggest that consensus comes easy. However, there is enough agreement on the critical measures of civic education that the education community can proceed to consider the evidence on differences between school sectors.

The first, and arguably least controversial, dimension of civic education is knowledge. It is difficult to imagine anyone seriously disagreeing with the proposition that students should acquire factual knowledge about government and politics. Significantly, the importance of factual knowledge is not merely an aspirational platitude. There is a large research literature on the unique importance of political knowledge as a precursor to political participation.[2] Admittedly, though, upon scratching below the surface of all this consensus there can be disagreement over just what students need to know—the cause of the controversy that has stymied the creation of national civics standards. Indeed, in this very volume, both Richard Niemi (chapter 1) and Peter Levine (chapter 2) have called for a reconsideration of what students need to know to be civically informed. Still, in spite of, or perhaps because of, the always-lurking potential for disagreement over what constitutes essential civic information, NAEP and other federal studies have managed to craft questions that do not appear to cause much controversy when testing young people's knowledge.

In addition to the cognitive dimension of knowledge (what people know), civic education is also often thought to have a behavioral dimension (what people do). One such civic activity is voluntarism or, as it is often labeled, service-learning. The primary justification for promoting voluntarism is that it reflects public-spiritedness. Indeed, this sort of concern for the well-being of one's community is what the very term *civic* connotes.

Like the importance of knowledge, voluntarism has a virtuous veneer. It is hard to argue that there is anything wrong with encouraging teens to volunteer in soup kitchens, blood drives, charity fund-raisers, and the like. Rather, the debate over volunteering centers on whether schools should mandate such community service (in which case it obviously ceases to be voluntary) and whether community service is merely used as a credential by upper-middle-class youth to burnish their college applications. From the perspective of education to prepare youth to be politically active, an especially potent argument against service-learning is that its emphasis on apolitical activity subtly teaches young people that they should shun political solutions to societal problems. Meira Levinson expresses concern that service-learning teaches "a weak, even eviscerated, conception of civic engagement."[3] However, its critics notwithstanding, community service remains a common metric for gauging the civic involvement of young people.

Another behavioral aspect of civic education is the preparation of young people for civic and political involvement, namely, civic skills. Unfortunately, the term *civic skills* is so catchy that it has been bandied about to mean many things, but I use the term in the same way that its originators, Sidney Verba, Kay Schlozman, and Henry Brady, meant.[4] They use it to refer to the capacity to perform activities common to virtually all civic involvement: write a letter, give a speech, or run a meeting. Their research shows the importance of learning such skills as a precondition for political activity. The skills are especially critical for ensuring a politically active citizenry because, unlike many other factors feeding political participation, civic skills can be taught. One important venue for learning such skills, especially for young people, is the classroom.

The final dimension of civic education on which I will focus is also the most controversial—tolerance. While some conservatives cringe at the term *tolerance* as symptomatic of a values-free, nonjudgmental worldview, this caricature is unfair. As noted above, tolerance, a longtime term of art within empirical social science, refers to a person's willingness to grant civil liberties to unpopular minorities. Recall my story about the defused disagreement with the former member of Congress over tolerance: when put in terms of First Amendment protections, questions about tolerance are really questions about applied constitutional principles.

While I submit that these are measurable dimensions of civic education on which the existing literature has settled because of an informal consensus among scholars and practitioners, neither are they the final word. As I discuss below, debate continues on what the content of civic education ought to be, and so perhaps other dimensions could, and will, be added in future evaluations. These dimensions of civic education are a starting point for the conversation about the civic education provided in different types of schools.

HOW DO PUBLIC, CHARTER, AND PRIVATE SCHOOLS COMPARE?

To date, the most comprehensive account of civic education in different school types is a 2007 article by Patrick Wolf in *Education Next*.[5] In this article, Wolf summarizes fifty-nine empirical findings from twenty-one studies (disclosure: I wrote or cowrote five of those studies). By aggregating across multiple studies, Wolf highlights their commonalities—much like the Web site Rotten Tomatoes, which aggregates movie reviews. As with any such meta-analysis, some of the specific results vary from study to study—just as not everyone hates a box-office bomb or loves a blockbuster. There is, however, a consistent theme that runs through the bulk of the studies assembled by Wolf. In his words, "the 59 findings from existing studies suggest that the effect of private schooling or school choice on civic values is most often neutral or positive . . . Only one finding from the rigorous evaluations indicates that *traditional* public schooling arrangements enhance a civic value."[6] In short, Wolf's meta-analysis shows that at best, private schooling provides a "civic advantage," and at worst, there is no difference between the public and private sectors. In his article, Wolf is careful to differentiate studies according to their analytical rigor, and thus persuasiveness. He gives the greatest weight to studies that employ the power of random assignment, a research design often described as the gold standard.

Wolf was drawing on the available research circa 2007, which was largely focused on comparing public and private schools. Less research had been done on the civic education of charter schools. Also in 2007—but too late for inclusion in Wolf's article—Jack Buckley and Mark Schneider published their book *Charter Schools: Hope or Hype?*, which includes a sophisticated examination of civic outcomes for charter school students in Washington, D.C.[7] While Buckley and Schneider do not rely on data from a true randomized experiment, they nonetheless use a system of statistical matching that approximates an experimental research design. Their conclusions regarding charter schools are consistent with the extant research on private schools, as they find no negative civic effects for charter school students compared with their peers in traditional public schools, and some positive effects.

While the overall picture painted by the study of students in private and charter schools is that these schools hold their own against, and often outdo, their public school counterparts in civic education, the broad brush strokes of this general conclusion hide the details. We can learn more about the consequences of different school types by examining how students in traditional public, charter, and private schools (of different types) differ on each dimension of civic education.

Knowledge

When it comes to political knowledge, no study has found that students in traditional public schools score higher than students in private or charter schools. However, the evidence on whether private or charter schools boost students' political knowledge is mixed.

My analysis of data from the National Household Education Survey (NHES)—a high-quality, nationally representative study conducted by the U.S. Department of Education—shows that, when a wide array of potentially confounding variables are controlled for, students in Catholic schools score higher on a short quiz of political knowledge than their counterparts in traditional public schools. But students in other types of private schools, and those enrolled in public schools of choice, show no statistically significant differences from traditional public school students.[8] On the other hand, in a more limited study, R. Kenneth Godwin and Frank Kemerer found a positive boost for the political knowledge of all private school students compared with those enrolled in traditional public schools.[9]

I have also analyzed data from the most rigorous type of study, a randomized experiment whereby a nationwide lottery determined which students received a voucher to attend a private school, and found no increased political knowledge for private school students.[10] But since this analysis could only draw on a two-question quiz administered by telephone and was conducted after the student attended just one year in a private school, it is hardly definitive. In their charter school study, Buckley and Schneider did not examine any cognitive outcomes, so no rigorous evidence is available on whether there is a charter school effect on political knowledge.

Voluntarism

A number of studies have found that students in private and charter schools have higher rates of community volunteering than their peers in traditional public schools. For example, Richard Niemi, Mary Hepburn, and Chris Chapman found that students in religious schools are more likely to engage in volunteer service than traditional public school students.[11] In my analysis of the NHES, Catholic school students were the most likely to volunteer. And this effect is not just because Catholic schools are more likely to mandate service by their students, as the results hold even when omitting students who attend schools with compulsory service requirements.[12] Wolf notes that "four voluntarism findings emerged from rigorous studies, with three of them favoring school choice" (by which he means private school students).[13]

In their study of charter schools in the Washington, D.C., area, Buckley and Schneider found that charter school students are more likely to participate in volunteer work than young people in traditional public schools. Holding everything else constant, just over 10 percent of students in the D.C. Public Schools participate in community service once a week or more, compared with over 40 percent of charter school students.[14]

Buckley and Schneider note that, like many private schools, charter schools often require their students to participate in service. Such requirements are a good example of what is still unknown about civic education. Does required service promote an ethic of service within a school, leaving a lasting imprint of civic engagement (presumably, the objective of such requirements)? Or, as some critics contend, does mandatory service breed resentment among young people, making them cynical about the merits of volunteering? At this point, no one knows the answers to questions like these.

Civic Skills

Buckley and Schneider also found that charter school students are more likely to report learning civic skills—specifically, taking part in a debate and making comments in a public meeting.[15] My analysis of the NHES indicates a civic skill advantage for Catholic school students over those enrolled in traditional public schools. Catholic school students are more likely to have written a letter in class, given a speech or oral report, and taken part in a debate.[16]

Tolerance

The findings regarding political tolerance are the most contested on normative grounds, for this is where advocates for public education have long argued that public schools excel. The data, however, suggest otherwise. To quote Wolf's meta-analysis once more, "with one exception, the findings regarding the effect of school choice on political tolerance are confined to the neutral-to-positive range."[17] In my analysis of the aforementioned randomized, nationwide school voucher experiment, I found a positive effect on political tolerance after one year in a private school.[18] But just as I earlier downplayed a null finding for political knowledge from the same study, I must also do the same for this result. The limited number of questions plus the short duration of the study mean that the results are suggestive but not conclusive. Bolstering this conclusion, results from a voucher program in Washington, D.C., also finds a positive effect for private schooling on political tolerance. Likewise, Godwin and Kemerer found that students in secular and nonevangelical private schools have a higher level of political tolerance than do their public school peers.[19]

Tempering these findings, my analysis of the NHES also suggests a lower level of political tolerance for students in non–Catholic religious schools—largely evangelical Protestant or Christian fundamentalist schools—than for traditional public school students, although the lack of a key statistical control (frequency of religious attendance) makes this finding tentative.[20] Buckley and Schneider found no charter school effect on political tolerance, although theirs is, notably, a single study in a single city and thus is far from the final word.[21]

With this plethora of data, it is easy to lose the forest for the trees. Studies differ in their methodology and measures, but the central thrust of the empirical evidence is clear. Compared with a public education, attending a private or charter school does not mean that civic education is diminished; instead, it is enhanced. In particular, students in Catholic schools often lead the pack.

THE SECOND GENERATION

Regrettably, what is known about the differences in civic education across school sectors ends here, with comparisons of various civic outcomes. Scholars know very little about *why* traditional public, charter, and private schools might provide a different type of civic education. One reason such explanations are lacking is the motivation for the "boomlet" of research on civic education in public, charter, and private schools. Much of the research on civic education across school sectors has been spurred by the heated debate over school choice, vouchers especially. Critics of vouchers have made some strong claims about the danger to democracy posed by private, particularly religious, schools. Consider the words of Justice John Paul Stevens, in his dissent to *Zelman v. Simmons-Harris* (2002), the Supreme Court case that found vouchers constitutional. He warned that vouchers would "weaken the foundation of our democracy."[22] Such strong words cry out for empirical confirmation. Thus, the research on civic education in different sectors has largely been conducted with the relatively narrow but highly policy-relevant question of determining whether private schools lag behind in civic education. Accordingly, Wolf frames his influential article as an examination of whether school choice harms democratic values, rather than an exploration of why public and private schools might differ in the civic education they provide.

I do not mean to imply the insignificance of asking whether school choice has implications, positive or negative, for citizenship education. To the contrary, I was one of the scholars seeking to answer this question. I would like to think that this research has done what more social science ought to do—employ the tools of its trade to address a question of policy significance. And while, as with all social science, the case is not fully closed, the burden of proof has shifted to those who argue that public schools are the exemplars of civic education. I consider this literature the first generation of research on civic education across school sectors.

The time has come for a second generation of research, when scholars move from comparing to *understanding* outcomes. Today, society's understanding of civic education in private and charter schools is like willow bark tea. For centuries, people drank the tea as a pain reliever. It worked, but no one knew why. Then, scientists discovered the active ingredient in willow bark, salicylic acid. Even more significantly, the Bayer Company figured out how to make a compound with that same active ingredient and distribute it widely. It was called aspirin.

As has been detailed in earlier chapters, civic education in America could use some aspirin. Even Peter Levine, more sanguine than most about the state of civics in our schools, acknowledges that improvement is needed. But improvement will only come when educators find the active ingredient or, more likely, ingredients. I submit that careful study of why civic education differs across traditional public, charter, and private—including religious—schools can help society in the search for civic aspirin. It is not that differences between private, charter, and traditional public schools will explain everything Americans want to know about what makes for effective civic education. Rather, examining differences across sectors should ideally be just one aspect of multidimensional research into what works, and what does not, in teaching young people the principles and practices of democratic citizenship.

WHY SCHOOLS MIGHT DIFFER

There are myriad explanations for the differences in civic outcomes observes across school types. Here I propose two that seem most promising to study.

Classroom Instruction

For decades, the conventional wisdom about civic education had been that taking a civics class (whether given that label or not) had little to no effect on civic outcomes. In the 1990s, that conventional wisdom was updated when Richard Niemi and Jane Junn analyzed NAEP data and concluded that civics classes did have an effect after all, although that effect is small.[23] More recently, Donald Green and his colleagues conducted a controlled experiment to test the effect of a new civics curriculum and found that it does indeed have an effect on students' political knowledge.[24]

This is not to say that educators should conclude that all civics instruction is equally effective. Other research, including my own, suggests that simply taking a high school course is too crude a measure to detect any effects. Similarly, the specific content of the curriculum does not seem to be the critical factor. Instead, what seems to matter is the style of instruction. In an analysis of a major multinational study of civic education, I have found that civics classrooms with an open airing of contentious issues in a respectful environment correspond to greater student knowledge and students' greater intention to participate in politics as an adult.[25] Perhaps even more importantly, an open classroom climate is especially effective with lower-class youth, as it closes the participation gap between teens of higher and lower socioeconomic status.[26] Using a different methodology, Diana Hess also describes the effectiveness of an open classroom climate for sparking young people's democratic engagement.[27]

Given the apparent effect of classrooms where students are able to participate in democratic debate and discussion, classroom instruction is a logical place to look to explain differences between traditional public, charter, and private schools. Does variation in the openness of the classroom climate explain those differences? If so, why are some schools better able to foster healthy debate within their classrooms than others? Answering that question and pollinating all schools with whatever it takes to promote more classroom discussion would take us a long way toward improving civic education.

School Ethos

In addition to classroom instruction, another important contributing factor is what I call the *ethos* of a school. By ethos, I mean the norms encouraged, shared, and "enforced" within a school community—such as interpersonal trust and an expectation of public engagement. While perhaps not as easy to observe as classroom instruction, extant research indicates that a school's ethos has a substantial, and enduring, effect on the civic engagement of its students.

Attention to a school's ethos dates at least as far back as James Coleman's seminal research on public and private high schools. Coleman sought to explain the higher academic achievement in private, especially Catholic, high schools. How could students in these schools have relatively high academic achievement in spite of limited resources? His answer was *social capital*, a term that has spread widely throughout the social sciences to have many applications. For Coleman and his colleague

Thomas Hoffer, to have high social capital meant that these schools, and the communities in which they were embedded, had strong, positive social norms encouraging academic achievement.[28] Putnam then borrowed the concept of social capital and applied it specifically to civic engagement—high social capital results in high civic engagement.[29] It thus makes sense that schools high in social capital would also provide effective civic education.

Anthony Bryk, Valerie Lee, and Peter Holland have examined the Catholic schools that, in Coleman and Hoffer's account, are rich in social capital. In their masterful book *Catholic Schools and the Common Good*, they dig deep to understand what makes Catholic schools successful.[30] They conclude that Catholic schools promote a strong sense of community, centered on trust. In other words, they too point to the schools' ethos as a key contributor to their academic success. And while the authors do not speak of civic education per se, there is every reason to think that the esprit de corps found within many Catholic schools produces positive civic outcomes. Thomas Dee finds convergent evidence that Catholic schools foster a "civic inclination." As adults, people educated in Catholic schools are more likely to vote than are public school alumni.[31]

Terry Moe explicitly makes the connection between a school's ethos and the consequences for civic attitudes (although, a propos of the above discussion, Moe notably does so in the context of the debate over school choice):

> As parents choose their own schools, they are more likely to identify with them, to share their values and missions, to trust one another, to participate, and to have respect for teachers and principals. And to the extent that schools are free from restrictive rules, they are free, among other things, to hire the kinds of teachers who share the school's mission, do their jobs well, get along with one another, have mutual respect, and share power. These are all hallmarks of community, characteristics that arise naturally in an environment of choice and autonomy but that stand little chance under a bureaucratic regime.[32]

There is thus good reason to consider schools' ethos a promising avenue for an effective, even holistic, civic education. But the $64,000 question is whether the ethos of Catholic schools, or of private schools generally, can be replicated in public schools. My own research suggests that the ethos within public schools matters, too. In *Why We Vote: How Schools and Communities Shape Our Civic Life*, I detail how adolescents who attended public high schools with a strong civic ethos were more likely to be civically engaged—voting and volunteering—fifteen years after graduating from high school.[33] The school ethos, I find, has more long-term impact on civic engagement than an individual's personal sense of civic duty as an adolescent. In other words, imagine that I wanted to predict whether an adolescent will, upon reaching adulthood, be civically engaged. In making my prediction, I can know only one of the following: the individual's personal sense of civic obligation, or the collective sense of civic obligation within the individual's high school (that is, the school ethos). I would be more likely to make an accurate prediction knowing the school ethos. In fact, an individual's own sense of civic responsibility as a teenager has no bearing on his or her civic engagement as an adult.

These results are promising, but, I will be the first to admit, leave as many questions as answers. My measure of civic ethos is thin, consisting of a survey question about whether voting is the hallmark of good citizenship. The data I used stretched from 1965 to 1980, leaving open whether these findings from an earlier era apply today. Perhaps most importantly, the data were not equipped to tell me what fosters a strong civic ethos. *Why* are some schools better able to encourage a strong sense of civic commitment? To what extent do schools create these norms versus serving as repositories of civic attitudes formed outside their walls?

If I am right, and a school's ethos has a long-term impact, there is still the question of exactly where that impact will be felt. How might school ethos affect the aforementioned dimensions of civic education? A norm encouraging civically oriented behavior could foster voluntarism and the practice of civic skills, while a norm encouraging awareness of current events could lead to greater political knowledge. For many, however, political tolerance raises a red flag. After all, the sort of school community Moe describes—formed by like-minded parents banding together—would seem to run the risk of promoting intolerance toward those outside that community. Exacerbating such concerns, religiosity is generally associated with lower levels of political tolerance, imply-ing that religious schools may breed intolerance.[34] Recall, though, that the empirical data on this score are mixed. Some data suggest that stu-dents in non-Catholic religious schools have lower tolerance, but that Catholic school students come out ahead (as do students in secular pri-vate schools). Frankly, it is not known the extent to which these differ-ences in political tolerance are owing to a school's ethos. Bryk, Lee, and Holland's careful study of Catholic schools gives every indication that a school's religious mission need not run counter to open-mindedness and tolerance and can provide the foundation for such attitudes.

Recalling the above discussion of classroom instruction, a school's ethos likely shapes discourse in the classroom. It seems plausible that an ethos of trust opens space for teachers to feel comfortable introducing contentious issues into their lessons and allowing debate and discussion of those issues among the students. Absent an environment of trust, I suspect most teachers would sooner shy away from potential conflict at the risk of raising the ire of students, parents, and administrators alike.

In short, while there is promising evidence that a school's ethos has a meaningful, measurable, and long-term impact on civic education, there is only limited understanding of why, how, and what it affects. Educators may have found their willow bark tea, but they do not yet know how to make aspirin.

Some of the most exciting, but vastly underutilized, places to study school ethos are charter schools. As schools of choice, they would seem to embody the sort of community Moe advocates. But since they are public and thus without a religious character, they present the opportu-nity to study a school's ethos in the absence of a religious mission. For the purpose of determining causal effects, the admissions lotteries of many charter schools make randomized experiments possible. Anecdotally, there is good reason to think that at least some charter schools succeed in fos-tering a strong civic ethos. For example, consider how Seth Andrew de-scribes Democracy Prep, a charter school he operates in Harlem:

> In the classroom, we provide our citizen-scholars with a rigorous civics
> curriculum that integrates the theory and processes of American govern-
> ment into social studies and debate classes. We hold students and teachers

accountable through frequent student assessments. And to deepen our scholars' knowledge, we facilitate inspiring hands-on activities that demonstrate how civic skills enable them to be purposeful agents of change.

To learn about voting, our citizen-scholars participate in mock elections every year. On the ballot are candidates for city, state, and federal government, as well as Democracy Prep ballot initiatives.[35]

This school certainly seems as if it is infused with a strong civic ethos. In the same volume as the essay quoted above, Mike Feinberg, a cofounder of the Knowledge Is Power Program schools, similarly describes the emphasis on civic education within the KIPP curriculum.[36] However, only a rigorous, data-driven evaluation can show the actual effects on what students know and do. Even more importantly, assuming there are measurable effects on students, educators would want to know whether they can be replicated elsewhere.

CONCLUSION

Understanding why some schools succeed at civic education and others fail requires two things to happen. First, there needs to be more and better data both on civic outcomes and on the school-level factors—like classroom climate and school ethos—that are likely to affect those outcomes. Second, the researchers studying school type need to move beyond demonstrating differences between traditional public, charter, and private schools and instead ask why those differences exist.

This chapter began by celebrating the information revolution in American education over the last twenty or so years. Scholars, policymakers, and parents alike have access to a wealth of data on the country's schools. Yet these data rarely include civic indicators. Only when interested Americans shine as much light on civics as they do on other subjects can we expect to learn what works, and how to replicate it.

The first step to collecting data is deciding what needs to be collected. That, in turn, requires consensus on what is worth knowing. I have briefly outlined here some dimensions of civic education on which consensus seems possible, beginning with knowledge. It may be that, as Levine suggests (chapter 2), the Department of Education must limit itself to measuring knowledge, as it does already with the periodic NAEP civics exam. If so, then the data on civic knowledge must be collected on a much larger scale. Data on the other dimensions of civic education would have to come from studies funded through alternative sources, presumably private foundations. These, too, need to be done on a large scale. Wherever possible, they should employ randomization to test for causal effects and be longitudinal to examine long-term effects on civic education. In short, evaluations of civic education need to include traditional public, charter, and private schools, while evaluations of school choice need to carefully measure civic inputs and outputs.

However, while more data are necessary for improving what is known about civic education, it is not sufficient. Equally important will be what is done with the data. Researchers must move beyond simply comparing civic outcomes across different school types and instead seek to understand the sources of those differences, all with an eye toward practices that are replicable across sectors.

It probably seems self-serving for an academic like me to write an essay calling for more research, more data, and thus presumably more grants. My call for more data is really a call to take civic education seriously. Public school advocates need to acknowledge the scholarship on the positive civic effects observed in private and charter schools, as this research questions the platitudinous celebration of public schools as the wellsprings of civic virtue. Advocates of choice, whether in the form of vouchers or charters, need to give civic education more than just lip service and recognize that improving civic education for all young people requires attention to the dominant form of secondary education—the traditional local school assigned on the basis of where one lives.

In conclusion, it is fair to ask whether my recommendations are feasible. In these politically polarized times, can interested Americans really expect any consensus on what a civic education should entail, let alone a commitment of the substantial resources required to study civic education well? I submit that it is precisely *because* of these polarized times— and the political disaffection caused by polarization—that all Americans must pay attention to civic education. We in the research community must not let ideology blind us to discovering ways that civic success in one type of school can be implemented in another.

CONCLUSION

THE THIRD C

College, Career, and *Citizenship*

Meira Levinson

The case for improving and expanding civic education in U.S. schools in the early twenty-first century feels both self-evident and doomed. It's self-evident because we can all agree—left, right, or centrist; policy wonk, antigovernment crusader, or news avoider; youth or adult; Occupier or Tea Partier; isolationist or internationalist—that American politics is broken. At this writing, Congress has an 11 percent approval rating—a number that leads one to ask not why it's so low, but what on earth those 11 percent who still approve of Congress could be thinking.[1] The United States is facing domestic and international challenges of massive proportions, yet seems unable to take basic steps to put its economic, social, or diplomatic house in order. State and even local politics are also increasingly riven by seemingly unbridgeable partisan divides, leading to municipal bankruptcies, shutdowns in state governments, collapses in services, and even vigilante legislation and justice.

At the same time, advocacy for high-quality civic learning feels doomed because civic educators may be seen as just one more special interest jockeying for school leaders' and policymakers' attention. Advocates of physical and health education introduce the threatening specter of the obesity epidemic, warning of skyrocketing health-care costs and the progressive disabling of the workforce. Arts education advocates speak of the importance of creativity, intercultural understanding, and whole-child development. Foreign-language boosters make dire forecasts about U.S. children's lack of preparedness to succeed in a globalized, multilingual economy. What good are science and history education, they ask, in the absence of a capacity to speak Mandarin or to cross other cultural and linguistic boundaries? Amid this cacophony of voices all trying to be heard above the brass band of reading and math instruction, civic education advocates may seem to be just another set of special pleaders contributing to the din. States' overriding focus on the Common Core Standards in English Language Arts and Mathematics risks further sidelining civic learning. Furthermore, contemporary concerns about education in underserved communities, the closure of "dropout factories," and the elimination of the academic achievement gap may crowd out apparently tangential calls for better civic education.

Given these concerns, how can advocates of high-quality civic education get beyond preaching to the choir? Civic education boosters face the same challenge in the contemporary education policy landscape that Keith Barton explicates in his analysis of teacher education programs in chapter 7: "Not only must teachers know how to teach for democracy, but they must also *want* to do so." The consensus that emerges across the chapters in this book—a consensus that was not foreordained, given that they were written by authors from ideologically diverse vantage points, from a wide variety of disciplines, and on a range of topics in civic education—suggests that educators and scholars know quite a bit about how to teach for democracy. So why is it not happening? Could it be that people don't *want* to do so?

THE CASE FOR THE "THIRD C"

As David Campbell mentions in the introduction, schools and policymakers over the past fifty years have not wanted to spend time on civic education, because school-based civic education was thought to be irrelevant to students' civic learning. Scholars and educators now know that this was wrong. Experiential civic education, classroom discussion, student participation in school governance, digital civic media production, current-events lessons, media literacy curricula, and service-learning are all effective means by which schools can increase students' civic knowledge, engagement, and identity (chapters 1, 2, 5, 6, 9). Students also learn democratic skills and habits in response to school context. Schools that create intentional civic spaces teach students how to interact respectfully and productively with diverse others, since this learning does not occur naturally on its own (chapter 4). Possibly as a result, different kinds of schools (private, parochial, charter, and traditional public) have measurably disparate impacts on their students' civic knowledge, skills, attitudes, and present and future action (chapter 10). Students' civic learning is also directly dependent on the quality of teaching they experience (chapter 8). These findings confirm that schools have an essential role to play in ensuring that all Americans develop the capacities and inclination for effective, thoughtful, public-spirited civic engagement.

This emphasis on *all* Americans is important because it provides a powerful response to those who claim that the math and reading achievement gap should remain the primary, even sole, focus of educators and policymakers. I fully agree that educational equity is a matter of grave concern, as equality of educational opportunity is both a civil and a moral obligation in any democracy. But this actually reinforces my point. Democracies demand equality of opportunity not solely because they value citizens' equal access to college and career, although they may well do so, but also because democracies are based on the premise of *civic* equality. This premise is instantiated in such democratic principles as "One person, one vote," and "All are equal before the law." The Campaign for the Civic Mission of Schools report *Guardian of Democracy: The Civic Mission of Schools* stresses this point: "We cannot be said to live in a true democracy if individuals or members of groups systematically possess unequal civic and political power, if some votes and voices count more or less than others, or if some stand either above or below the law . . . Without civic knowledge, skills, identity, and propensity toward engagement, some students are essentially disenfranchised and disempowered. Civic learning opportunities are thus essential for promoting civic equity as a democratic ideal."[2]

Hence, democratic nations like the United States must educate for college, career, *and* citizenship. Civic readiness is the essential "third C" in a democracy. This isn't a distraction from the real work of schools and educational policymakers; it is a crucial part of that work. In this respect, too, the inequities in opportunities for civic learning and engagement that many of this volume's authors highlight in their chapters are as important to combat as are inequities in other academic domains. The United States is challenged by a civic empowerment gap as much as an academic achievement gap, and schools have a responsibility to help citizens overcome both assaults on democracy and individual freedom.[3]

In addition, Peter Levine points to provocative evidence that education for civic empowerment actually increases students' likely academic achievement. Civics and academics are not in competition with one another; rather, they symbiotically reinforce one another. Political scientists have known for a very long time that higher levels of educational achievement map directly onto higher levels of civic knowledge, skills, and engagement.[4] Academic achievement definitely feeds civic empowerment. The relationship seems to go the other way as well. Levine cites studies showing that civic and historical knowledge may increase students' reading comprehension skills; service-learning has a positive effect on students' graduation rate; and civic engagement experiences increase young people's prosocial beliefs and actions in ways that are directly correlated with likely subsequent academic performance. I don't want to push this argument too strongly. The data are still suggestive rather than dispositive; high-quality studies are relatively few and far between. Even more to the point, I don't want to suggest that civic education has value only if it also serves academic ends. Citizenship is a third pillar of education, not merely a handmaiden to college and career goals. It is nonetheless useful, and encouraging, to see evidence that attention to one might advance the cause of the others.

SCHOOLS WITHIN A LARGER CIVIC ECOLOGY

As the contributors to this book attempt to convince educators, policymakers, and members of the public to *want* high-quality civic education, it is essential to point out that such education looks radically different from traditional civics classes. The knowledge, skills, attitudes, actions, and pedagogies called for above—in other words, for which there is robust evidence of their effectiveness in preparing young people to be active, informed participants in democratic life—are far removed from the dusty flowcharts, lists, and lectures that pass for civics in many schools and districts. High-quality civic education is dynamic, responsive to the present, committed to equity, capable of moving among virtual and offline worlds, attentive to identity and difference, and supportive of student action. The Spencer Foundation has recently dubbed such approaches "the new civics," which is an apt description of civic learning's need to move in a new direction.

The individual authors featured in this volume have been at the forefront of advocating for new-civics approaches over the past decade or more. There is often wisdom to be gained in the collective, however, that does not emerge as readily from individual members. Reading these chapters as a whole, I was especially struck by their collective illumination of schools' positioning within a larger *civic ecology*. This insight generates at least three important implications for why, how, and how much schools should take on responsibility for civic education.

First, schools are members of a larger set of institutions that have historically inducted young people into American civic and political life. These include churches and other religious organizations, neighborhood and fraternal associations, unions, youth groups such as scouting and 4-H, other voluntary associations, and news media. Levine elucidates the ways in which many of these nonschool institutions both served to promote civic learning and engagement in the past and have withered in contemporary civil society. Membership in voluntary associations, neighborhood groups, and unions has plummeted. The public sphere has become dominated by professional citizens—those who make their living in government, media, lobbying, or nonprofit work—rather than serving as an egalitarian and inclusive meeting ground for the public as a whole. Newspaper readership and hard-news viewership has dropped precipitously over the past few decades; it has not systematically been replaced by other serious sources of information such as news-oriented Web sites.

Admittedly, other forms of media may promote civic learning as a by-product of their actions. In chapter 1, for example, Niemi notes that over 90 percent of twelfth-graders accurately answered test questions about "the right to a lawyer, the right to remain silent, and the meaning of the right to counsel." He notes that students may be highly knowledgeable about these rights because they are mentioned in the Constitution—or maybe because these rights are "what students see on television and in the movies." I wager that if the National Assessment of Educational Progress similarly included questions about forensic pathology, virtually every teenager with a television set (and hence with access to *CSI*) would nail the test. Unlike hard-news shows, however, these television dramas are not designed to promote civic learning. This is not to castigate the civic knowledge that may be gained on occasion from watching these shows. Rather, it is to point out that the civic ecology of contemporary American institutions is both more attenuated and less intentional than it has been in the past.

Similarly, Joseph Kahne, Jacqueline Ullman, and Ellen Middaugh point to new forms of democratic association that are springing up online in the form of interest-driven digital communities, online forums for political and civic dialogue and action, and even civically oriented video games. Many young people are excited by these opportunities and become more civically knowledgeable and engaged as a result. Nonetheless, these authors also point out that many other youth are occupying "empty chambers" online in which no civic learning or engagement takes place. Yes, Facebook may have facilitated the Arab Spring of 2011. But no, hanging out on Facebook and posting comments on friends' walls does not in itself advance young people's civic development.

Given these declines in the associations that historically promoted civic learning and engagement, and the uncertain contribution of new forms of digital media and networking, schools are left to pick up the slack. Citizens' knowledgeable and effective participation in public life is as important as ever. No longer, however, can schools merely complement and reinforce the civic lessons imparted by the daily newspaper, the church ladies' society, the union stewards' meeting, or the Welcome Wagon. The erosion of these organizations leaves a more barren plain in which schools stand out as one of the few institutions positioned to impart the knowledge, skills, attitudes, and experiences to prepare active, informed participants in democratic life. This makes the achievement of high-quality, school-based civic education more important than ever.

Second, schools function within a broader civic ecology insofar as they must mediate students' and teachers' incoming civic beliefs, habits, and values. Schools don't operate in a civic vacuum. They instead must deal with the already-developed perspectives of those who walk through their doors. Chapter 4, in which I discuss the treatment of "undesirable," "deviant," or even "illegal" group members within schools, addresses these challenges most directly. External conflicts about the civic and legal standing of gays, immigrants, Muslims, drug users, and others can spill into schools, despite educators' desperate wishes to remain neutral and above the fray. In chapter 7, Barton suggests that teachers' very desire for conflict avoidance reveals their adherence to non- and even anti-democratic values. They see themselves as surrogate mothers with private, parental duties of protection, for instance, not as representatives of the state with public duties to develop children's civic capacities. As a result, even schools that have a strong democratic ethos may find themselves undermined by teachers who are unable or unwilling to "subject" their students to democratic deliberation and disagreement. Diana Hess and John Zola point out that sometimes, students themselves are the only ones who can dislodge teachers' assumptions about what degree of civic education is possible: "It is not uncommon for the student work to actually *raise* teachers' expectations about what students can and should be expected to learn." As Levine and Kahne, Ullman, and Middaugh argue, however, this laudable attempt is often complicated when patterns of civic inequality are replicated within the classroom and school. Again, the ecology of civic patterns, opportunities, and values outside schools come to shape what is seen as civically feasible inside schools.

The relationship between civil society and schools, however, is not monodirectional. This leads to the third insight about schools' role within the larger civic ecology: namely, that schools themselves are civic actors. They—and the students they teach—can and should interact with the world beyond their walls. In chapter 3, Michael Johanek offers three fascinating past examples of schools' acting within and upon the community as self-conscious civic institutions. "Civic education was understood to encompass the school's role as an *actor* within neighborhood life," he explains. His historical case studies reveal schools and districts that attempted to revive rural communities in West Virginia through community programming, that organized self-governing adult centers and civic clubs in Rochester, and that engaged East Harlem students in community-based research projects and civic action campaigns to address a wide variety of social, economic, and political issues. Shifting from historical to contemporary analysis, Anna Saavedra and James Youniss each provide intriguing present-day models of schools and students as civic actors. Through examples of middle school science students whose research and public advocacy work led to changes in Iowa's waste disposal laws, or Youth Council members in Chicago whose violence-reduction recommendations were adopted district-wide, these scholars provide ample evidence that, as Youniss declares, "schools can make a difference that reaches into communities, government, and the political system." In emphasizing the importance of teaching current events, Levine and Niemi also reinforce the idea that schools should engage young people in civic life now, not just in the future as adults. Finally, Kahne, Ullman, and Middaugh provide provocative anticipation of schools' and students' direct civic engagement in the future through online communities, digitally mediated action in the real world, and authentic civic work that earns students recognition for civic accomplishments.

CIVIC EDUCATION ON THE LEADING EDGE

I have thus far discussed three ways to understand schools as positioned within the larger civic ecology of society. I have suggested that schools may step into the breach to make up for the diminution of other civically educative institutions. I showed how schools will necessarily find themselves needing to respond to broader civic disputes and values as these enter the walls of the school. Finally, I have also suggested that historical, present-day, and future-oriented examples demonstrate multiple ways in which schools and students may act upon civil society. Perhaps the most consistent insight deriving from this collection of essays, however, is that schools can create their *own* civic ecology—and that this may be the most effective and important thing they do in service of student civic learning.

Time and again, these chapters show that schools' communities and cultures matter. Youniss reveals the crucial roles of an open classroom climate, student participation in school governance, and participation in service that reflects schools' "conscious" intent to induct students into particular civic identities and traditions. Saavedra illuminates the ways in which "dynamic civic education strategies" create classrooms and schools that engage students' heads and hearts in civic participation. My own chapter shows how schools can help students learn to respect one another and work together across lines of difference by intentionally and transparently leveraging diversity within the school community. At the same time, I argue, the school community must be constructed so as to offer all students and families a "warm, inclusive embrace"; to do otherwise would be to betray the school's civic and moral responsibilities. Campbell in chapter 10 similarly emphasizes that a school's "ethos," or "the norms encouraged, shared, and 'enforced' within a school community" has "a substantial, and enduring, effect on the civic engagement of its students." Hess and Zola reveal potentially similar mechanisms at work with teachers. It is when teachers themselves experience civically engaging and empowering pedagogies like a Socratic seminar that they become inclined and equipped to use such techniques with their own students.

Taken together, these intersections and overlaps reveal the permeability of schools and society. Schools permeate civil society. Civil society permeates schools. Neither schools nor social institutions function as separate, independent entities. This insight should be obvious, but educational reform discourse currently assumes a rigid dichotomy between the two. Citizens often fail to recognize schools even as social institutions, let alone as institutions reflective of, responsive to, embedded within, and effective upon society.

Insofar as civic education scholarship cuts through such false dichotomies, it can and should be a leader in education reform, not an also-ran. Civic education is essential for democracy's health, communities' well-being, and students' engagement and empowerment. As the chapters in this book reveal, high-quality civic education practices also demonstrate the power of teaching and learning within, through, and beyond the school walls. These practices pull contemporary society into the school, for example, by incorporating the study of current events, and push the school into society through such means as service-learning, community organizing, action civics, and digital media production. Furthermore, civic education also requires that educators turn schools into the kind of model civic communities that any American would hope to see instantiated in the larger society. This is necessary as a means of building students' civic capacities now and influencing their vision of the kind of society youth will help create in the future. Saavedra points out that this is not "your father's" civics. Instead, it is exactly the kind of dynamic, contextualized learning and teaching that is called for across all subject areas in twenty-first-century schools.

In addition to providing cutting-edge models of intellectual content and pedagogical practice, civic education has the potential to lead the way into a new generation of educational assessment. Until recently, civics was arguably among the hardest disciplines to assess meaningfully, because children were legally prevented from enacting many of the public roles of citizens: serving on juries, voting, running for office, or even volunteering in an organization without a parent in tow. Those interested in civic education were therefore reduced to measuring students' decontextualized knowledge and skills. In all other school-based subjects, educators can in theory assess children's capacities to enact the disciplines that they teach (even if this occurs only sporadically in practice. Assessments can have students read, do math, conduct science experiments, create art, or play sports. But how could one assess young people's capacities to *be* citizens?

Thanks to the insights of the collected scholars, it is now possible for educators, policymakers, and interested citizens to see that civics may offer some of the most authentic and exciting opportunities in educational assessment and pedagogical practice—ones that could serve as models for other disciplines. Multiplayer real-time simulations, digital civic portfolios and badges, authentic online civic engagement, and demonstrated off-line civic action are all promising avenues for civics instruction and assessment. Even the simulated versions of these enable children to *do* civics and interact *as* citizens in the process of acquiring and demonstrating their learning. But perhaps even more excitingly, many of these approaches enable children to make a real, meaningful, lasting contribution to the world from a very young age. Frankly, most youth won't write original poems or essays of lasting value to others. Nor are they likely to do original mathematics that engages adults other than their teachers and parents. But young people *can* make authentic civic contributions that influence or even transform individuals' and communities' lives for years to come. This is an incredible opportunity for all concerned. Let's make the "third C" of citizenship education a reality.

NOTES

Introduction

David E. Campbell

1. These statistics are based on the Current Population Survey, November Supplements. See "Population Characteristic (P20) Reports and Detailed Tables," U.S. Census Bureau, available at www.census.gov/hhes/www/socdemo/voting/publications/p20/index.html.

2. Robert D. Putnam, *Bowling Alone: The Collapse and Revival of American Community* (New York: Simon and Schuster, 2000).

3. Morris Fiorina, Samuel J. Abrams, and Jeremy C. Pope, *Culture War? The Myth of a Polarized America*, 3rd ed. (New York: Longman, 2010).

4. Marc J. Hetherington, *Why Trust Matters: Declining Political Trust and the Demise of American Liberalism* (Princeton, NJ: Princeton University Press, 2006).

5. John R. Hibbing and Elizabeth Theiss-Morse, *Stealth Democracy: Americans' Beliefs about How Government Should Work* (New York: Cambridge University Press, 2002), 225–226.

6. Thomas Jefferson to William C. Jarvis, 1820, in *The Writings of Thomas Jefferson, Memorial Edition*, ed. Andrew Adgate Lipscomb and Albert E. Bergh, vol. 15 (Washington, DC: 1903–1904), 278.

Chapter 1
What Students Know About Civics and Government

Richard G. Niemi

1. This tradition goes back to at least 1951, when a reporter in Wisconsin solicited signatures for a document composed of passages from the Bill of Rights and the Declaration of Independence. He was turned down 111 times and was able to obtain only one signature. John Patrick Hunter, "4th of July Celebrants Afraid to Sign the Declaration and Bill of Rights," *Madison (WI) Capital Times*, July 5, 1951.

2. Barbara A. Bardes, Mack C. Shelley, and Steffen W. Schmidt, *American Government and Politics Today 2008: The Essentials* (Belmont, CA: Cengage/Wadsworth, 2009).

3. James Michener, *Presidential Lottery* (New York: Random House, 1969), 43.

4. Michael X. Delli Carpini and Scott Keeter, *What Americans Know about Politics and Why It Matters* (New Haven, CT: Yale University Press, 1996), 92.

5. Ibid., 101.

6. Angus Campbell et al., *The American Voter* (New York: Wiley, 1960). On knowledge

about Congress, see John R. Hibbing and Elizabeth Theiss-Morse, *Congress as Public Enemy: Public Attitudes Toward American Political Institutions* (New York: Cambridge University Press, 1995).

7. "American Public Vastly Overestimates Amount of U.S. Foreign Aid," November 29, 2010, available at www.worldpublicopinion.org/pipa/articles/brunitedstatescanadara/670.php.

8. Carnegie Corporation of New York and CIRCLE, *The Civic Mission of Schools* (New York: Carnegie Corporation of New York; College Park, MD: CIRCLE, 2003), 19; Sandra Day O'Connor, quoted in Sam Dillon, "Failing Grades on Civics Exam Called a Crisis," *New York Times*, May 4, 2011.

9. William A. Galston, "Political Knowledge, Political Engagement, and Civic Education," *Annual Review of Political Science* 4 (2001): 217–234.

10. All NAEP results are from the NAEP civics Web site, National Center for Education Statistics, http://nces.ed.gov/nationsreportcard/civics/, and National Center for Education Statistics, *Civics 2010: National Assessment of Educational Progress at Grades 4, 8, and 12* (Washington, DC: U.S. Department of Education, 2011).

11. Intercollegiate Studies Institute, *The Coming Crisis in Citizenship* (Wilmington, DE: Intercollegiate Studies Institute, 2006); Intercollegiate Studies Institute, *Our Fading Heritage* (Wilmington, DE: Intercollegiate Studies Institute, 2008).

12. "Pop Quiz: What Do Students Know?" *Newsweek on Campus*, March 1988, 18.

13. "Polling on the Holocaust: The Decline of Historical Knowledge?" *Public Perspective* (July–August 1993): 34.

14. Delli Carpini and Keeter, "Explaining Political Knowledge," in *What Americans Know*, 178–218.

15. Delli Carpini and Keeter, "Stability and Change in Political Knowledge," in *What Americans Know*, 105–135.

16. Richard G. Niemi, Mitchell S. Sanders, and Dale Whittington, "Civic Knowledge of Elementary and Secondary School Students, 1933–1998," *Theory & Research in Social Education* 33 (2005): 185.

17. National Center for Education Statistics, *Civics 2010*.

18. Martin P. Wattenberg, *Is Voting for Young People? With a Postscript on Citizen Engagement* (New York: Pearson Longman, 2008), 79.

19. Ibid.; Paul Howe, *Citizens Adrift: The Democratic Disengagement of Young Canadians* (Vancouver: UBC Press, 2010).

20. Howe, *Citizens Adrift*, 71–72.

21. Delli Carpini and Keeter, *What Americans Know*, 172.

22. Ibid., 145, 345; M. Kent Jennings, "Political Knowledge over Time and Across Generations," *Public Opinion Quarterly* 60 (1996): 228–252.

23. Wattenberg, *Is Voting for Young People?* 79.

24. Judith Torney-Purta et al., *Citizenship and Education in Twenty-Eight Countries: Civic Knowledge and Engagement at Age Fourteen* (Amsterdam: International Association for the Evaluation of Educational Achievement, 2001).

25. That is, they differed by a statistically significant amount.

26. The items used in this study are also subject to the criticism that "[r]ather than testing factual knowledge, the questionnaire tested vocabulary, logic, and appreciation of democratic values." Henry Milner, *The Internet Generation: Engaged Citizens or Political Dropouts* (Lebanon, NH: University Press of New England, 2010), 179.

27. Torney-Purta et al., *Citizenship and Education*, 44.

28. W. A. Schaper, "What Do Students Know about American Government, Before Taking College Courses in Political Science?" in *Proceedings of the American Political Science Association*, vol. 2 (Lancaster, PA: Wickersham Press, 1906), 218.

29. In mathematics and the sciences, international comparisons to some degree validate the specification of proficiency levels. In civics and history, such comparisons are of more limited value, given the enormous difficulty of designing valid cross-national tests. See note 26 above.

30. Niemi, Sanders, and Whittington, "Civic Knowledge," 186.

31. Richard Rothstein, "We Are Not Ready to Assess History Performance," *Journal of American History* 90 (2004): 1381–1391; Sam Wineberg, "Crazy for History," *Journal of American History* 90 (2004): 1401–1414; Richard J. Paxton, "Don't Know Much About History—Never Did," *Phi Delta Kappan* 85 (2003): 265–273.

32. Dale Whittington, "What Have 17-Year-Olds Known in the Past?" *American Educational Research Journal* 28 (1991): 759–780.

33. Richard G. Niemi and Jane Junn, *Civic Education: What Makes Students Learn?* (New Haven, CT: Yale University Press, 1998), chap. 2.

34. Herbert H. Hyman, Charles R. Wright, and John Shelton Reed, *The Enduring Effects of Education* (Chicago: University of Chicago Press, 1975), appendix; Delli Carpini and Keeter, "Who's Informed? Individual, Group, and Collective Patterns of Political Knowledge," in *What Americans Know*, chap. 4; Elisabeth Gidengil et al., *Citizens* (Vancouver: UBC Press, 2004).

35. Delli Carpini and Keeter, *What Americans Know*, 183, 245.

36. Ibid., 144–145, 183.

37. Stephen P. Nicholson, Adrian Pantoja, and Gary M. Segura, "Political Knowledge and Issue Voting Among the Latino Electorate," *Political Research Quarterly* 59 (2006): 259–271.

38. See Jeffery J. Mondak and Mary R. Anderson, "A Reexamination of Gender-Based Differences in Political Knowledge," *Journal of Politics* 66 (2004): 492–512, and the sources cited therein.

39. Mondak and Anderson, "A Reexamination."

40. Gidengil et al., *Citizens*, 53; Dietlind Stolle and Elisabeth Gidengil, "What Do Women Really Know? A Gendered Analysis of Varieties of Political Knowledge," *Perspectives on Politics* 8 (2010): 93–110. See also Niemi and Junn, *Civic Education*, 105–109.

41. Robert D. Hess and Judith V. Torney, *The Development of Political Attitudes in Children* (Chicago: Aldine, 1967), 176; M. Kent Jennings and Richard G. Niemi, *Generations and Politics* (Princeton, NJ: Princeton University Press, 1981), 281.

42. Niemi and Junn, *Civic Education*, 104–109; National Center for Education Statistics, *Civics 2010*.

43. National Center for Education Statistics, *U.S. History 2010: National Assessment of Educational Progress at Grades 4, 8, and 12* (Washington, DC: U.S. Department of Education, 2011).

44. In Anja Neundorf, Kaat Smets, and Gema García-Albacete, "Bringing It Together: The Development of Political Interest in Light of Parental Socialization and Life-Cycle Events" (unpublished paper, Oxford University, Oxford), the authors, using German data, find that political interest increases considerably up to about age twenty-five and then flattens out. Markus Prior, "You've Either Got It or You Don't? The Stability of Political Interest over the Life Cycle," *Journal of Politics* 72 (2010): 747–766, based on U.S. data, finds relative stability throughout adulthood.

45. Russell J. Dalton, Ian McAllister, and Martin J. Wattenberg, "The Consequences of Partisan Decline," in *Parties Without Partisans*, ed. Russell Dalton and Martin J. Wattenberg (Oxford: Oxford University Press, 2001), 57.

46. "The ANES Guide to Public Opinion and Electoral Behavior," American National Election Studies, (Ann Arbor: University of Michigan, Center for Political Studies), available at http://electionstudies.org/nesguide/nesguide.htm.

47. John H. Pryor et al., *The American Freshman: Forty Year Trends* (Los Angeles: Cooperative Institutional Research Program, University of California, Los Angeles, 2007), 126–127. The percentage has now bounced back somewhat to the mid- to high 30s.

48. Howe, *Citizens Adrift*, 75.

49. Martin P. Wattenberg, *Where Have All the Voters Gone?* (Cambridge, MA: Harvard University Press, 2002), 89; Howe, *Citizens Adrift*, 74–76.

50. "The ANES Guide."

51. Harold W. Stanley and Richard G. Niemi, *Vital Statistics on American Politics 2011–2012* (Washington, DC: CQ Press, 2011), 159–160.

52. "The ANES Guide."

53. Wattenberg, *Where Have All the Voters Gone?* chap. 1; Howe, *Citizens Adrift*, 79–84.

54. Howe, *Citizens Adrift*, 84.

55. Wattenberg, *Where Have All the Voters Gone?* chap. 2.

56. Howe, *Citizens Adrift*, 85–101.

57. Matthew Baum and Angela S. Jamison, "The Oprah Effect: How Soft News Helps Inattentive Citizens Vote Consistently," *Journal of Politics* 68 (2006): 946–959; Marcus Prior, "Any Good News in Soft News? The Impact of Soft News Preference on Political Knowledge," *Political Communication* 20 (2003): 149–171.

58. Markus Prior, "News vs. Entertainment: How Increasing Media Choice Widens Gaps in Political Knowledge and Turnout," *American Journal of Political Science* 49 (2005): 577–592.

59. *Audience Segments in a Changing New Environment: Pew Research Center Biennial News Consumption Survey* (Washington, DC: Pew Research Center for the People and the Press, 2008), 64–67, available at http://people-press.org/files/legacy-pdf/444.pdf.

60. Richard G. Niemi and Julia Smith, "Enrollments in High School Government Classes: Are We Short-Changing Both Citizenship and Political Science Training?" *PS: Political Science & Politics* 34 (2001): 281–287.

61. An excellent study of changes in the content of civics coursework is found in an

undergraduate thesis: Nathaniel Leland Schwartz, "Civic Disengagement: The Demise of the American High School Civics Class," (Harvard University, 2002).

62. Niemi and Smith, "Enrollments in High School"; Stephen Roey et al., *The 2000 High School Transcript Study Tabulations* (Washington, DC: National Center for Education Statistics, U.S. Department of Education, 2007), Table 34D, http://nces.ed.gov/nationsreportcard/hsts/tabulations/.

63. National Center for Education Statistics, *Civics 2010*, 39. The percentage self-reporting a civics or government class in high school in 1988 was 93 percent; see Lee Anderson et al., *The Civics Report Card* (Washington, DC: National Center for Education Statistics, U.S. Department of Education, 1990), 72.

64. Howe, *Citizens Adrift*, 72, makes the further point that civics teaching did not decline at the same time across all the countries he analyzed.

65. Richard E. Gross, "The Status of the Social Studies in the Public Schools of the United States: Fact and Impressions of a National Survey," *Social Education* 41 (1977): 194–200, 205.

66. Howe, *Citizens Adrift*, 101, 264.

67. Henry Milner, *Civic Literacy: How Informed Citizens Make Democracies Work* (Medford, MA: Tufts University Press, 2002), 188; Howe, *Citizens Adrift*, 266–271; Milner, *Civic Literacy*, chap. 8; Benjamin I. Page, *Choices and Echoes in Presidential Elections* (Chicago: University of Chicago Press, 1978), 91; James S. Fishkin, *Democracy and Deliberation* (New Haven, CT: Yale University Press, 1991); Milner, *Civic Literacy*, chap. 9; Delli Carpini and Keeter, *What Americans Know*, 279–280.

68. In addition to proposals from individual academics, see calls from various blue-ribbon commissions: *Civic Mission of the Schools*; *A Nation of Spectators* (Washington, DC: National Commission on Civic Renewal, 1998); *New Millennium Project, Part I* (Lexington, KY: National Association of Secretaries of State, 1999).

69. Howe, *Citizens Adrift*, 275–277.

70. David E. Campbell, "Voice in the Classroom: How an Open Classroom Climate Fosters Political Engagement among Adolescents," *Political Behavior* 30 (2008): 437–454; Judith Torney, Abraham N. Oppenheim, and Russell F. Farnen, *Civic Education in Ten Countries* (New York: Wiley, 1975); Torney-Purta et al., *Citizenship and Education*, 150–151; Wolfram Shulz et al., *ICCS 2009 International Report: Civic Knowledge, Attitudes and Engagement among Lower-secondary Students in 38 Countries* (Amsterdam: International Association for the Evaluation of Educational Achievement, 2010), 228; Susan MacManus, "What Florida's College Students Say They Didn't Learn in Their High School Government Class," *Journal of the James Madison Institute*, May/June (1999): 4–10; National Conference of State Legislatures, "America's Legislators Back to School Program," available at http://www.ncsl.org/default.aspx?TabID=746&tabs=1116,88,407#1116.

71. John R. Hibbing and Elizabeth Theiss-Morse, "Civics Is Not Enough: Teaching Barbarics in K-12," *PS: Political Science and Politics* 29 (1996): 57–62; Delli Carpini and Keeter, *What Americans Know*, 279.

72. See National Center for Education Statistics, "NAEP Questions Tool," available at

http://nces.ed.gov/nationsreportcard/itmrlsx/search.aspx?subject=civics; *National Standards for Civics and Government* (Calabasas, CA: Center for Civic Education, 1994).

73. The five questions are: "What are civic life, politics, and government?" "What are the foundations of the American political system?" "How does the government established by the Constitution embody the purpose, values, and principles of American democracy?" "What is the relationship of the United States to other nations and to world affairs?" "What are the roles of citizens in American democracy?"

74. These were questions that were asked more than once with substantially the same wording between the late 1940s and early 1990s. See Delli Carpini and Keeter, *What Americans Know*, app. 3; In the interest of full disclosure, it should be noted that I was a participant in the development of the focus and questions used in the 1998 NAEP Civics Assessment.

75. Diana E. Hess, "Teaching Controversial Public Issues Discussions: Learning from Skilled Teachers," *Theory and Research in Social Education* 30 (2002): 10–41.

76. The phrase is from W. Russell Neuman, *The Paradox of Mass Politics* (Cambridge, MA: Harvard University Press, 1986). Others use terms such as "the rules of the game" or "what government is." See Delli Carpini and Keeter, *What Americans Know*, 63–65.

77. Bernard R. Berelson, Paul F. Lazarsfeld, and William N. McPhee, *Voting* (Chicago: University of Chicago Press, 1954), see esp. 308; Michael Schudson, *The Good Citizen* (New York: Free Press, 1999), 310–314.

78. Eric Plutzer, "Becoming a Habitual Voter: Inertia, Resources, and Growth in Young Adulthood," *American Political Science Review* 96 (2002): 41–56.

79. See Milner, *The Internet Generation*, 175 for a similar point.

80. For a useful study of when young people begin to grasp political concepts, see Joseph Adelson and Robert P. O'Neil, "Growth of Political Ideas in Adolescence: The Sense of Community," *Journal of Personality and Social Psychology* 4 (1966): 295–306.

Chapter 2
Education for a Civil Society

Peter Levine

1. Sam Dillon, "Failing Grades on Civics Exam Called a 'Crisis,'" *New York Times*, May 4, 2011, available at www.nytimes.com/2011/05/05/education/05civics.html.

2. "Making History and Civics a Priority," editorial, *Washington Post*, June 17, 2011, available at www.washingtonpost.com/opinions/making-history-and-civics-a-priority/2011/06/17/AGb1tYZH_story.html.

3. Catherine Rampell, "A Generation of Slackers? Not So Much," *New York Times*, May 28, 2011, available at www.nytimes.com/2011/05/29/weekinreview/29graduates.html.

4. Stephane Baldi et al., *What Democracy Means to Ninth-Graders: U.S. Results from the International IEA Civic Education Study* (Washington, DC: National Center for Education Statistics, U.S. Department of Education, 2001), 21.

5. National Center for Education Statistics, *Civics 2010: National Assessment of Educational Progress at Grades 4, 8, and 12* (Washington, DC: U.S. Department of Education, 2011).

6. Data drawn from "NAEP Questions Tool."

7. Council of Chief State School Officers, Center for Civic Education, and the American Institutes for Research, *NAEP Civics Assessment Specifications* (Washington, DC: National Assessment Governing Board, 1996). The five major headings of the NAEP are "What Are Civic Life, Politics, and Government?" "What Are the Foundations of the American Political System?" "How Does the Government Established by the Constitution Embody the Purposes, Values, and Principles of American Democracy?" "What Is the Relationship of the United States to Other Nations and World Affairs?" and "What Are the Roles of Citizens in American Democracy?"

8. "NAEP Questions Tool."

9. According to Tiffany Lennon, *ECS Policy Brief: Citizenship Education* (Denver: Education Commission of the States, July 2006), available at www.ecs.org/clearinghouse/71/30/7130.pdf, every state except Iowa had civics standards. But Iowa does have social studies standards with a strong civics component. See Iowa Department of Education, "Iowa Core," 2012, available at www.corecurriculum.iowa.gov.

10. National Center for Education Statistics, *Civics 2010*, 39.

11. The mean credits earned in social studies rose from 3.52 in 1990 to 4.19 in 2009. National Center for Education Statistics, *America's High School Graduates: Results of the 2009 NAEP High School Transcript Study* (Washington, DC: U.S. Department of Education, 2011), available at http://nces.ed.gov/pubsearch/pubsinfo.asp?pubid=2011462. See also Peter Levine, Mark Hugo Lopez, and Karlo Barrios Marcelo, *Getting Narrower at the Base: The American Curriculum After NCLB* (Medford, MA: CIRCLE, 2008), available at www.civicyouth.org/PopUps/Narrowing_Curriculum.pdf; National Center for Education Statistics, "Summary of Major Findings," available at http://nationsreportcard .gov/civics_2010/summary.asp.

12. Richard G. Niemi and Julia Smith, "Enrollments in High School Government Classes: Are We Short-Changing Both Citizenship and Political Science Training?" *PS: Political Science and Politics* 34, no. 2 (June 2001): 282.

13. Service-learning was offered in 24 percent of K–12 schools in 2008, down from 32 percent in 1999, but up from a very low rate twenty or thirty years ago. Corporation for National and Community Service, *Community Service and Service-Learning in America's Schools: Issue Brief* (Washington, DC: Corporation for National and Community Service, 2008), available at www.nationalservice.gov/about/role_impact/performance_research.asp.

14. Arne Duncan, "The Next Generation of Civics Education" (speech) given at iCivics Educating for Democracy in a Digital Age Conference, March 29, 2011.

15. "NAEP Questions Tool."

16. Joseph Kahne and Ellen Middaugh, "Democracy for Some: The Civic Opportunity Gap in High School," in *Engaging Young People in Civic Life*, ed. James Youniss and Peter Levine (Nashville: Vanderbilt University Press, 2009), 29–58.

17. Nell K. Duke, "The Case for Informational Text," *Educational Leadership* 61, no. 6 (2004): 40–44.

18. Alberto Dávila and Marie T. Mora, *Civic Engagement and High School Academic Progress: An Analysis Using NELS Data* (working paper 52, CIRCLE, Medford, MA, 2007), available at www.civicyouth.org/circle-working-paper-52-civic-engagement-and-high-school-academic-progress-an-analysis-using-nels-data.

19. Andrew Hahn et al., *Life After YouthBuild: 900 YouthBuild Graduates Reflect on Their Lives, Dreams, and Experiences* (Somerville, MA: YouthBuild USA, 2004), available at www.youthbuild.org/atf/cf/%7B22B5F680-2AF9-4ED2-B948-40C4B32E6198%7D/GraduateResearchReport_ExecSum.pdf.

20. A helpful short introduction to the relevant aspects of Habermas's voluminous thought is his own "The Public Sphere: An Encyclopedia Article," *New German Critique* 3 (1974): 49–55. An accessible overview is James Gordon Finlayson, *Habermas: A Very Short Introduction* (New York: Oxford University Press, 2005).

21. Data compiled from American National Election study database and analyzed by the author. Database available at http://www.electionstudies.org/.

22. Jean Johnson, Jonathan Rochkind, and Samantha DuPont, *Don't Count Us Out: How an Overreliance on Accountability Could Undermine the Public's Confidence in Schools, Business, and More* (Dayton, OH: Public Agenda Foundation and Kettering Foundation, 2011).

23. Bill Bishop with Robert G. Cushing, *The Big Sort: Why the Clustering of Like-Minded America Is Tearing Us Apart* (Boston: Houghton Mifflin, 2008).

24. Diana Hess, *Controversy in the Classroom: The Democratic Power of Discussion* (New York: Routledge, 2009).

25. National Council for the Social Studies, "NCSS National Standards for Social Studies Teachers," n.d., available at www.socialstudies.org/standards/teacherstandards; Center for Civic Education, "National Standards for Civics and Government," 2009, available at www.civiced.org/index.php?page=stds_preface.

26. Paul Gagnon, *Educating Democracy: State Standards to Ensure a Civic Core* (Washington, DC: Albert Shanker Institute, 2003).

27. Ibid., 6–7.

28. Andrew P. Kelly, Daniel K. Lautzenheiser, and Cheryl Miller, *Contested Curriculum: How Teachers and Citizens View Civics Education* (Washington, DC: American Enterprise Institute, 2011).

29. Arold William Brown, *The Improvement of Civics Instruction in Junior and Senior High Schools* (Ypsilanti, MI: Standard Printing Co., 1928), 28.

30. Carl D. Glickman, *Holding Sacred Ground: Essays on Leadership, Courage and Endurance in Our Schools* (San Francisco: Jossey-Bass, 2003), 266–268.

31. Center for Action Civics, "Action Civics Declaration," 2012, available at www.centerforactioncivics.org/action-civics-declaration/.

32. Michael McDevitt and Spiro Kiousis, *Experiments in Political Socialization: Kids Voting USA as a Model for Civic Education Reform* (working paper 49, CIRCLE, Medford, MA, August 2006), available at www.civicyouth.org/PopUps/WorkingPapers/WP49McDevitt.pdf; Hess, *Controversy in the Classroom*; David E. Campbell, *Voice in the Classroom: How an Open Classroom Environment Facilitates Adolescents' Civic Development*,

(working paper 28, CIRCLE, Medford, MA, 2005), 1–22; David E. Campbell, "Voice in the Classroom: How an Open Classroom Climate Fosters Political Engagement Among Adolescents," *Political Behavior* 30, no. 4 (2008): 437–454.

33. David E. Campbell, *Why We Vote: How Schools and Communities Shape Our Civic Life* (Princeton, NJ: Princeton University Press, 2006), 147–169.

34. Shelley Billig, Sue Root, and Dan Jesse, *The Impact of Participation in Service-Learning on High Schools Students' Civic Engagement* (working paper 33, CIRCLE, Medford, MA, 2005).

35. Reuben J. Thomas and Daniel A. McFarland, *Joining Young, Voting Young: The Effects of Youth Voluntary Associations on Early Adult Voting* (working paper 73, CIRCLE, Medford, MA, 2010), available at www.civicyouth.org/featured-extracurricular-activities-may-increase-likelihood-of-voting.

36. M. Kent Jennings and Laura Stocker, "Generations and Civic Engagement: A Longitudinal Multiple-Generation Analysis" (paper presented at the 2001 American Political Science Association Convention, San Francisco, 2001).

37. Center for Education Policy, *From the Capital to the Classroom: Year 4 of the No Child Left Behind Act* (Washington, DC: Center for Education Policy, March 2006), xi, 20.

38. Duncan, "The Next Generation of Civics Education."

39. David Williamson Shaffer, *How Computer Games Help Children Learn* (New York: Palgrave MacMillan, 2008).

40. Michael Berson, Kerry Poole, and Peter Levine, "On Becoming a Legislative Aide: Enhancing Civic Engagement Through a Digital Simulation," *Action in Teacher Education* 32, no. 4 (2011): 70–82.

41. John D. and Catherine T. MacArthur Foundation, "Digital Media & Learning Competition Provides $2 Million for Innovations in Digital Badges," news release, September 15, 2011, available at www.macfound.org/site/c.lkLXJ8MQKrH/b.4196225/apps/s/content.asp?ct=11221065.

42. Another important aspect of the Boston effort is its origin. Students on the Boston Student Advisory Council developed it—both the outline and the details—and succeeded in persuading the Boston School Committee to approve it. Those students are supported by Youth on Board (a nationally recognized nonprofit) and by the school system's Office of High School Renewal, so they perform excellent, well-informed, and effective work as public leaders.

43. Mark Hugo Lopez et al., "Schools, Education Policy and the Future of the First Amendment," *Political Communication* 26, no. 1 (2009).

Chapter 3
Preparing Pluribus for Unum: Historical Perspectives on Civic Education

Michael C. Johanek

1. Or, as historian Carl Kaestle asks, does anyone really want "a skeptical, slow complexifier at the table when you're trying to sort through important policy dilemmas?"

(quote; Kenneth K. Wong and Robert Rothman, eds., *CLIO at the Table: Using History to Inform and Improve Education Policy* (New York: Peter Lang, 2009); Paul Theobald, *Education Now: How Rethinking America's Past Can Change Its Future* [Boulder: Paradigm Publishers, 2009]).

2.   R. Freeman Butts, *The Civic Mission in Educational Reform* (Stanford, CA: Hoover Institution Press, 1989); M. Schudson, "The Informed Citizen in Historical Context," *Research in the Teaching of English* 30, no. 3 (1996): 361–369; David F. Labaree, "Public Goods, Private Goods: The American Struggle over Educational Goals," *American Educational Research Journal* 34, no. 1 (1997): 39–81; M. Schudson, *The Good Citizen: A History of American Civic Life* (New York: Free Press, 1998).

3.   For a wonderful recent history examining civic engagement in the early days of the republic, see Nancy Beadie, *Education and the Creation of Capital in the Early American Republic* (New York: Cambridge University Press, 2010).

4.   The quote in the section heading comes from Benjamin Rush, *Of the Mode of Education Proper in a Republic: Essays, Literary, Moral & Philosophical* (Philadelphia: Thomas and Samuel F. Bradford, 1798).

5.   Bernard Bailyn, *Education in the Forming of American Society* (Chapel Hill: University of North Carolina Press–Chapel Hill, 1960), 48.

6.   Regarding Rush's rhetoric, C. E. Terrell cautions against an ahistorical reading of the rhetoric, from an era in which the human body was understood as a machine, and "connoted illimitable beauty and wonder, revealing, like the universe itself, a divine master craftsmanship." C. E. Terrell, "'Republican Machines': Franklin, Rush, and the Manufacture of Civic Virtue in the Early Republic," *Early American Studies: An Interdisciplinary Journal* 1, no. 2 (2003): 100–132.

7.   Rogers M. Smith, *Civic Ideals: Conflicting Visions of Citizenship in U.S. History* (New Haven and London: Yale University Press, 1997); Julie A. Reuben, "Patriotic Purposes: Public Schools and the Education of Citizens" in *The Public Schools*, ed. Susan Fuhrman and Marvin Lazerson (New York: Oxford University Press, 2005), 1–24.

8.   Smith, *Civic Ideals*, 15.

9.   Amy Gutmann, "Democratic Education in Difficult Times," *Teachers College Record* 92, no. 1 (1990): 7–20.

10.   Hazel W. Hertzberg, *Social Studies Reform 1880–1980* (Boulder: Social Science Education Consortium, 1981); David Warren Saxe, *Social Studies in Schools: A History of the Early Years* (Albany: State University of New York Press, 1991); George W. Chilcoat and Jerry A. Ligon, "Developing Democratic Citizens: The Mississippi Freedom Schools As a Model for Social Studies Instruction," *Theory and Research in Social Education* 22, no. 2 (1994): 128–175; Michael Whelan, "Albert Bushnell Hart and the Origins of Social Studies Education," *Theory and Research in Social Education* 22, no. 4 (1994): 423–440; Christine Woyshner, Joseph Watras, and Margaret Smith Crocco, eds., *Social Education in the Twentieth Century: Curriculum and Context for Citizenship* (New York: Peter Lang, 2004).

11.   The term *social studies* was reportedly coined from settlement house work in New York City.

12. Dennis Shirley, "A Brief History of Public Engagement in American Public Education," in *Public Engagement for Public Education*, ed. Marion Orr and John Rogers (Stanford, CA: Stanford University Press, 2011).

13. Cited in Chara Haeussler Bohan, "Early Vanguards of Progressive Education: The Committee of Ten, the Committee of Seven, and Social Education," in *Social Education in the Twentieth Century: Curriculum and Context for Citizenship*, ed. Christine Woyshner, Joseph Watras, and Margaret Smith Crocco (New York: Peter Lang, 2004), 10.

14. U.S. Bureau of Education, *Report of the Committee on Social Studies of the Commission on the Reorganization of Secondary Education of the National Education Association*, U.S. Bureau of Education bulletin 28 (Washington, DC: Government Printing Office, 1916), 53. See also National Education Association, *Report of the Commission on the Reorganization of Secondary Education: Cardinal Principals of Secondary Education—1918*, U.S. Bureau of Education bulletin 35 (Washington, DC: National Education Association, 1918).

15. Ronald W. Evans, "Problems of Democracy: A Case Study in Curricular Change," Annual Meeting of the New England Educational Research Organization, Stratton Mountain, VT, 1987, 37; Andra Makler, "'Problems of Democracy' and the Social Studies Curriculum During the Long Armistice," in *Social Education in the Twentieth Century: Curriculum and Context for Citizenship*, ed. Christine Woyshner, Joseph Watras, and Margaret Smith Crocco (New York: Peter Lang, 2004), 20–41; Linda Greenhouse, "Problems of Democracy," *New York Times*, January 12, 2011, available at http://opinionator.blogs.nytimes.com/2011/01/12/problems-of-democracy/?scp=4&sq=Greenhouse&st=nyt.

16. John T. Greenan, "The Case Method in the Teaching of Problems of Democracy," *School Review* 38, no. 3 (1930): 200–205.

17. By 1923, twenty-three states mandated U.S. Constitution courses; many also required state constitution and history. Texts generally communicated a triumphal history of the U.S. republic (Frances FitzGerald, *America Revised: History Schoolbooks in the Twentieth Century* [New York: Vintage Books, 1980], 27; Makler, "'Problems of Democracy'").

18. In the process, claims Julie Reuben, the curriculum accommodated culturally the legal reality of a recently broadened citizenship still accompanied by restricted suffrage in an era of state expansion into social welfare. "The new curriculum confirmed that voting and political rights were not the defining features of citizenship. It also extended the inclusive view of citizenship to encompass not only African Americans and women, but also a new group, children. Citizenship no longer required independence, but it also no longer entailed political rights. All could be citizens; only some would fulfill their citizenship responsibilities in the public sphere." J. A. Reuben, "Beyond Politics: Community Civics and the Redefinition of Citizenship in the Progressive Era," *History of Education Quarterly* 37, no. 4 (1997): 410, 413.

19. Ibid. Community civics was generally targeted to elementary years, though at times ninth grade as well.

20. Reuben, "Beyond Politics," 399–400, 420.

21. Michael C. Johanek and John L. Puckett, *Leonard Covello and the Making of Ben-*

jamin Franklin High School: Education As if Citizenship Mattered (Philadelphia: Temple University Press, 2007), 6.

22. Joel Westheimer and Joseph Kahne, "What Kind of Citizen? The Politics of Educating for Democracy," *American Educational Research Journal* 41, no. 2 (2004): 237–269; Michael C. Johanek and John Puckett, "The State of Civic Education: Preparing Citizens in an Era of Accountability," in *The Public Schools*, ed. Susan Fuhrman and Marvin Lazerson (New York: Oxford University Press, 2005): 130–159. See esp. p. 154, n. 19; the continuum adapts a typology of Westheimer and Kahne.

23. Positioning the school to coordinate with other community-serving agencies also makes sense for current school improvement: Michael C. Johanek, "School Reform That Matters," *Penn GSE: A Review of Research* (2009).

24. By 1913, seventy-one cities in twenty-one states reported having schools that functioned as social centers, and by the following year, seventeen states had passed laws allowing school facilities to be used for other purposes by the community (Edward W. Stevens Jr., "Social Centers, Politics, and Social Efficiency in the Progressive Era," *History of Education Quarterly* 12, no. 1 [1972]: 16–33).

25. A. Gove, "The Proper Use of Schoolhouses," *Journal of Proceedings and Addresses of the NEA* (1897): 253–257.

26. John Dewey, *The School As Social Centre* (Carbondale & Edwardsville: Southern Illinois University Press, 1902).

27. Ibid.

28. William J. Reese, *Power and the Promise of School Reform: Grassroots Movements During the Progressive Era* (Boston: Routledge & Kegan Paul, 1986; New York: Teachers College, Columbia University: 2002), 169–170. Citations are to the Teachers College edition.

29. Edward J. Ward, *The Social Center* (New York and London: D. Appleton and Company, 1913 and 1915; Charleston, SC: Nabu Press, 2010). Citations are to the Nabu Press edition.

30. Ibid., 187.

31. School Methods Company, *Public School Methods* (Chicago: School Methods Publishing Co., 1922), 37.

32. Johanek and Puckett, *Leonard Covello*; Reese, *Power and the Promise of School Reform*; Kevin Mattson, *Creating a Democratic Public: The Struggle for Urban Participatory Democracy During the Progressive Era* (University Park: Pennsylvania State University Press, 1998).

33. Ward, *The Social Center*, 4–5, 324.

34. Ibid., 9, 13, 17.

35. Ibid., 326.

36. Ibid., 334. Ward attributes the term *magnified school* to his colleague at University of Wisconsin, Edward Elliott.

37. Ibid., 327.

38. Reese, *Power and the Promise of School Reform: Grassroots Movements During the Progressive Era*, 175.

39. Ward suggested that aligning local political boundaries to school district boundaries would further enhance the vitality of schools as social centers. In addition to

citizenship training and participation in civic issues, an active local citizenry would also counter what was a recurring danger to education: the influence of "general ideas" about schooling, applied "blindly and extravagantly." He says, "That there is a great need for a more careful study of the details of the public schools by our citizenship, especially the citizenship that is composed of parents, is pressing, if not apparent." Ward, *The Social Center*, 331.

40. Efforts to address dramatic inequities in school finance, however, did not succeed.

41. U.S. Commission on Country Life, *Report of the Commission on Country Life* (New York: Sturgis & Walton Co., 1911; reprint, 1917). Citations are to the 1917 edition.

42. William L. Bowers, *The Country Life Movement in America, 1900–1920* (Port Washington, NY: Kennikat Press, 1974).

43. William L. Sherman and Paul Theobald, "Progressive Era Rural Reform: Creating Standard Schools in the Midwest," *Journal of Research in Rural Education* 17, no. 2 (2001): 84–91.

44. U.S. Commission on Country Life, *Report of the Commission on Country Life*, 24, 30.

45. Ibid., 121, 122.

46. L. J. Hanifan, "The 'Hesperia Movement' in West Virginia," *West Virginia School Journal* 39, no. 5–6 (1910): 23–24.

47. Kenyon L. Butterfield, "Neighborhood Cooperation in School Life: The 'Hesperia Movement,'" *American Monthly Review of Reviews* 23 (April 1901): 444.

48. A. E. Winship, "The Hesperia Movement," *Journal of Education* (1906): 686–687.

49. D. E. McClure, quoted in Kenyon L. Butterfield, "The Hesperia Movement," in *Social Aspects of Education*, ed. Irving King (New York: Macmillan Company, 1912), 36, 31; see also Irving King, *Education for Social Efficiency: A Study in the Social Relations of Education* (New York and Chicago: D. Appleton and Company, 1913), 36–38; Butterfield, "Neighborhood Cooperation in School Life," 443–446.

50. D. E. McClure, "The Hesperia Plan," *Educational Foundations* 16 (1904): 284–285.

51. L. J. Hanifan, "The Rural School and Rural Life," *West Virginia School Journal* 4 (1912): 204–207.

52. Ibid, 204–207.

53. Ibid.

54. L. J. Hanifan, *The Community Center* (Boston: Silver, Burdett & Company, 1920), 5. See also Howard C. Hill, "Recent Literature on Civics and Other Social Studies," *School Review* 26, no. 9 (1918): 705–714.

55. Hanifan, *The Community Center*, 10.

56. Edward J. Ward, "Summary of the Report of the School Extension Committee" (presented at the Sixteenth Annual Meeting of the National Municipal League, Eighteenth National Conference for Good City Government, Buffalo, NY, 1910), 356.

57. L. J. Hanifan, *A Handbook Containing Suggestions and Programs for Community Social Gatherings at Rural School Houses*, 3rd rev., 6th ed. (Charleston, WV: Department of Free Schools, State of West Virginia, 1916).

58. Robert D. Putnam, "Community-Based Social Capital and Educational Performance,"

in *Making Good Citizens: Education and Civil Society*, ed. Diane Ravitch and Joseph P. Viteritti (New Haven, CT: Yale University Press, 2001), chap. 3.

59. Hanifan, *The Community Center*, 49, 29.

60. L. J. Hanifan, "The Rural School Community Center," *Annals of the American Academy of Political and Social Science* 67 (1916): 130–138. Political philosopher James Farr, in his insightful conceptual history of the term *social capital*, locates Hanifan squarely in the critical pragmatism of his day, in kinship with John Dewey, Edward Ward, and Mabel Carney, and others. Farr even makes an intriguing speculation regarding Hanifan's possible debt to Dewey for the invention of the term (James Farr, "Social Capital: A Conceptual History," *Political Theory* 32, no. 1 [2004]: 6–33). Kevin Mattson locates Hanifan among the "localist" democratic progressives of the period, alongside Ward, John Collier, and Charles Zeublin, all of whom Mattson cites in his work *Creating a Democratic Public*.

61. Hanifan, *The Community Center*, 107.

62. Ibid., 108.

63. Ibid., 24.

64. In Hanifan's exercises in *The Community Center*, one suspects the influence of such figures as W. I. Thomas of Chicago, as well as other early sociologists.

65. Hanifan, *The Community Center*, 107, 108, 24.

66. L. J. Hanifan, *A Handbook Containing Suggestions and Programs for Community Social Gatherings at Rural School Houses*, 2nd ed. (Charleston: West Virginia State Department of Education, Tribune Print Co., 1913), 3.

67. See various revisions and editions of ibid., all published by the Department of Free Schools, State of West Virginia, in Charleston: rev. ed. (1914); 2nd rev., 5th ed. (1915); 3rd rev., 6th ed. (1916).

68. L. J. Hanifan and the Department of Free Schools, *District Supervision—Bulletin No. 7—Containing Information and Suggestions on Supervision of Rural Schools* (Charleston: State of West Virginia, 1915).

69. Mattson, *Creating a Democratic Public*.

70. Johanek and Puckett, *Leonard Covello*, 102.

71. The schools' largest constituency was East Harlem's Italian population. The problems of these poor immigrants played a defining role in the high school's developing phase. See ibid., chap. 2.

72. Leonard Covello, "A High School and Its Immigrant Community: A Challenge and an Opportunity," *Journal of Educational Sociology* 9, no. 6 (1936): 331–346.

73. Johanek and Puckett, *Leonard Covello*.

74. In a 1938 article for the journal *Progressive Education*, Covello wrote that the school aimed to provide (1) "adequate service to the community along educational civic, social, and welfare lines"; (2) restoration of communal living, as far as may be possible, in a congested city neighborhood; (3) creation of "more harmonious" relationships between Americans of foreign stock and older Americans; (4) training of local leaders qualified to guide and serve within the community itself in creating the "finest background possible

for the life of the community as a whole"; and (5) development of a complete neighborhood program. See Leonard Covello, "Neighborhood Growth Through the School," *Progressive Education* 15 (1938): 126–139.

75. For more on public work, see Nancy Fraser, "Rethinking the Public Sphere: A Contribution to the Critique of Actually Existing Democracy," in *Habermas and the Public Sphere*, ed. Craig Calhoun (Cambridge, MA: MIT Press, 1992), 109–142; Harry Chatten Boyte and Nancy N. Kari, *Building America: The Democratic Promise of Public Work* (Philadelphia: Temple University Press, 1996); Benjamin R. Barber, *A Place for Us: How to Make Civil Society and Democracy Strong* (New York: Hill and Wang, 1998); and Harry Chatten Boyte, *Everyday Politics: Reconnecting Citizens and Public Life* (Philadelphia: University of Pennsylvania Press, 2004).

76. Johanek and Puckett, *Leonard Covello*, chap. 6.

77. Ibid.

78. Ibid., 213–214.

79. Ibid., 102.

80. Ibid., 125, 170.

81. Ibid., chs. 3–5.

82. Ibid., chs. 5–7. Sections adapted from L. Benson et al., "The Enduring Appeal of Community Schools," *American Educator* (Summer 2009): 22–29; 47.

83. Lawrence A. Cremin, "Public Education and the Education of the Public," *Teachers College Record* 77, no. 1 (1975): 5. In the fall of 1998, Google filed for incorporation and MoveOn.org formed as a political action committee. See Google Company, "Google History," available at www.google.com/about/corporate/company/history.html; and MoveOn.org, "About the MoveOn Family of Organizations," n.d., available at http://moveon.org/about.html. The history of civic education requires interweaving the histories of voluntary organizations, the press, religious organizations, families, and so on. A notable effort to synthesize a summary of these educating histories was Cremin's masterful three-volume history of American education: Lawrence A. Cremin, *American Education: The Colonial Experience, 1607–1783* (New York: Harper & Row, 1970); Lawrence A. Cremin, *American Education: The National Experience, 1783–1876* (New York: Harper & Row, 1980); and Lawrence A. Cremin, *American Education: The Metropolitan Experience, 1876–1980* (New York: Harper & Row, 1988).

84. Making an explicit link across the historical and political science worlds regarding civic education, Amy Gutmann notes that "since the democratic ideal of education is that of conscious social reproduction, a democratic theory focuses on practices of deliberate instruction by individuals and on the educative influences of institutions designed at least partly for educational purposes." Democratic education cannot be subsumed under political socialization, or it will "lose sight of the distinctive virtue of a democratic society, that it authorizes citizens to influence how their society reproduces itself." In turn, citizens can also "appreciate the centrality of schooling to democratic education and still recognize that there is much more to democratic education than schooling." Amy

Gutmann, *Democratic Education* (Princeton, NJ: Princeton University Press, 1987), 14–15.

85. The terms *relational trust* and *collective efficacy*, apparently, being are of much more recent usage.

86. Skocpol, Ganz, and Munson, "A Nation of Organizers"; Theda Skocpol, *Diminished Democracy: From Membership to Management in American Civic Life* (Norman: University of Oklahoma Press, 2003); Theda Skocpol, Rachael V. Cobb, and Casey Andrew Klofstad, "Disconnection and Reorganization: The Transformation of Civic Life in Late-Twentieth-Century America," *Studies in American Political Development* 19 (2005): 137–156.

87. Frederick A. Fickardt, "The Order of the Sons of Temperance of North America, As a School for Popular Debate and Eloquence," in *The National Temperance Offering, and Sons and Daughters of Temperance Gift*, ed. Samuel Fenton Cary (New York: R. Vandien, 1850), as cited in Skocpol, *Diminished Democracy*, 102–103.

88. Alexis de Tocqueville, *Democracy in America*, vol. 2, 3rd ed., trans. Henry Reeve (Cambridge, MA: Sever and Francis, 1863), 134.

89. Arthur M. Schlesinger, "Biography of a Nation of Joiners," *American Historical Review* 50, no. 1 (1944): 1–25.

90. Skocpol, Ganz, and Munson, "A Nation of Organizers," 541.

91. Ibid., 542. The social capital versus civic reorganization debates force consideration of historical and current drivers, whether generational, governmental, media, or institutional. For current civic educators, finding places for youth and adult experience in public deliberative processes remains the immediate challenge, in whatever form that organization may need to take today. For more, see Robert D. Putnam, "The Strange Disappearance of Civic America," *American Prospect* 7, no. 24 (1996): 34–38; Theda Skocpol, "Unravelling [*sic*] from Above," *American Prospect* 25 (March–April 1996): 20–25; Robert D. Putnam, *Bowling Alone: The Collapse and Revival of American Community* (New York: Simon & Schuster, 2000); Skocpol, Ganz, and Munson, "A Nation of Organizers"; Putnam, "Community-Based Social Capital"; Robert D. Putnam, "Bowling Together: The United State of America," *American Prospect* 13, no. 3 (2002): 20–22; Skocpol, *Diminished Democracy*; Robert D. Putnam, *Education, Diversity, Social Cohesion and "Social Capital"* (paper presented at Raising the Quality of Education for All, meeting of Organization for Economic Cooperation and Development [OECD] education ministers, Dublin, Ireland, 2004); and Skocpol, Cobb, and Klofstad, "Disconnection and Reorganization."

92. Jeffrey E. Mirel, *Patriotic Pluralism: Americanization Education and European Immigrants* (Cambridge, MA: Harvard University Press, 2010).

93. Ibid., 10.

94. Maxine Seller, quoted in ibid., 102.

95. Ibid., 226.

96. Ibid., 240.

97. Summary data, author's calculation, of federal voting average 1960–2010; see source table at Infoplease, "National Voter Turnout in Federal Elections: 1960–2010"; 2011 data available at www.infoplease.com/ipa/A0781453.html.

98. For the latest in a string of reports, see Jonathan Gould, ed., *Guardian of Democracy:*

The Civic Mission of Schools (Philadelphia: Leonore Annenberg Institute for Civics of the Annenberg Public Policy Center, University of Pennsylvania; Silver Spring, MD: The Campaign for the Civic Mission of Schools, 2011).

99. George S. Counts, *Dare the School Build a New Social Order?* (Carbondale, IL: Southern Illinois University Press, 1978).

100. Essentially, psychologist Edward Thorndike trumps philosopher John Dewey, per Ellen Condliffe Lagemann's insightful study, *An Elusive Science: The Troubling History of Education Research* (Chicago: University of Chicago Press, 2000). We measure massively now in education and fret a good deal less—in policy circles, at least—about enhancing our democratic capacities through public schooling.

Chapter 4
Diversity and Civic Education

Meira Levinson

I would like to thank Michelle Bellino, Andrew Scott Conning, Jacob Fay, David Groshoff, Rick Hess, Patrick Keegan, Jal Mehta, James Noonan, Brendan Randall, Yun-Kyoung Park, Laurel Stolte, and Jennifer Worden for useful conversations about the ideas contained in this chapter. I am also grateful to Patrick Keegan, David Knight, and Celina Benavides for their research assistance.

1. These rights are guaranteed in a combination of the Civil Rights Act of 1964; *Plyler v. Doe*, 457 U.S. 202 (1982); *Lau v. Nichols*, 414 U.S. 563 (1974); the Elementary and Secondary Education Act; and the Individuals with Disabilities Education Act, among other legislative and court-ordered mechanisms.

2. See Tony Fabelo et al., *Breaking Schools' Rules: A Statewide Study of How School Discipline Relates to Students' Success and Juvenile Justice Involvement* (New York: Council of State Governments Justice Center, 2011); Advancement Project, *Test, Punish, and Push Out: How 'Zero Tolerance' and High-Stakes Tests Funnel Youth into the School-to-Prison Pipeline* (Washington, DC, and Los Angeles: Advancement Project, 2010); *Morse v. Frederick*, 551 U.S. 393 (2007). One year when I was teaching eighth grade, for example, one of my homeroom students was suspended and ultimately prevented from attending her middle school graduation, because she left a bicycle chain lock she occasionally wore as a necklace hanging in her locker. It was treated as a potentially dangerous—and concealed—weapon.

3. *Bethel School District No. 403 v. Fraser*, 478 U.S. 675, 683 (1986).

4. Cornelia G. Kennedy, Concurring Opinion, *Mozert v. Hawkins County School Board*, 827 F.2d 1058 (1987), available at www.soc.umn.edu/~samaha/cases/mozert_v_hawkins_schools.html.

5. See Meira Levinson, "Common Schools and Multicultural Education," *Journal of Philosophy of Education* 41, no. 4 (2007): 625–642, for a more expansive discussion of this challenge.

6. Michel Martin, "Racial Tensions Grow Violent at Philly High School," *Tell Me More*, December 16, 2009, available at www.npr.org/templates/story/story.php?storyId=

121506559; Jesse Washington, "Racial Violence Changes Student—and School," msnbc.com, September 5, 2010, available at www.msnbc.msn.com/id/39017234/ns/us_news/t/racial-violence-changes-student-school/#.

7. Laurie Olsen, "Racialization: The Contemporary Americanization Project," in *E Pluribus Unum? Contemporary and Historical Perspectives on Immigrant Political Incorporation,* ed. Gary Gerstle and John Mollenkopf (New York: Russell Sage Foundation, 2001), 371–411 (quotation from p. 388). Olsen's study provides a fascinating example of immigrant bilingual students' social maps of their school as compared to those of native-born "American" students; the former are far more detailed than the latter, which tend to lump all immigrant students together in an undifferentiated mass.

8. Robert D. Putnam, "E Pluribus Unum: Diversity and Community in the Twenty-First Century—the 2006 Johan Skytte Prize Lecture," *Scandinavian Political Studies* 30, no. 2 (2007): 137–174. See also David E. Campbell, "Sticking Together: Classroom Diversity and Civic Education," *American Politics Research* 35, no. 1 (2007): 57–78; Levinson, "Common Schools and Multicultural Education."

9. Diverse communities can bring about noncivic benefits, too; I'm just focusing on civic issues in this chapter.

10. Josiah Ober, *Democracy and Knowledge: Innovation and Learning in Classical Athens* (Princeton, NJ: Princeton University Press, 2010); James Surowiecki, *The Wisdom of Crowds* (New York: Random House, 2005).

11. John R. Hibbing and Elizabeth Theiss-Morse, *Stealth Democracy: Americans' Beliefs About How Government Should Work* (New York: Cambridge University Press, 2002).

12. Bill Bishop, with Robert G. Cushing, *The Big Sort: Why the Clustering of Like-Minded America Is Tearing Us Apart* (New York: Houghton Mifflin Harcourt, 2008).

13. Judith Torney-Purta et al., *Citizenship and Education in Twenty-Eight Countries: Civic Knowledge and Engagement at Age Fourteen* (Amsterdam: IEA, 2001),137. See also Diana E. Hess, "Teaching About Same-Sex Marriage As a Policy and Constitutional Issue," *Social Education* 73, no. 7 (2009): 344–349.

14. See Meira Levinson, *No Citizen Left Behind* (Cambridge, MA: Harvard University Press, 2012) for a comprehensive summary and analysis of this research.

15. A 2011 Alabama House of Representatives bill is an exception to this. The Beason-Hammon Alabama Taxpayer and Citizen Protection Act (HB56) requires all public schools to collect data on students' and families' citizenship status. The social chaos that has ensued, however—including overnight increases of 5–10 percent in student absentee rates in some districts—has led to a bipartisan call for repeal of at least pieces of the law.

16. Hirokazu Yoshikawa, *Immigrants Raising Citizens: Undocumented Parents and Their Young Children* (New York: Russell Sage, 2011); Jeffrey S. Passel and D'Vera Cohn, *A Portrait of Unauthorized Immigrants in the United States* (Washington, DC: Pew Hispanic Center, 2009), available at http://pewhispanic.org/files/reports/107.pdf.

17. Jayne Jaramillo, "Children of the Undocumented," *The Student Voice,* Syracuse University, April 10, 2010, available at http://studentvoicesu.wordpress.com/2010/04/10/childrenof-the-undocumented/.

18. This is notably a relatively recent occurrence; it was only in 2003 that the Supreme Court invalidated all remaining adult antisodomy laws, for instance.

19. Joseph G. Kosciw et al., *The 2009 National School Climate Survey: The Experiences of Lesbian, Gay, Bisexual and Transgender Youth in Our Nation's Schools* (New York: GLSEN, 2010); Suicide Prevention Resource Center, *Suicide Risk and Prevention for Lesbian, Gay, Bisexual, and Transgender Youth* (Newton, MA: Education Development Center, Inc., 2008); Gay, Lesbian & Straight Education Network, "Background and Information About Gay-Straight Alliances," n.d., available at www.glsen.org/cgi-bin/iowa/all/library/record/2336.html?state=media&type=media; National Center for Education Statistics, "Public Elementary and Secondary Schools, by Type of School: Selected Years, 1967–1968 through 2008–2009," table 97 in *Digest of Education Statistics, 2010 (NCES 2011-015)* (Washington, DC: U.S. Department of Education, 2011).

20. Silence would actually be a luxury in some states. An Arizona statute prohibits schools from employing material that "portrays homosexuality as a positive alternative lifestyle." See Arizona Revised Statutes, § 15-716(C)(1)–(3), available at www.azleg. state.az.us/ars/15/00716.htm. Texas requires schools to tell minors that "homosexual conduct is not an acceptable lifestyle and is a criminal offense under Section 21.06, Penal Code," even though Section 21.06 was invalidated by *Lawrence v. Texas*. See Texas Health and Safety Code, Section 85.007(b)(2), available at www.statutes.legis.state. tx.us/Docs/HS/htm/HS.85.htm. South Carolina's health education classes "may not include a discussion of alternate sexual lifestyles from heterosexual relationships, including, but not limited to, homosexual relationships except in the context of instruction concerning sexually transmitted diseases." See South Carolina Code of Laws, Section 59-32-30(A)(5), available at www.scstatehouse.gov/code/t59c032.php.

21. Anoka-Hennepin District No. 11, "Sexual Orientation Curriculum Policy" (Coon Rapids, MN: Anoka-Hennepin District No. 11, 2009).

22. Erik Eckholm, "In Suburb, Battle Goes Public on Bullying of Gay Students," *New York Times*, September 13, 2011, available at www.nytimes.com/2011/09/13/us/13bully.html.

23. Ibid.

24. Lydia Saad, "Americans Rate the Morality of 16 Social Issues," Gallup, June 4, 2007, available at www.gallup.com/poll/27757/Americans-Rate-Morality-Social-Issues.aspx.

25. Pamela Constable, "For Some Muslim Wives, Abuse Knows No Borders," *Washington Post*, May 8, 2007, available at www.washingtonpost.com/wpdyn/content/article/2007/05/07/AR2007050701936.html; Barbara Bradley Hagerty, "Some Muslims in U.S. Quietly Engage in Polygamy," *All Things Considered*, May 27, 2008, available at www.npr.org/templates/story/story.php?storyId=90857818&ps=rs. See also *Wikipedia*, s.v. "Legal status of polygamy," last modified March 1, 2012, available at http://en.wikipedia.org/wiki/Legal_status_of_polygamy.

26. Sue Austreng, "Respectful Learning Environment Focus of Anoka-Hennepin's New Curriculum Policy," *(Minnesota) Press & News*, February 15, 2012, available at www.pressnews.com/articles/2012/02/26/regional_headlines/00ahrlecp.txt.

27. Maria Elena Baca, "Anoka-Hennepin School District Settles Bullying Lawsuit," *Minneapolis Star Tribune*, March 6, 2012, available at www.startribune.com/local/north/141427303.html?page=all&prepage=1&c=y#continue; Sabina Rubin Erdely, "One Town's War on Gay Teens," *Rolling Stone*, February 2, 2012, available at www.rollingstone.com/politics/news/one-towns-war-on-gay-teens-20120202.

28. Putnam, "E Pluribus Unum."

29. I develop these arguments in much greater detail in Levinson, *No Citizen Left Behind*, chap. 3.

30. Tucson Unified School District, "Mexican American Studies—About Us," last updated December 29, 2010, available at www.tusd1.org/contents/depart/mexicanam/about.asp.

31. Curtis Acosta, "Developing Critical Consciousness: Resistance Literature in a Chicano Literature Class," *English Journal* 97, no. 2 (2007): 37–38, 41.

32. Cambium Learning Inc., *Curriculum Audit of the Mexican American Studies Department Tucson Unified School District* (Miami Lakes, FL: Cambium Learning, 2011), 5–6.

33. Tom Horne, "An Open Letter to the Citizens of Tucson," State of Arizona Department of Education, Office of the Superintendent of Public Instruction, June 11, 2007, available at www.scribd.com/doc/32001977/An-Open-Letter-to-the-Citizens-of-Tucson.

34. Arizona H.B. 2281: 1, § 15-112, lines 8–16 (May 2010).

35. Arizona Department of Education, "Superintendent of Public Instruction John Huppenthal Rules Tucson Unified School District Out of Compliance with A.R.S. § 15-112," news release, July 15, 2011, available at www.azed.gov/public-relations/files/2011/08/pr06-15-11.pdf.

36. Dylan Smith, "Huppenthal: TUSD's Ethnic Studies Violate Law; Audit Says Otherwise," *Tucson Sentinel*, June 16, 2011, available at www.tucsonsentinel.com/local/report/061511_ethnic_studies/huppenthal-tusds-ethnic-studies-violate-law-audit-says-otherwise/.

37. Cambium Learning Inc., "Curriculum Audit." Subsequent independent research has also found that MAS students have significantly higher reading, writing, and math test scores than their peers, and that two-thirds enter college, a rate much higher than the overall national average, let alone the average for Latino students. Shawn Ginwright and Julio Cammarota, "Youth Organizing in the Wild West: Mobilizing for Educational Justice in Arizona!" *Voices in Urban Education* 30 (2011): 13–21.

38. Curtis Acosta, "Tucson Mex-Am Studies News," e-mail post to Association of Raza Educators, Yahoo! Groups, January 14, 2012, available at http://groups.yahoo.com/group/razaeducator/message/1157.

39. "MAS Ban in TUSD: Everything Has Been Taken Away, and It's Awful," California State at Northridge (CSUN) Delegation Meeting, Tucson, Arizona, February 25, 2012, YouTube video, posted by ThreeSonorans, February 28, 2012, available at www.youtube.com/watch?v=U1h0k2zU3Iw.

40. See, for example, a litany of outrageous statements by Horne, Huppenthal, and citizens protesting ethnic studies captured in *Precious Knowledge*, directed by Ari Luis Palos (Tucson, AZ: Dos Vatos Productions, 2011), DVD.

41. Cambium Learning Inc., "Curriculum Audit," figure 10.

42. See Levinson, *No Citizen Left Behind*, chap. 2, for a review of this literature.

43. Franc Contreras, "Arizona Bill Targets Ethnic Studies," Al Jazeera English, January 28, 2011, available at www.youtube.com/watch?v=cM1NPH2Ii3Y.

44. Meira Levinson, "The Civic Empowerment Gap: Defining the Problem and Locating Solutions," in *Handbook of Research on Civic Engagement in Youth*, ed. Lonnie R. Sherrod, Judith Torney-Purta, and Constance A. Flanagan (Hoboken, NJ: John Wiley & Sons, 2010).

45. Thelma Gutierrez, "Arizona Teacher: 'We Don't Teach Racism,'" *CNN*, September 14, 2011, available at edition.cnn.com/video/standard.html#/video/us/2011/09/14/pkg-az-ethnic-studies-ban.cnn. In a separate CNN interview, Tom Horne repeatedly condemned teaching about racism and oppression as a "downer" to which students should not be subjected. Tom Horne and Michael Eric Dyson, interview by Anderson Cooper, "Ethnic Studies Ban Racist?" *Anderson Cooper 360°*, CNN, May 13, 2011, available at ac360.blogs.cnn.com/2010/05/13/must-see-ac360-az-ethnic-studies-discussion.

46. Levinson, *No Citizen Left Behind*, chaps. 1–3. See also Roy Rosenzweig and David Thelen, *The Presence of the Past: Popular Uses of History in American Life* (New York: Columbia University Press, 1998); Terrie Epstein, *Interpreting National History: Race, Identity, and Pedagogy in Classrooms and Communities (Teaching/Learning Social Justice)* (New York: Routledge, 2009).

47. Dylan Smith, "Horne: TUSD Ethnic Studies Illegal," *Tucson Sentinel*, January 3, 2011, available at www.tucsonsentinel.com/local/report/010311_ethnic_studies.

Chapter 5
How to Enrich Civic Education and Sustain Democracy

James Youniss

1. Hector Ibarra, correspondence with author, April–May 2011. The achievements of Ibarra's students are a matter of record, as they have repeatedly received recognition in the eCybermission national science awards (available at www.ecybermission.org) and other science competitions.

2. Debbie Viertel, interviews with author, April–May, 2011. The achievements of Viertel's students are on record through their repeated recognition in the eCybermission national science awards (available at www.ecybermission.org) and other science competitions.

3. Cited in Gar Alperowitz, *America Beyond Capitalism: Reclaiming Our Wealth, Our Liberty, and Our Democracy* (New York: Wiley, 2005), 44.

4. Report of the Committee of Five of the American Political Science Association on Instruction in American Government in Secondary Schools, *Proceedings of the American Political Science Association* 5 (1908); Hildy Schacter, "Civic Education: Three Early American Political Science Association Committees and Their Relevance for Our Times," *PS: Political Science and Politics* 31 (2009): 631–635.

5. William Galston, "Political Knowledge, Political Engagement, and Civic Education," *Annual Review of Political Science* 4 (2002): 217–234; Peter Levine, *The Future of Democ-*

racy: Developing the Next Generation of American Citizens (Medford, MA: Tufts University Press, 2007); Henry Milner, *The Internet Generation: Engaged Citizens or Political Dropouts?* (Medford, MA: Tufts University Press, 2010).

6. Martin P. Wattenberg, *Is Voting For Young People?* (New York: Person-Longman, 2009).

7. Constance Flanagan, Peter Levine, and Richard Settersten, *The Civic Opportunity Gap* (Medford, MA: Center for Information and Research on Civic Learning and Engagement [hereafter cited as CIRCLE], 2009); Jon Zaff, James Youniss, and Cynthia Gibson, *An Inequitable Invitation to Citizenship* (Washington, DC: Philanthropy for Active Civic Engagement, 2009).

8. Meira Levinson, "The Civic Empowerment Gap" (working paper 51, CIRCLE, Medford, MA, 2007.)

9. Wolfgang Edelstein, "Education for Democracy: Reasons and Strategies," *European Journal of Education* 46 (2011): 127–137; Matthew Miller, "Lower the Voting Age to 10," *Washington Post*, August 5, 2010, available at http://www.washingtonpost.com/wp-dyn/content/article/2010/08/04/AR2010080403468.html.

10. See also Carnegie Corporation of New York and CIRCLE, *The Civic Mission of Schools* (New York: Carnegie Corporation of New York; College Park, MD, CIRCLE, 2003); Jonathan Gould, ed., *Guardian of Democracy: The Civic Mission of Schools* (Philadelphia: Leonore Annenberg Institute for Civics of the Annenberg Public Policy Center, University of Pennsylvania; Silver Spring, MD: The Campaign for the Civic Mission of Schools, 2011), available at www.civicmissionofschools.org.

11. Walter Laqueur, *Young Germany: A History of the German Youth Movement* (New York: Basic Books, 1967), 48.

12. James Youniss and Miranda Yates, *Community Service and Social Responsibility in Youth* (Chicago: University of Chicago Press, 1997). The actual dialogue has been paraphrased here by the author for clarity.

13. Calculations of averages were made by the author using the NAEP 2010 Web site calculator. Test scores and proficiency levels are from U.S. Department of Education, Institute of Education Sciences, National Center for Education Statistics, "Civics 2010: National Assessment of Educational Progress at Grades 4, 8, and 12," in *The Nation's Report Card*, NCES 2011-466, May 2011, pp. 28 and 41, available at http://nces.ed.gov/nationsreportcard/pdf/main2010/2011466.pdf.

14. Judith Torney-Purta et al., *Citizenship and Education in Twenty-Eight Countries: Civic Knowledge and Engagement at Age Fourteen* (Amsterdam: IEA, 2001).

15. Michael McDevitt and Spiro Kiousis, "Education for Deliberative Democracy: The Long-Term Influence of Kids Voting USA" (working paper 22, CIRCLE, Medford, MA, 2004).

16. Hugh McIntosh, James Youniss, and Daniel Hart, "The Influence of Family Political Discussion on Youth Civic Development: Which Parent Qualities Matter Most?" *PS: Political Science and Politics* 40 (2007): 495–499.

17. Diana Hess, *Controversy in the Classroom: The Democratic Power of Discussion* (New York: Routledge, 2009).

18. Nina Eliasoph, *How Americans Produce Apathy in Everyday Life* (New York: Cambridge University Press, 1998).

19. Hugh McIntosh and James Youniss, "Toward a Political Theory of Political Socialization," in *Handbook of Research on Civic Engagement in Youth*, ed. Lonnie R. Sherrod, Judith Torney-Purta, and Constance Flanagan (Hoboken, NJ: John Wiley, 2010), 23–41.

20. Deanna Kuhn and Wadiya Udell, "The Development of Argument Skills," *Child Development* (September–October 2003): 1245–1260; Deanna Kuhn, Victoria Shaw, and Mark Felton, "Effects of Dyadic Interaction on Argumentative Reasoning," *Cognition and Instruction* 15, no. 3 (1997): 287–315.

21. William Gamson, *Talking Politics* (Cambridge, MA: Harvard University Press, 1992); Lawrence I. Jacobs, Fay Lomax Cook, and Michael X. Delli Carpini, *Talking Together: Public Deliberation and Political Participation* (Chicago: University of Chicago Press, 2009).

22. James Gimpel, J. Celeste Lay, and Jason E. Schuknecht, *Cultivating Democracy: Civic Environments and Political Socialization in America* (Washington, DC: Brookings Institution Press, 2003).

23. Richard E. Labunski, *James Madison and the Struggle for the Bill of Rights* (New York: Oxford University Press, 2006).

24. Gimpel, Lay, and Schuknecht, *Cultivating Democracy.*

25. Matthew Hindman, *The Myth of Digital Democracy* (Princeton, NJ: Princeton University Press, 2009); Milner, *The Internet Generation.*

26. Joseph E. Kahne and Susan E. Sporte, "Developing Citizens: The Impact of Civic Learning Opportunities on Students' Commitment to Civic Participation," *American Educational Research Journal* 45, no. 3 (2008); Joseph Kahne and Ellen Middaugh, "Democracy for Some: The Civic Opportunity Gap in High School," in *Engaging Young People in Civic Life*, ed. James Youniss and Peter Levine (Nashville: Vanderbilt University Press, 2009), 29–58; Joseph Kahne, David Crow, and Nam-Jin Lee, "Different Pedagogy, Different Politics: High School Learning Opportunities and Youth Political Engagement," *Political Psychology* (forthcoming).

27. David E. Campbell, "Voice in the Classroom: How an Open Classroom Climate Fosters Political Engagement Among Adolescents," *Political Behavior* 30 (2008): 437–454.

28. Michael Hanks and Bruce K. Eckland, "Adult Voluntary Associations and Adolescent Socialization," *Sociological Quarterly* (Summer 1978): 481–490.

29. Sidney Verba, Kay L. Schlozman, and Henry E. Brady, *Voice and Equality: Civic Voluntarism in American Politics* (Cambridge, MA: Harvard University Press, 1995), 425.

30. Nancy L. Rosenblum, *Membership and Morals: The Personal Uses of Pluralism in America* (Princeton, NJ: Princeton University Press, 1998); Theda Skocpol, *Diminished Democracy: From Membership to Management in American Civic Life* (Norman: University of Oklahoma Press, 2003).

31. Howard Ladewig and John K. Thomas, *Assessing the Impact of 4-H on Former Members* (College Station: Texas Tech University, 1987). See also Penny Pennington and M. Craig Edwards, "Former 4-H Key Club Members' Perceptions of the Impact of 'Giving' Life Skills Preparation on Their Civic Engagement," *Journal of Extension* (February 2006).

32. Daniel A. McFarland and Carlos Starrnanns, "Inside Student Government: The Variable Quality of High School Student Councils," *Teachers College Record* 111 (2009): 27–54.

33. Reed W. Larson and David Hansen, "The Development of Strategic Thinking: Learning to Impact Human Systems in a Youth Activist Program," *Human Development* 48 (2005): 327–349; Reed W. Larson and Rachel M. Angus, "Adolescents' Development of Skills for Agency in Youth Programs: Learning to Think Strategically," *Child Development* (January–February 2011): 277–294.

34. Florida Association of School Administrators, www.fasa.net.

35. Carmen Sirianni and Diana Marginean Schor, "City Government as Enabler of Youth Civic Engagement: Policy and Design Implications," *Engaging Young People in Civic Life*, ed. James Youniss and Peter Levine (Nashville: Vanderbilt University Press, 2009), 121–163; Carmen Sirianni, *Investing in Democracy: Engaging Citizens in Collaborative Government* (Washington, DC: Brookings Institution Press, 2009).

36. Shepherd Zeldin et al., *Youth Decision-Making: A Study on Impacts of Youth on Adults and Organizations* (Chevy Chase, MD: Innovation Center for Community and Youth Development, 2000).

37. Emily Foxhall and Daniel Sisgoreo, "High School Students Lobby for Change," *Yale Daily News*, April 19, 2011, www.yaledailynews.com/news/2011/apr/19/high-school-students-lobby-for-change/.

38. Daniel Hart et al., "High School Community Service As a Predictor of Adult Voting and Volunteering," *American Educational Research Journal* 44, no. 1 (March 2007): 197–219.

39. Harry Boyte, *Everyday Politics: Reconnecting Citizens and Public Life* (Philadelphia: University of Pennsylvania Press, 2005); Marc A. Musick and John Wilson, *Volunteers: A Social Profile* (Bloomington: University of Indiana Press, 2008); Joel Westheimer and Joseph Kahne, "What Kind of Citizen? The Politics of Educating for Democracy," *American Educational Research Journal* 41, no. 2 (Summer 2004): 237–269.

40. Musick and Wilson, *Volunteers: A Social Profile*, 520.

41. Michael X. Delli-Carpini, "Gen.com: Youth, Civic Engagement, and the New Information Environment," *Political Communication* 17 (2000): 345.

42. Lloyd D. Johnston, John G. Bachman, and Peter O'Malley, *Monitoring the Future: Questionnaire Responses from the Nation's High School Seniors* (Ann Arbor: Institute for Social Research, 2010); John H. Pryor et al., *The American Freshman: National Norms Fall 2009* (Los Angeles: Higher Education Research Institute, January 2010).

43. Charles C. Moskos, *A Call to Service: National Service for Country and Community* (New York: Free Press, 1988).

44. *A Nation at Risk: An Imperative for Educational Reform* (Washington, DC: National Commission on Excellence in Education, April 1983); for the counter view, see David C. Berliner and Bruce J. Biddle, *The Manufactured Crisis: Myths, Fraud, and the Attack on American Public Schools* (New York: Addison-Wesley, 1995).

45. Campus Compact, "Who We Are," Campus Compact, n.d., www.campuscompact.org/about/history-mission-vision/.

46. Lewis A. Friedland and Shauna Morimotto, "Why Young People Are Volunteering in Record Numbers," *Around the CIRCLE* 3, no. 2 (November 2005).

47. Kimberly Spring, Nathan Dietz, and Robert Grimm Jr., *Leveling the Path to Participation: Volunteering and Civic Engagement Among Youth from Disadvantaged Circumstances* (Washington, DC: Corporation for National and Community Service, 2007); see also Kahne and Sporte, "Developing Citizens."

48. Jeffery A. McLellan and James Youniss, "Two Systems of Youth Service: Determinants of Voluntary and Required Youth Community Service," *Journal of Youth and Adolescence* 32, no. 1 (2003): 47–58; National Center for Education Statistics, *National Household Education Survey, 1999* (Washington, DC: National Center for Education Statistics, 1999).

49. Youniss and Yates, *Community Service.*

50. Rebecca A. Allahyari, *Visions of Charity: Volunteer Workers and Moral Community* (Berkeley: University of California Press, 2000).

51. McLellan and Youniss, "Two Systems of Youth Service"; Edward Metz and James Youniss, "Longitudinal Gains in Civic Development Through School-Based Required Service," *Political Psychology* 26 (2005): 413–437; Heinz Reinders and James Youniss, "School-Based Required Community Service and Civic Development in Adolescents," *Applied Developmental Science* 10 (2006): 2–12.

52. James Youniss, "When Morality Meets Politics in Development," *Journal of Moral Education* 38, no. 2 (2009): 129–144; James Youniss and Miranda Yates, "Youth Service and Moral Identity," *Educational Psychology Review* 11, no. 4 (1999): 361–376.

53. Louis A. Penner, "Dispositional and Organizational Influences on Sustained Volunteerism: An Interactionist Perspective," *Journal of Social Issues* 58 (2002): 447–467; Jane A. Piliavin, Jean A. Grube, and Peter L. Callero, "Role As Resource in Public Service," *Journal of Social Issues* 58 (2002): 469–486.

54. Ann Colby and William Damon, *Some Do Care: Lives of Moral Commitment* (New York: Free Press, 1995); Nathan Teske, *Political Activists in America: The Identity Construction Model of Political Participation* (Cambridge, UK: Cambridge University Press, 1997).

55. Hector Ibarra, correspondence with author, April–May 2011.

56. James M. Fendrich, *Ideal Citizens: The Legacy of the Civil Rights Movement* (Albany: State University of New York Press, 1993); Doug McAdam, *Freedom Summer* (New York: Oxford University Press, 1988).

57. James Youniss, Jeffrey A. McLellan, and Miranda Yates, "What We Know About Generating Civic Identity," *American Behavioral Scientist* 40 (1997): 620–631.

58. Doug McAdam and Cynthia Brandt, "Assessing the Effects of Voluntary Youth Service: The Case of Teach for America," *Social Forces* 88 (December 2009): 945–970; James Youniss, "Why We Need to Learn More Youth Civic Engagement," *Social Forces* 88 (December 2009): 971–975.

59. M. Kent Jennings, "Generation Units and the Student Protest Movement in the United States: An Intra- and Intergenerational Analysis," *Political Psychology* 23 (June 2002): 322.

60. Milner, *The Internet Generation*, 224.

Chapter 6
Dry to Dynamic Civic Education Curricula
Anna Rosefsky Saavedra

1. For example, see Jonathan Gould, ed., *Guardian of Democracy: The Civic Mission of Schools* (Philadelphia: Leonore Annenberg Institute for Civics of the Annenberg Public Policy Center, University of Pennsylvania; Silver Spring, MD: The Campaign for the Civic Mission of Schools, 2011), available at www.civicmissionofschools.org/site/guardianofdemocracy; Joseph Kahne, Bernadette Chi, and Ellen Middaugh, "Building Social Capital for Civic and Political Engagement: The Potential of High School Civics Courses," *Canadian Journal of Education* 29, no. 2 (2006): 387–409; Joseph Kahne and Ellen Middaugh, "High Quality Civic Education: What Is It and Who Gets It?" *Social Education* 72, no. 1 (January 2008): 34–39; Joseph Kahne, David Crow, and Nam-Jin Lee, "Different Pedagogy, Different Politics: High School Learning Opportunities and Youth Political Engagement" *Political Psychology* (forthcoming); Joseph Kahne and Sue Sporte, "Developing Citizens: The Impact of Civic Learning Opportunities on Students' Commitment to Civic Participation," *American Educational Research Journal* 45, no. 3 (September 2008): 738–766.

2. All information and quotes in this paragraph from Brian Brady (executive director, the Mikva Challenge), telephone interview with author, August 2011.

3. Education Commission of the States, "ECS National Center for Learning and Citizenship's State Policies for Citizenship Education Database," 2012, www.ecs.org/html/educationIssues/CitizenshipEducation/CitEdDB_intro.asp.

4. Ibid.

5. Arizona Department of Education, "K–12 Academic Standards: The Social Studies Standards Articulated by Grade Level, Social Studies Strand 3—Civics/Government," updated May 22, 2006, www.azed.gov/standards-practices/social-studies-standard/.

6. New York State Department of Education, "Learning Standards for Social Studies," last updated October 5, 2009, www.p12.nysed.gov/ciai/socst/socstand/home.html.

7. Education Commission of the States, "ECS National Center."

8. Ibid.

9. Ibid.

10. National Center for Education Statistics, "National Assessment of Educational Progress 2010 Civics Assessment Database," U.S. Department of Education, last updated April 20, 2011, http://nces.ed.gov/nationsreportcard/civics/.

11. Ibid.

12. Ibid.

13. Organization for Economic Cooperation and Development, "OECD Program for International Student Assessment," n.d., www.pisa.oecd.org/pages/0,2987,en_32252351_32235731_1_1_1_1,00.html.

14. Drasgow Consulting, "The Need for Innovation in Personality Testing," 2008, http://drasgowassessments.com/Assessments/Personality/Background.aspx.

15. Peter Levine and Mark Hugo Lopez, "Themes Emphasized in Social Studies and Civics Classes: New Evidence," CIRCLE, College Park, MD, February 2004, www .civicyouth.org/PopUps/FactSheets/FS_Themes_Emphasized_SocStudies_Civics.pdf; Emily Hoban Kirby and Karlo Barrios Marcelo, "Young Voters in the 2006 Elections: Fact Sheet," CIRCLE, College Park, MD, December 2006, www.civicyouth.org/ PopUps/FactSheets/FS-Midterm06.pdf.

16. Joel Westheimer and Joseph Kahne, "What Kind of Citizen? The Politics of Educating for Democracy," *American Educational Research Journal* 41, no. 2 (Summer 2004): 237–269.

17. National Center for Education Statistics, "National Assessment of Educational Progress 2010 Civics Assessment Database."

18. William Hartley and William Vincent, *American Civics* (Austin, TX: Holt, Rinehart and Winston, 2005); James Davis, Phyllis Fernlund, and Peter Woll, *Civics: Government and Economics in Action*, teacher's ed. (Upper Saddle River, NJ: Pearson Prentice Hall, 2005); Richard Remy et al., *Civics Today: Citizenship, Economics and You* (New York: McGraw Hill Glencoe, 2005).

19. Hartley and Vincent, *American Civics*, 7.

20. Ibid., 1.

21. Remy et al., *Civics Today*, 1.

22. David N. Perkins and Tina A. Grotzer, "Teaching Intelligence," *American Psychologist* 52, no. 10 (October 1, 1997): 1125–1133.

23. Hartley and Vincent, *American Civics*, 7.

24. Remy et al., *Civics Today*, x.

25. Pages cited from Davis, Fernlund, and Woll, *Civics: Government and Economics in Action*.

26. Ibid., 678.

27. Meira Levinson, *No Citizen Left Behind* (Cambridge, MA: Harvard University Press, 2012). See also Joel Westheimer and Joseph Kahne, "Reconnecting Education to Democracy: Democratic Dialogues," *Phi Delta Kappan* 85, no. 1 (September 2003): 9–14.

28. Westheimer and Kahne, "Reconnecting Education"; David Campbell, "Voice in the Classroom: How an Open Classroom Climate Fosters Political Engagement Among Adolescents," *Political Behavior* 70 (2008): 437–454; Diana Hess and Julie Posselt, "How High School Students Experience and Learn from the Discussion of Controversial Public Issues," *Journal of Curriculum and Supervision* 17, no. 4 (Summer 2002): 283–314; Diana Hess and P. McAvoy, *The Political Classroom: Ethics and Evidence in Democratic Education* (New York: Routledge, 2012).

29. Gould, *Guardian of Democracy*.

30. Joe Geraghy, ed., *Current Issues*, 35th ed. (Washington, DC: Close Up Press, 2011).

31. According to National Center for Education Statistics, "National Assessment of Educational Progress 2010 Civics Assessment Database," 63 percent of twelfth-grade students report discussing current events at least once a week.

32. Jeffrey L. Bernstein, "Cultivating Civic Competence: Simulations and Skill-Building in an Introductory Government Class," *Journal of Political Science Education* 4, no. 1

(January 1, 2008): 1–20; Joseph Kahne, Bernadette Chi, and Ellen Middaugh, "Building Social Capital for Civic and Political Engagement: The Potential of High-School Civics Courses," *Canadian Journal of Education* 29, no. 2 (2006): 387–409; Celeste J. Lay and Kathleen J. Smarick, "Simulating a Senate Office: The Impact on Student Knowledge and Attitudes," *Journal of Political Science Education* 2, no. 2 (August 2006): 131–146; National Center for Education Statistics, "National Assessment of Educational Progress 2010 Civics Assessment Database"; Michael McDeitt and Spiro Kiousis, "Education for Deliberative Democracy: The Long-Term Influence of Kids Voting USA" (working paper 22, CIRCLE, College Park, MD, 2004).

33. Discovering Justice, "Our Programs," n.d., www.discoveringjustice.org/?p= programs; Meryl Kessler (legal director, Discovering Justice), telephone interview with author, March 2011.

34. Mary Witte, "Through Another's Eyes: Engaging Students in Interdisciplinary Curricula," *Gifted Child Today* 27, no. 2 (Spring 2004): 52–53.

35. Sherry Schwartz, "Mock Trial: A Window to Free Speech Rights and Abilities," *Social Studies* 101, no. 6 (November 2010): 242–249.

36. Discovering Justice Web page, www.discoveringjustice.org/.

37. Elisabeth J. Medvedow (executive director, Discovering Justice), telephone interview with author, August 2011.

38. Amy Linimon and Mark R. Joslyn, "Trickle Up Political Socialization: The Impact of Kids Voting USA on Voter Turnout in Kansas," *State Politics & Policy Quarterly* 2, no. 1 (Spring 2002): 24.

39. Kids Voting Ohio, *Kids Voting Voice, Spring 2007* (Columbus, OH: Kids Voting Ohio, 2007), www.kidsvotingoh.org/insidefiles/newsletter/2011SpringFinalLetter.pdf.

40. Ibid.

41. Patrick C. Meirick and Daniel B. Wackman, "Kids Voting and Political Knowledge: Narrowing Gaps, Informing Votes," *Social Science Quarterly* 85, no. 5 (December 15, 2004): 1161–1177.

42. Jeff Cabot (central Ohio executive director, Kids Voting USA [KVUSA]), telephone interview with author, August 2011. According to Cabot, the fee varies according to the number of KVUSA participating schools in the region. Regional associations often find support from local election boards and the affiliation fees "are not oppressive."

43. Mathew Goldwasser, "Evaluation of Chicago Youth Policymaking Initiatives in Year II," report prepared for the Mikva Challenge and the Kellogg Foundation, July 2010.

44. All information in this paragraph from ibid.

45. Learn and Serve America, "What Is Service-Learning?" n.d., www.learnandserve .gov/about/service_learning/index.asp.

46. Emily Hoban Kirby, Kei Kawashima-Ginsberg, and Surbhi Godsay, "Youth Volunteering in the States: 2002 to 2009," CIRCLE, Medford, MA, February 14, 2011, www.civicyouth.org/featured-youth-volunteering-in-the-states-2002-to-2009/.

47. Maryland Department of Education, "Service-Learning in Maryland," 2003, http://marylandpublicschools.net/MSDE/programs/servicelearning/.

48. Kirby, Kawashima-Ginsberg, and Godsay, "Youth Volunteering in the States"; National Center for Education Statistics, "National Assessment of Educational Progress 2010 Civics Assessment Database."

49. National Center for Education Statistics, "National Assessment of Educational Progress 2010 Civics Assessment Database."

50. See this argument made, for example, in Joseph Kahne and Sue Sporte, "Developing Citizens: The Impact of Civic Learning Opportunities on Students' Commitment to Civic Participation," *American Educational Research Journal* 45, no. 3 (September 2008): 738–766; Kahne, Crow, and Lee, "Different Pedagogy, Different Politics."

Chapter 7
Expanding Preservice Teachers' Images of Self, Students, and Democracy

Keith C. Barton

This paper has benefitted immeasurably from conversations with Hilary G. Conklin, Diana Hess, Jennifer Hauver James, Rob Kunzman, Meira Levinson, and Stephanie van Hover.

1. Meira Levinson, *No Citizen Left Behind: Urban Schools, Youth Empowerment, and the New Civic Education* (Cambridge, MA: Harvard University Press, 2012).

2. See, for example, Elizabeth E. Heilman, *Social Studies and Diversity Education: What We Do and How We Do It* (New York: Routledge, 2010).

3. Walter C. Parker, *Teaching Democracy: United and Diversity in Public Life* (New York: Teachers College Press, 2002), xvii.

4. Ibid., 20.

5. Bruce A. VanSledright and S. G. Grant, "Citizenship Education and the Persistent Nature of Classroom Teaching Dilemmas," *Theory and Research in Social Education* 22, no. 3 (Summer 1994): 305–339.

6. Leisa A. Martin, "A Comparative Analysis of Teacher Education Students' Views About Citizenship Education," *Action in Teacher Education* 32, no. 2 (Summer 2010): 56–69.

7. A small but visible minority of preservice teachers are even directly opposed to democracy—not just in schools but everywhere. Some, for example, argue that democracy contradicts their religious beliefs. These students ascribe all direction and control of the world to a deity; they believe that any attempt to influence society or the environment is evidence of hubris, an unwarranted attempt to interfere in matters that must be left in God's hands. Such "theologically certain" students may reject such basic concepts as deliberation, reasoned judgment, and public policy. See Jennifer Hauver James, "'Democracy Is the Devil's Snare': Theological Certainty in Teacher Education," *Theory and Research in Social Education* 38, no. 4 (Fall 2010): 618–639.

8. Dorene D. Ross and Elizabeth Anne Yeager, "What Does Democracy Mean to Prospective Elementary Teachers?" *Journal of Teacher Education* 50, no. 4 (September–October

1999): 255–266; Stephanie van Hover, Dorene D. Ross, and Elizabeth Anne Yeager, "Contrasting Perspectives on Democracy? Similarities and Differences Among Three Undergraduate Majors," *Journal of Social Studies Research* 25, no. 1 (Spring 2011): 16–24; Elizabeth Anne Yeager and Stephanie van Hover, "Preservice Teachers' Understanding of Democracy: Toward a Conceptual Framework," in *Civic Learning in Teacher Education*, vol. 3, *International Perspectives on Education for Democracy in the Preparation of Teachers*, ed. Gregory E. Hamot, John J. Patrick, and Robert S. Leming (Bloomington, IN: Social Studies Development Center, 2004), 63–78.

9. Jason L. O'Brien and Jason M. Smith, "Elementary Education Students' Perceptions of 'Good' Citizenship," *Journal of Social Studies Education Research* 2, no. 1 (2011): 21–36; Leisa A. Martin, "Elementary and Secondary Teacher Education Students' Perspectives on Citizenship," *Action in Teacher Education* 30, no. 3 (Fall 2008): 54–63; Sarah A. Mathews and Paulette Patterson Dilworth, "Case Studies of Preservice Teachers' Ideas About the Role of Multicultural Citizenship Education in Social Studies," *Theory and Research in Social Education* 36, no. 4 (Fall 2008): 356–390.

10. National Education Association, *Status of the American Public School Teacher, 2005–2006* (Washington, DC: National Education Association, 2010), 83–93; Dan Lortie, *Schoolteacher* (Chicago: University of Chicago Press, 1975), 111–114.

11. Joel Westheimer and Joseph Kahne, "What Kind of Citizen? The Politics of Educating for Democracy," *American Educational Research Journal* 41, no. 2 (Summer 2004): 237–269.

12. Lortie, *Schoolteacher*, 27–29; National Education Association, *Status of the American Public School Teacher*, 83–93.

13. Jennifer Hauver James, "Teachers As Mothers in the Elementary Classroom," *Gender and Education* 22, no. 5 (September 2010): 521–534; Jennifer Hauver James, "Embracing Controversy, Enacting Motherhood: Social Education in the Primary Classroom," paper presented at the Annual Meeting of the American Educational Research Association, Denver, April 2010.

14. Jennifer Hauver James, "Teachers As Protectors: Making Sense of Preservice Teachers' Resistance to Interpretation in Elementary History Teaching," *Theory and Research in Social Education* 36, no. 3 (Summer 2008): 172–205.

15. Lortie, *Schoolteacher*, 29–30, 114; National Education Association, *Status of the American Public School Teacher*, 83–93.

16. Stephanie van Hover, "Implications of the DCI Findings on Teacher Preparation," comments at the Annual Meeting of the American Educational Research Association, New Orleans, April 2011.

17. Todd Dinkelman, "Reflection and Resistance: Challenges of Rationale-Based Teacher Education," *Journal of Inquiry and Action in Education* 2, no. 1 (2009): 91–108.

18. Lortie, *Schoolteacher*, 113; Jennifer Hauver James, "Caring for 'Others': Examining the Interplay of Mothering and Deficit Discourses in Teaching," *Teaching and Teacher Education* 28, no. 2 (February 2012): 165–173, available at http://myscidir.cjb.net/science/article/pii/S0742051X11001041; Guadalupe Valdes, *Con Respeto: Bridging the*

Distances Between Culturally Diverse Families and Schools (New York: Teachers College Press, 1996); Angela Valenzuela, *Subtractive Schooling: U.S.-Mexican Youth and the Politics of Caring* (Albany: State University of New York Press, 1999).

19. Lortie, *Schoolteacher*, 111–114; James, "Embracing Controversy, Enacting Motherhood"; Stephanie van Hover and Elizabeth Yeager, "'Making Students Better People'? A Case Study of a Beginning Teacher," *International Studies Forum* 3, no. 1 (2002): 219–232; Stephanie van Hover and Elizabeth Yeager, "'I Want to Use my Subject Matter to . . .': The Role of Purpose in One U.S. Secondary History Teacher's Instructional Decision Making," *Canadian Journal of Education* 30, no. 3 (2007): 670–690.

20. Graeme Aitken and Claire Sinnema, *Effective Pedagogy in Social Sciences / Tikanga ā Iwi: Best Evidence Synthesis Iteration* (Wellington, New Zealand: New Zealand Ministry of Education, 2008), 56–76.

21. Keith C. Barton, Alan W. McCully, and Melissa J. Marks, "Reflecting on Elementary Children's Understanding of History and Social Studies: An Inquiry Project with Beginning Teachers in Northern Ireland and the United States," *Journal of Teacher Education* 55, no. 1 (January 2004): 70–90; Elizabeth R. Hinde and Nancy Perry, "Elementary Teachers' Application of Jean Piaget's Theories of Cognitive Development During Social Studies Curriculum Debates in Arizona," *Elementary School Journal* 108, no. 1 (September 2007): 63–79; James, "Teachers As Protectors."

22. Hilary G. Conklin et al., "Learning from Young Adolescents: The Use of Structured Teacher Education Coursework to Help Beginning Teachers Investigate Middle School Students' Intellectual Capabilities," *Journal of Teacher Education* 61, no. 4 (September–October 2010): 314.

23. Barton, McCully, and Marks, "Reflecting on Elementary Children's Understanding."

24. Terrie Epstein, *Interpreting National History: Race, Identity, and Pedagogy in Classrooms and Communities* (New York: Routledge, 2009).

25. Beth C. Rubin, "'There's Still not Justice': Youth Civic Identity Development amid Distinct School and Community Contexts," *Teachers College Record* 109, no. 2 (February 2007): 449–481.

26. See, for example, the programs profiled in Linda Darling-Hammond, *Powerful Teacher Education: Lessons from Exemplary Programs* (San Francisco: Jossey-Bass, 2006).

27. Ibid.; Linda Darling-Hammond and John Bransford, eds., *Preparing Teachers for a Changing World* (San Francisco: Jossey-Bass, 2005); Linda Darling-Hammond and Gary Sykes, eds., *Teaching As the Learning Profession: Handbook of Policy and Practice* (San Francisco: Jossey-Bass, 2009).

28. Donald P. Green et al., "Does Knowledge of Constitutional Principles Increase Support for Civil Liberties? Results from a Randomized Field Experiment," *Journal of Politics* 73, no. 2 (April 2011): 463–476.

29. Keith C. Barton and Linda S. Levstik, *Teaching History for the Common Good* (New York: Routledge, 2004), 244–265; Conklin et al., "Learning from Young Adolescents"; Bruce Fehn and Kim E. Koeppen, "Intensive Document-Based Instruction in a Social Studies Methods Course," *Theory and Research in Social Education* 26, no. 4 (Fall 1998):

461–484; G. Williamson McDiarmid, "Understanding History for Teaching: A Study of the Historical Understanding of Prospective Teachers," in *Cognitive and Instructional Processes in History and the Social Sciences*, ed. James F. Voss and Mario Carretero (Hillsdale, NJ: Lawrence Erlbaum Associates, 1994), 159–186; van Hover and Yeager, "Making Students Better People?"

30. For example, Prentice T. Chandler, "Academic Freedom: A Teacher's Struggle to Include 'Other' Voices in History," *Social Education* 70, no. 6 (October 2006): 354–357.

31. Jan Nespor, "The Role of Beliefs in the Practice of Teaching," *Journal of Curriculum Studies* 19, no. 4 (July–August 1987): 321.

32. Dinkelman, "Reflection and Resistance"; Mathews and Dilworth, "Case Studies of Preservice Teachers' Ideas"; Nel Noddings, *Happiness and Education* (New York: Cambridge University Press, 2003), 76.

33. Paula Wasley, "Education School Revises Policy on 'Dispositions,'" *Chronicle of Higher Education*, March 10, 2006.

34. Robert Dahlgren and Stephen Masyada, "Ideological Dissonance: A Comparison of the Views of Eight Conservative Students with the Recruitment Document from a Southeastern College of Education," *Social Studies Research and Practice* 4, no. 1 (March 2009): 1–12; Paula Wasley, "Accreditor of Education Schools Drops Controversial 'Social Justice' Language," *Chronicle of Higher Education*, June 16, 2006.

35. Noddings, *Happiness and Education*, 74–93; Stephen J. Thornton, *Teaching Social Studies That Matters: Curriculum for Active Learning* (New York: Teachers College Press, 2005), 45–56.

36. Diana E. Hess, "Discussion in Social Studies: Is it Worth the Trouble?" in *Social Studies Today: Research and Practice*, ed. Walter C. Parker (New York: Routledge, 2009), 205–214.

37. Yeager and van Hover, "Preservice Teachers' Understanding of Democracy."

38. Diana E. Hess, *Controversy in the Classroom: The Democratic Power of Discussion* (New York: Routledge, 2009), 77–96.

Chapter 8
Professional Development as a Tool for Improving Civic Education
Diana Hess and John Zola

Thanks to Meira Levinson, Lauren Gatti, Melissa Sherfinski, Jaye Zola, Barbara Miller, Megan Hanson, and Lee Arbetman for their help with this chapter, and to Beth Ratway, Keith Barton, and Carolyn Pereira for a number of helpful conversations about professional development.

1. Beth C. Rubin, *Making Citizens: Transforming Civic Learning for Diverse Social Studies Classrooms* (New York: Routledge, 2011); Diana Hess, *Controversy in the Classroom: The Democratic Power of Discussion* (New York: Routledge, 2009); Janet S. Bixby and Judith L. Pace, eds., *Educating Citizens in Troubled Times: Qualitative Studies of Current Efforts* (Albany: SUNY Press, 2008); Brian D. Schultz, *Spectacular Things Happen Along the Way: Lessons from an Urban Classroom* (New York: Teachers College Press, 2008).

2. Linda Darling Hammond et al., *Professional Learning in the Learning Profession: A Status Report on Teacher Development in the U.S. and Abroad* (Dallas, TX: National Staff Development Council, 2009); Hilda Borko, "Professional Development and Teacher Learning:

Mapping the Terrain," *Educational Researcher* 33, no. 8 (2004): 3–15; Elham Kazemi and Amanda Hubbard, "New Directions for the Design and Study of Professional Development: Attending to the Coevolution of Teachers' Participation Across Contexts," *Journal of Teacher Education* 59, no. 5 (2008): 428–441; Stephanie van Hover, "The Professional Development of Social Studies Teachers," in *Handbook of Research in Social Studies Education*, ed. Linda S. Levstik and Cynthia A. Tyson (New York: Routledge, 2008), 352–372.

3. For an important recent study of the positive effect of high-quality professional development on the practice of civic education teachers, see Dennis J. Barr, *Continuing a Tradition of Research on the Foundations of Democratic Education: The National Professional Development and Evaluation Project* (Brookline, MA: Facing History and Ourselves National Foundation, Inc., 2010), available at www.facinghistory.org/system/files/Continuing_a_Tradition_v93010_0.pdf.

4. Bill Bishop, *The Big Sort: Why the Clustering of Like-Minded Americans Is Tearing Us Apart* (New York: Houghton Mifflin, 2008).

5. Thomas R. Guskey, "Closing the Knowledge Gap on Effective Professional Development," *Educational Horizons* 87, no. 4 (2009): 224–233.

6. For information on CELD, see Center for Education in Law and Democracy Web page, www.lawanddemocracy.org/.

7. As just one example of a curricular resource, there are elaborate, unusually well-crafted, and thoroughly field-tested lesson plans about many important Supreme Court cases at Street Law, "Landmark Cases of the U.S. Supreme Court," Street Law, Inc., Web page, n.d., available at www.landmarkcases.org.

8. Our assessment of the Supreme Court Summer Institute stems from personal experience. John attended the institute in 1995, when he was a high school teacher, and Diana has been a teacher in the institute for many years. Moreover, both John and Diana have participated in follow-up activities with local teachers. The activities are designed to provide assistance as teachers work to put into practice what was learned at the institute.

9. The materials that have been created about the selected cases (including the two mentioned here) are available at Street Law, "Supreme Court Case Studies: Alphabetically," Street Law, Inc., Web page, n.d., www.streetlaw.org/en/page.sccasesalpha.aspx.

10. See Street Law, "Supreme Court Summer Institute for Teachers," Street Law, Inc., Web page, n.d., www.streetlaw.org/scsi.

11. Walter C. Parker et al., "Rethinking Advanced High School Coursework: Tackling the Depth/Breadth Tension in the AP 'US Government and Politics Course,'" *Journal of Curriculum Studies* 43, no. 4 (2011): 533–559.

Chapter 9
Digital Opportunities for Civic Education

Joseph Kahne, Jacqueline Ullman, and Ellen Middaugh

We are enormously grateful to the MacArthur Foundation and to the Center for Information and Research on Civic Learning and Education (CIRCLE) for funding and support that enabled this work. Namjin Lee, Jessica Timpany Feezell, and Chris Evans were all coauthors on studies published elsewhere and summarized here. Of course, we take full responsibility for the findings and interpretations presented here.

1. Stephen Macedo with Yvette Alex-Assensoh et al., *Democracy at Risk: How Political Choices Undermine Citizen Participation, and What We Can Do About It* (Washington, DC: Brookings Institution, 2005); National Conference on Citizenship, *Civic Health Index: Beyond the Vote* (Washington, DC: National Conference on Citizenship, 2008).

2. Andrew Kohut, *Cable and Internet Loom Large in Fragmented Political News Universe* (Washington, DC: Pew Internet and American Life Project, Pew Research Center, 2004).

3. Andrew Kohut and Lee Rainie, *Youth Vote Influenced by Online Information: Internet Election News Audience Seeks Convenience, Familiar Names* (Washington, DC: Pew Internet and American Life Project, Pew Research Center, 2000); Andrew Kohut, *Social Networking and Online Videos Take Off: Internet's Broader Role in Campaign, 2008* (Washington, DC: Pew Internet and American Life Project, Pew Research Center, 2008).

4. Kohut and Rainie, *Internet Election News Audience Seeks Convenience.*

5. Wade Valainis, "One Quarter (27%) of American Teens Use Facebook Continuously Throughout the Day," *Ipsos,* January 5, 2011, www.ipsos-na.com/news-polls/pressrelease .aspx?id=5095.

6. Amanda Lenhart et al., *Teens and Social Media* (Washington, DC: Pew Internet and American Life Project, Pew Research Center, 2007).

7. James Youniss and Miranda Yates, *Community Service and Social Responsibility in Youth* (Chicago: University of Chicago Press, 1997).

8. Kristen Purcell and Michael Dimock, *Americans Under Age 40 Are Just as Likely to Donate to Japan Disaster Relief Through Electronic Means as Traditional Means* (Washington, DC: Pew Internet and American Life Project, Pew Research Center, 2011).

9. Ellen Middaugh and Joseph Kahne, "Youth Internet Use and Recruitment into Civic and Political Participation" (working paper, Civics Education Research Group, Mills College, Oakland, CA, 2011); Kay Lehman Schlozman, Sidney Verba, and Henry E. Brady, "Weapon of the Strong? Participatory Inequality and the Internet," *Perspectives on Politics* 8, no. 2 (2010): 487–509.

10. Amanda Lenhart et al., *Social Media and Young Adults* (Washington, DC: Pew Internet and American Life Project, Pew Research Center, 2010); comScore, *The 2010 Mobile Year in Review* (Reston: comScore, Inc., 2011).

11. Though they did not work on this particular chapter, Namjin Lee, Jessica Timpany Feezell, and Christine Evans also played significant roles in the data collection, analysis, and writing of the research discussed here.

12. Additional panel data for one of the studies were drawn from the Mobilization, Change, and Political and Civic Engagement (MCPCE) Project from the University of Chicago.

13. Mizuko Ito et al., *Living and Learning with New Media: Summary of Findings from the Digital Youth Project* (Cambridge, MA: MIT Press, 2008).

14. Howard Rheingold, *The Virtual Community: Homesteading on the Electronic Frontier*

(Cambridge, MA: MIT Press, 2000); Henry Jenkins et al., *Confronting the Challenges of Participatory Culture: Media Education for the 21st Century* (Cambridge, MA: MIT Press, 2009).

15. Quantcast, "GaiaOnline.com," www.quantcast.com/gaiaonline.com.

16. Joseph Kahne, Namjin Lee, and Jessica Timpany Feezell, "The Civic and Political Significance of Online Participatory Cultures Among Youth Transitioning to Adulthood," *Journal of Information Technology and Politics* (forthcoming).

17. Jenkins et al., *Confronting the Challenges of Participatory Culture.*

18. Although the InterroBang game has ended, you can learn about its mission at Microsoft News Center, "Mission Possible: Make a Difference on Global Youth Service Day," Microsoft press release, April 2, 2011, www.microsoft.com/presspass/press/2011/apr11/04-06interrobangma.mspx. See also InterroBang, "About," www.playinterrobang.com/about#.

19. Emily Webb, "Loudoun County High School Teachers Bring Service-Learning Game into Curriculum to Drive Student Success," *PRNewswire*, March 18, 2011, www.education.virginia.gov/News/viewRelease.cfm?id=640.

20. John Dewey, *Democracy and Education* (New York: Macmillan, 1916); Hannah Arendt, *Between Past and Future: Eight Exercises in Political Thought* (New York: Viking, 1968); J. Jurgen Habermas, *The Structural Transformation of the Public Sphere* (Cambridge, MA: MIT Press, 1989).

21. Cass R. Sunstein, *Republic.com* (Princeton, NJ: Princeton University Press, 2001).

22. Eli Pariser, "Beware Online 'Filter Bubbles,'" *TED Blog*, May 2, 2011, http://blog.ted.com/2011/05/02/beware-online-filter-bubbles-eli-pariser-on-ted-com/.

23. Joseph Kahne, Ellen Middaugh, Namjin Lee, and Jessica Timpany Feezell, "Youth Online Activity and Exposure to Diverse Perspectives," *New Media and Society* 14, no. 3 (2012): 492–512.

24. Dewey, *Democracy and Education.*

25. Diana C. Mutz, *Hearing the Other Side: Deliberative Versus Participatory Democracy* (Cambridge: Cambridge University Press, 2006); Vincent Price, Joseph N. Cappella, and Lilach Nir, "Does Disagreement Contribute to More Deliberative Opinion?" *Political Communication* 19, no. 1 (2002): 95–112.

26. Magdalena Wojcieszak and Diana Mutz, "Online Groups and Political Discourse: Do Online Discussion Spaces Facilitate Exposure to Political Disagreement?" *Journal of Communication* 59, no. 1 (2009): 40–56.

27. Eszter Hargittai, "Digital Na(t)ives? Variation in Internet Skills and Uses Among Members of the 'Net Generation,'" *Sociological Inquiry* 80, no. 1 (February 2010): 92–113.

28. Eszter Hargittai, "How Wide a Web? Inequalities in Accessing Information Online" (PhD diss., Princeton University, Princeton, NJ, 2003); Pippa Norris, *Digital Divide: Civic Engagement, Information Poverty, and the Internet in Democratic Societies* (New York: Cambridge University Press, 2001).

29. Joseph Kahne, Jessica Timpany Feezell, and Namjin Lee, "Digital Media Literacy Education and Online Civic and Political Participation," *International Journal of Communication* 6 (2012): 1–24.

30. Jane David, "Teaching Media Literacy," *Educational Leadership* 66 (March 2009): 84–86; Renee Hobbs, "A Review of School-Based Initiatives in Media Literacy Education," *American Behavioral Scientist* 48, no. 1 (September 2004); Paul Mihailidis, "Beyond Cynicism: Media Education and Civic Learning Outcomes in the University," *International Journal of Learning and Media* 1, no. 3 (Summer 2009).

31. Joseph Kahne, Ellen Middaugh, and Chris Evans, *The Civic Potential of Video Games* (Cambridge, MA: MIT Press, 2009).

32. Carnegie Corporation of New York and Center for Information and Center for Information and Research on Civic Learning (hereafter cited as CIRCLE), *The Civic Mission of Schools* (New York: Carnegie Corporation of New York; College Park, MD: CIRCLE, 2003).

33. Joseph Kahne and Ellen Middaugh, "Democracy for Some: The Civic Opportunity Gap in High School" (working paper 59, CIRCLE, College Park, MD, 2008).

34. Janice L. Anderson, "Developing Ecological Stewardship in Elementary School Through Student Participation in Virtual Worlds" (paper presented at the National Association for Research in Science Teaching conference, Philadelphia, March 21–24, 2010).

35. Educational Simulations, "Real Lives 2010," n.d., www.educationalsimulations.com/products.html.

36. Games for Change, "Play: Become a Game Critic," 2012, www.gamesforchange.org/play.

37. Renee Hobbs, "The State of Media Literacy: A Response to Potter," *Journal of Broadcasting and Electronic Media* 55, no. 3 (2011): 419–430.

38. Ibid.; U.S. Department of Education, Office of Educational Technology, *Transforming American Education: Learning Powered by Technology* (Washington, DC, 2010), www.ed.gov/sites/default/files/NETP-2010-final-report.pdf; National Governors Association and the Council of Chief State School Officers, *Common Core Standards*, 2010, www.corestandards.org/.

39. Common Sense Media (2010) as cited in: Hobbs, "The State of Media Literacy."

40. American Political Science Association (ASPA) Task Force on Inequality and American Democracy, "American Democracy in an Age of Rising Inequality," *Perspectives on Politics* 2, no. 4 (December 2004).

41. Economics and Statistics Administration and the National Telecommunications and Information Administration, *Exploring the Digital Nation: Home Broadband Internet Adoption in the United States* (Washington, DC: U.S. Department of Commerce, 2010).

42. Victoria Rideout, Alexis Lauricella, and Ellen Wartella, *Children, Media and Race: Media Use Among White, Black, Hispanic, and Asian American Children* (Chicago: Center on Media and Human Development, Northwestern University, 2011); Craig Watkins, "Living on the Digital Margins: How Black and Latino Youth are Remaking the Participation Gap" (paper presented at the Diversifying Participation: Digital Media and Learning Conference, La Jolla, CA, February 18–20, 2010).

43. Jenkins et al., *Confronting the Challenges of Participatory Culture.*

44. Philadelphia Student Union, "Home Page," http://home.phillystudentunion.org/.

45. Jerusha O. Conner, "An Undeniable Force: The Influence of the Philadelphia Student Union on Youth Leaders, the Philadelphia School System, and Educational Policy" (working paper, Villanova University, Villanova, PA, 2011).

46. *Mozilla Wiki*, s.v. "Badges," last modified February 8, 2012, https://wiki.mozilla.org/Badges; DML central, "Featured Resource: Online Games and Interest-Driven Learning are Transformative for Today's Young Learners," n.d., http://dmlcentral.net/resources/4440source.

Chapter 10
Civic Education in Traditional Public, Charter, and Private Schools: Moving from Comparison to Explanation

David E. Campbell

1. See chapter 2 for a more sanguine assessment.

2. As just one example, see Michael Delli Carpini and Scott Keeter, *What Americans Know About Politics and Why It Matters* (New Haven, CT: Yale University Press, 1997).

3. Meira Levinson, *No Citizen Left Behind* (Cambridge, MA: Harvard University Press, 2012), 222.

4. Sidney Verba, Kay Lehman Schlozman, and Henry E. Brady, *Voice and Equality: Civic Voluntarism in American Politics* (Cambridge, MA: Harvard University Press, 1995).

5. Patrick J. Wolf, "Civics Exam: Schools of Choice Boost Civic Values," *Education Next* 7, no. 3 (Summer 2007): 66–72.

6. Ibid., 68.

7. Jack Buckley and Mark Schneider, *Charter Schools: Hope or Hype?* (Princeton, NJ: Princeton University Press, 2007).

8. David E. Campbell, "Making Democratic Education Work," in *Charters, Vouchers, and Public Education*, ed. Paul E. Peterson and David E. Campbell (Washington, DC: Brookings Institution, 2001). See also David E. Campbell, "Bowling Together: Private Schools, Serving Public Ends," *Education Next* (formerly *Education Matters*) 1, no. 3 (Summer 2001).

9. Kenneth Godwin and Frank Kemerer, *School Choice Tradeoffs: Liberty, Equality, and Diversity* (Austin: University of Texas Press, 2008).

10. David E. Campbell, "The Civic Side of School Reform: How Do School Vouchers Affect Civic Education?" unpublished manuscript, 2007, available at www.nd.edu/~dcampbe4/CIVICSIDE.pdf.

11. Richard G. Niemi, Mary A. Hepburn, and Chris Chapman, "Community Service by High School Students: A Cure for Civic Ills?" *Political Behavior* 23, no. 1 (2000): 45–69.

12. Campbell, "Making Democratic Education Work."

13. Wolf, "Civics Exam," 69.

14. Buckley and Schneider, *Charter Schools*.

15. Ibid.

16. Campbell, "Making Democratic Education Work."

17. Wolf, "Civics Exam," 68.

18. Campbell, "Civic Side."

19. Godwin and Kemerer, *School Choice Tradeoffs.*

20. Campbell, "Making Democratic Education Work."

21. Buckley and Schneider, *Charter Schools.*

22. *Zelman v. Simmons-Harris*, 536 U.S. 639 (2002).

23. Richard G. Niemi and Jane Junn, *Civic Education: What Makes Students Learn* (New Haven, CT: Yale University Press, 1998).

24. Donald P. Green et al., "Does Knowledge of Constitutional Principles Increase Support for Civil Liberties? Results from a Randomized Field Experiment," *Journal of Politics* 73, no. 2 (April 2011): 463–476.

25. David E. Campbell, "Voice in the Classroom: How an Open Classroom Climate Fosters Political Engagement Among Adolescents," *Political Behavior* 30 no. 4 (2008): 437–454.

26. Specifically, in classrooms with an open climate, students with both high and low levels of expected education (a good marker for social class) are equally likely to say that they expect to vote when given the opportunity.

27. Diana Hess, *Controversy in the Classroom: The Democratic Power of Discussion* (New York: Routledge, 2009).

28. James S. Coleman and Thomas Hoffer, *Public and Private High Schools: The Impact of Communities* (New York: Basic Books, 1987).

29. Robert D. Putnam, *Making Democracy Work: Civic Traditions in Modern Italy* (Princeton, NJ: Princeton University Press, 1994); Robert D. Putnam, *Bowling Alone: The Collapse and Revival of American Community* (New York: Simon and Schuster, 2000).

30. Anthony Bryk, Valerie Lee, and Peter Holland, *Catholic Schools and the Common Good* (Cambridge, MA: Harvard University Press, 1993).

31. Thomas S. Dee, "The Effects of Catholic Schooling on Civic Participation," *International Tax and Public Finance* 12 (2005): 605–625.

32. Terry M. Moe, "The Two Democratic Purposes of Schooling," in *Rediscovering the Democratic Purposes of Education*, ed. Lorraine M. McDonnell, P. Michael Timpane, and Roger Benjamin (Lawrence: University Press of Kansas, 2000), 145.

33. David E. Campbell, *Why We Vote: How Schools and Communities Shape Our Civic Life* (Princeton, NJ: Princeton University Press, 2006).

34. Robert D. Putnam and David E. Campbell, *American Grace: How Religion Divides and Unites Us* (New York: Simon and Schuster, 2010).

35. Seth Andrew, "Fighting Civic Malpractice: How a Harlem Charter School Closes the Civic Achievement Gap," in *Teaching America: The Case for Civic Education*, ed. David Feith (Lanham, MD: Rowman and Littlefield, 2011), 104.

36. Mike Feinberg, "The KIPP Approach: Be the Change You Wish to See in the World," in *Teaching America: The Case for Civic Education*, ed. David Feith (Lanham, MD: Rowman and Littlefield, 2011).

Conclusion
The Third *C*: College, Career, and Citizenship

Meira Levinson

1. "Congressional Job Approval," Real Clear Politics Web page, accessed March 19, 2012, www.realclearpolitics.com/epolls/other/congressional_job_approval-903.html.
2. Jonathan Gould, ed., *Guardian of Democracy: The Civic Mission of Schools* (Philadelphia: Leonore Annenberg Institute for Civics of the Annenberg Public Policy Center, University of Pennsylvania; Silver Spring, MD: Campaign for the Civic Mission of Schools, 2011), 18. Disclosure: the author was a contributor to this report.
3. For more on the civic empowerment gap, see Meira Levinson, *No Citizen Left Behind* (Cambridge, MA: Harvard University Press, 2012).
4. Sidney Verba, Kay Lehman Schlozman, and Henry E. Brady, *Voice and Equality: Civic Voluntarism in American Politics* (Cambridge, MA: Harvard University Press, 1995).

ACKNOWLEDGMENTS

Struck by the relative dearth of attention that policymakers, funders, and reformers devote to the challenges of citizenship education, the editors decided in the fall of 2010 to engage a number of leading thinkers in a project examining the current state of civic education and prospects for improvement. The collected analyses were first presented at an October 2011 conference at the American Enterprise Institute, where they were discussed by an all-star lineup of scholars, practitioners, and policymakers dedicated, in some way or another, to the field of civic education: William A. Galston, senior fellow at the Bookings Institution and professor at the University of Maryland; Veronica Boix-Mansilla, principal investigator for the Interdisciplinary Studies Project at the Harvard Graduate School of Education; Trey Grayson, director of Harvard's Institute of Politics; Juan Rangel, chief executive officer for the United Neighborhood Organization; Randi Weingarten, president of the American Federation of Teachers; Irasema Salcido, chief executive officer and founder of César Chávez Charter High School for Public Policy; Russlynn Ali, assistant secretary for civil rights at the U.S. Department of Education; Peter C. Groff, senior advisor at the Black Alliance for Educational Options; Ted McConnell, executive director of the Campaign for the Civic Mission of Schools; and Michael J. Petrilli, executive vice president of the Thomas B. Fordham Institute. We are grateful to these individuals for their participation and invaluable feedback, which helped shape the conference papers into the chapters you hold today.

This effort would not have been possible, of course, without the steadfast support provided by the American Enterprise Institute (AEI) and its president, Arthur Brooks. Financial support for this project was generously provided by the S. D. Bechtel, Jr. Foundation, and we express our deepest gratitude for it. We also thank the terrific staff at AEI, whose hard work in coordinating the October 2011 conference as well as compiling and editing the initial drafts herein made this volume possible. These include Jenna Talbot, Taryn Hochleitner, Daniel Lautzenheiser, Rebecca King, Barrett Bowdre, and Luke Sullivan, all of whom provided vital assistance. We also give a special thanks to Gary Schmitt and Cheryl Miller, whose work with the AEI Program on American Citizenship served as the launch pad for this effort. In addition, we express our gratitude to the Harvard Education Press team, in particular our publisher Doug Clayton and editor Nancy Walser.

We are most grateful, however, for the excellent assistance of Whitney Downs of AEI. She (gently) imposed order on the chaos of the busy coeditors' schedules, ensured that our authors kept to our ambitious schedule, served as quality control, and generally kept the ship afloat. Without Whitney, this book would not exist.

ABOUT THE EDITORS

David E. Campbell is professor of political science at the University of Notre Dame and the founding director of the Rooney Center for the Study of American Democracy. He is the coauthor of *American Grace: How Religion Divides and Unites Us* (2010, with Robert Putnam), which the *New York Times* describes as "intellectually powerful" and the *San Francisco Chronicle* as "the most successfully argued sociological study of American religion in more than half a century." Mr. Campbell is also the author of *Why We Vote: How Schools and Communities Shape Our Civic Life* (2006); the editor of *A Matter of Faith: Religion in the 2004 Presidential Election* (2007); and a coauthor of *Democracy at Risk: How Political Choices Undermine Citizen Participation and What We Can Do About It* (2005). As an expert on religion, politics, young people, and civic engagement, he has often been featured in the national media, including the *New York Times*, the *Economist*, *USA Today*, the *Washington Post*, the *Wall Street Journal*, *Time*, NBC News, CNN, NPR, Fox News, and C-SPAN.

Meira Levinson is an associate professor at the Harvard Graduate School of Education, following eight years working as a middle school teacher in the Atlanta and Boston Public Schools. She writes about the intersection of political theory, education policy, and pedagogical practice. She is the author of *No Citizen Left Behind* (2012); *The Demands of Liberal Education* (1999); and the coauthored *Democracy at Risk: How Political Choices Undermine Citizen Participation and What We Can Do About It* (2005), in addition to numerous articles and book chapters. She has served on the steering committees or boards of the American Political Science Association's Standing Committee on Civic Education and Civic Engagement, Campaign for the Civic Mission of Schools, CIRCLE/ Tisch College, Discovering Justice, Generation Citizen, the Civic Ed

Project, and the scholarly journal *Theory and Research in Education*. Ms. Levinson also co-convenes the Civic and Moral Education Initiative at the Harvard Graduate School of Education.

Frederick M. Hess is resident scholar and director of education policy studies at the American Enterprise Institute. He has authored influential books on education, including *The Same Thing Over and Over*; *Education Unbound*; *Common Sense School Reform*; *Revolution at the Margins*; and *Spinning Wheels* and pens the Education Week blog "Rick Hess Straight Up." His work has appeared in scholarly and popular outlets such as *Teachers College Record, Harvard Education Review, Social Science Quarterly, Urban Affairs Review, American Politics Quarterly, Chronicle of Higher Education, Phi Delta Kappan, Educational Leadership, U.S. News & World Report*, the *Washington Post*, and the *National Review*. He has edited widely cited volumes on education philanthropy, stretching the education dollar, the impact of education research, education entrepreneurship, and No Child Left Behind. He serves as executive editor of Education Next; as lead faculty member for the Rice Education Entrepreneurship Program; on the Review Board for the Broad Prize in Urban Education; and on the boards of directors of the National Association of Charter School Authorizers, 4.0 SCHOOLS, and the American Board for the Certification of Teaching Excellence. A former high school social studies teacher, he has taught at the University of Virginia, the University of Pennsylvania, Georgetown University, Rice University, and Harvard University.

ABOUT THE CONTRIBUTORS

Keith C. Barton is professor of curriculum and instruction and adjunct professor of history at Indiana University. He researches students' historical understanding, classroom teaching and learning contexts, and the history of the social studies curriculum. He has conducted several studies in the United States, Northern Ireland, and New Zealand and has been a visiting professor at Victoria University in Wellington, New Zealand, and at the UNESCO Centre for Education in Pluralism, Human Rights, and Democracy at the University of Ulster. He is the author, with Linda S. Levstik, of *Doing History: Investigating with Children in Elementary and Middle Schools* (2011); *Teaching History for the Common Good* (2004); and *Researching History Education: Theory, Method, and Context* (2004) and editor of *Research Methods in Social Studies Education: Contemporary Issues and Perspectives* (2006). He teaches courses on secondary social studies methods, educational research, and curriculum history.

Diana Hess is professor of curriculum and instruction at the University of Wisconsin–Madison. A former high school teacher, she currently teaches courses for undergraduate and graduate students in social studies education, social studies research, and democratic education. Since 1998, she has been researching what young people learn from deliberating highly controversial political and constitutional issues in schools. Ms. Hess is the author of *Controversy in the Classroom: The Democratic Power of Discussion* (2009), which received the 2009 exemplary research award from the National Council for the Social Studies. Beginning in the fall of 2011, she has been on leave from the university to serve as the senior vice president of the Spencer Foundation.

Michael C. Johanek is a senior fellow at the Graduate School of Education, University of Pennsylvania. As member of the Education Graduate

Group, he directs the Mid-Career Doctoral Program in Educational Leadership, codirects the Inter-American Educational Leadership Network, and is *profesor invitado internacional* at the Pontificia Universidad Católica de Chile. Previously, he was vice president of professional services for Teachscape; executive director for K–12 professional development for the College Board; and a high school teacher and administrator in Cleveland; New York; and Lima, Peru. Mr. Johanek's publications include *Leonard Covello and the Making of Benjamin Franklin High School: Education As If Citizenship Mattered* (2007, with J. Puckett) and *A Faithful Mirror: Reflections on the College Board and Education in America* (2001).

Joseph Kahne is the John and Martha Davidson Professor of Education at Mills College and chair of the MacArthur Foundation Research Network on Youth and Participatory Politics. His research focuses on ways that school practices and digital media influence youth civic and political development. Currently, he is writing up findings from a panel study of new media participation and civic education in students from nineteen districts in California. With Cathy Cohen, he is currently co-principal investigator of a national survey of youth civic and political engagement and of their digital media participation. Mr. Kahne sits on the steering committee of the National Campaign for the Civic Mission of Schools and on the advisory board of the Center for Information and Research on Civic Learning and Engagement.

Peter Levine is director of the Center for Information and Research on Civic Learning and Engagement (CIRCLE) and research director of Tufts University's Jonathan Tisch College of Citizenship and Public Service. He is the author of *The Future of Democracy: Developing the Next Generation of American Citizens* (2007), *Reforming the Humanities: Literature and Ethics from Dante to Modern Times* (2009), three other scholarly books on philosophy and politics, and a novel. He also coedited *The Deliberative Democracy Handbook* (2006) with John Gastil and *Engaging Young People in Civic Life* (2009) with Jim Youniss and co-organized the writing of "The Civic Mission of Schools," a report released by Carnegie Corporation of New York and CIRCLE in 2003 and leading to a national advocacy campaign. He has served on the boards or steering committees of AmericaSpeaks, Street Law, the Newspaper Association of America Foundation, the Campaign for the Civic Mission of Schools, the Kettering Foundation, the American Bar Association's Committee for Public Education, the Paul J. Aicher Foundation, the Democracy Imperative, and the Deliberative Democracy Consortium.

Ellen Middaugh currently serves as research director of the Civic Engagement Research Group. Her research focuses on the influence of variations in social context (online and off) on youth civic and political development. She recently published, with Joe Kahne, an NSSE Yearbook chapter, "Online Localities: Implications for Democracy and Education," and "Civic Development in Context" in a volume of qualitative studies of civic education. She is also author of the forthcoming white paper "Service and Activism in the Digital Age: Supporting Youth Engagement in Public Life." Previously, Ms. Middaugh served as a quantitative research and evaluation specialist for the Center for Research, Evaluation and Assessment at University of California–Berkeley's Lawrence Hall of Science, where she managed multiple research and evaluation projects examining the impact of teacher professional development on student learning in science, technology, engineering, and mathematics (STEM) education. She has also served as methodological consultant and analyst on numerous research and evaluation projects related to civic education, service-learning, and law-related education.

Richard G. Niemi is Don Alonzo Watson Professor of Political Science at the University of Rochester, where has taught for more than forty years, serving as department chair, associate dean, and interim dean. He is coauthor or coeditor of *Vital Statistics on American Politics, 2011–2012* (2011); *Comparing Democracies 3* (2010); *Controversies in Voting Behavior* (fifth ed., 2010); *Voting Technology: The Not-So-Simple Act of Casting a Ballot* (2008); *Civic Education: What Makes Students Learn* (1998); and numerous scholarly articles. His current research is on voting technologies and youth attitude development. In 2002, he was selected as a foreign member of the Finnish Academy of Science and Letters, and in 2007, he was elected to the American Academy of Arts and Sciences.

Anna Rosefsky Saavedra is a policy researcher at the RAND Corporation. Her expertise is in addressing questions relevant to civic, global, and twenty-first-century skills education, particularly in urban schools in the United States and in developing-country settings. Ms. Saavedra's current projects include studies of the International Baccalaureate program, district-sponsored summer learning programs, human-capital-based school reform initiatives, and the quality of higher education. Before her graduate studies, Ms. Saavedra taught world history to high school students and managed education-related projects in a corporate setting.

Jacqueline Ullman is a lecturer in adolescent development and well-being at the University of Western Sydney. Her research interests focus on adolescents' social relationships, in both school and digital contexts, as a motivating factor for socially and academically marginalized youth. She views these issues from a social justice lens, with the goal of promoting social responsibility and acceptance of diversity in young people and equitable academic access for all youth.

James Youniss is research professor of psychology at the Catholic University of America. He has studied normal development in children and youth since the 1960s. He is the author or editor of ten books and over 190 journal articles, chapters, and reviews. He has been on editorial boards of several journals and has received research grants from federal agencies (for example, National Institute of Child Health and Human Development, National Institute of Mental Health) and private foundations (e.g., William T. Grant, Carnegie Corporation of New York). He has received several awards for his research, including a lifetime achievement award from the Alexander von Humboldt Foundation, a senior fellowship from the Japanese Society for the Promotion of Science, and a fellowship from the Radcliffe Center for Advanced Studies at Harvard University.

John Zola spent thirty-two years as a high school social studies teacher, most recently at New Vista High School, a "break the mold" public high school in Boulder, Colorado, where he was part of the core design team. Throughout his career, Mr. Zola has developed interactive teaching materials, trained colleagues in active learning strategies and Socratic seminars, and presented workshops that help teachers make the voice and work of students central in the classroom. Many of these workshops were presented in countries of the former Soviet Union, where the programs helped to promote the skills and dispositions needed in the new democracies. Mr. Zola currently conducts professional development programs on civic education, Socratic seminars, and student-centered teaching strategies in a variety of locations in the United States, Central Europe, and Asia.

INDEX